A

JOURNEY

THROUGH

LIFE

by
Gordon Sabin

Best wishes,

Gordon.

A JOURNEY THROUGH LIFE

ISBN: 0 907616 87 9

First edition 1996

Published by
Able Publishing
13 Station Road, Knebworth.
Herts. SG3 6AP
Tel: 01438 814316 Fax: 01438 815232

Distributed by
Gordon Sabin
"Little Knoll" Common Road
Ightham, Kent TN15 9DY

CONTENTS

PART I - THE NAVY

Chapter   page no.

PART II - THE CIVILIAN WORLD

Chapter   page no.

Preface

The book covers the reminiscences and events of interest during the childhood and the Naval and Business life of the author covering the period 1930 to 1991. It is all about people and their environment, perhaps a form of social history?

It is based entirely upon experience and facts and opinions as recalled from the impressions at the time. It is not meant to be a technical book and there may, unwittingly, be some variance to the facts.

Acknowledgements

To my family and friends who were all anxious to read the draft but never did find the time. Will anybody else?

To my wife, Maureen, for listening painstakingly to my writing, as without her patience and encouragement the book would never have been written.

To Ted Walter, my tutor, who provided inspiration and encouragement, without which I could not have established the confidence to write the book, from which I have derived pleasure and the fascination to draw upon the incredible storage system of the "the mind" - Superior still to the Computer!!

PART I
THE NAVY

Chapter 1
The Environment

Father, Whose Creating hand
Made the Ocean and the land;
All thy creatures are Thy care,
Thou art present everywhere
Hear us, we beseech Thee.

A bird circles high gazing down on this panorama of colour; trees green with shades of red and brown as leaves gradually fade with approaching autumn; patches of green grass still with shades of brown from the summer sun; hedges surrounding the fields of barley, corn and wheat, a patchwork like an embroidered quilt. A movement near the hedgerow, a twisted turn and the bird plummets down, wings folded to swoop on the unsuspecting prey. These are everchanging patterns, with the contrasts of the season, peeping buds on trees, and hedgerows bursting into refreshing greens obliterating the dullness of the winter scene; the music of the birds with their dawn chorus heralding the awakening of spring; life in its many forms thrusting with a fierce energy without apparent control or cohesion in its conquest to survive and propagate.

The psychedelic colours reflected by the sun, the provider of life, as this golden orb sinks, below the horizon; clouds with their fascinating beauty a complex web of life desperate to survive and to propagate to preserve the species.

This earthly sphere following its path round the sun creates a complex mass of gases providing the medium for life. The delicate balance of nature provides life to the planet with a bonus of serenity and beauty of country and wildlife. Man is privileged in the process of surviving to enjoy this inspiring and stimulating scenario.

Life is a journey never straight forward contrasting like the sea from a shimmering calm and timidity to mountainous angry waves - driven with the ferocity of the wind.

Man in his journey often overlooks the beautiful gift created by this phenomenon.

Inexplicably every individual is different. Striving to survive and propagate forming part of this biological process.

During a lifetime the events of every description form the pattern of living. Even the squirrels have a built-in weighing machine discarding the bad nuts, selecting the sound only when ripe.

Whilst survival is our instinct the only known species with a developed brain, why therefore in its development must we relentlessly and systematically destroy the habitat with which we are endowed?

There have been many events in my life. Perhaps among them there may prove to be some of interest which will hopefully contribute to others in the course of their journey and perhaps answer that question.

Chapter 2
South Africa

The Sabin Family
History of High Jumpers
Poles to Business

My Grandfather beat the pole vaulting champion of England at an unofficial Contest.

A relative achieved a similar success in the U.S.A.

My father, a commissioned officer, having risen from the ranks, and been awarded a distinction in the 1914-1918 war, served in the Royal Naval hospital at Simonstown, South Africa, from 1930 to 1934. It was an important strategic naval base at the foot of Africa where the Indian and Atlantic oceans meet.

It was in this wonderful country that my childhood from the age of eight to twelve proved indelible. These were the years of enthusiasm and innocence. My father and I climbed mountains, enjoyed the rich wildlife, the flowers and the scenery. Swimming, fishing and cricket with my chum on a rough bit of old ground formed the ingredients of a healthy outdoor life for a boy. There was no radio or T.V., and cars only for the very rich.

A trip of twenty miles on the train to Capetown was a tremendous adventure maybe three times a year, with a visit to the Bioscope (cinema) to see a black and white film such as Harold Lloyd, Buster Keaton or Tarzan. Simonstown a 'a mini Pompey' flourished because of the Navy. The Jewish fraternity ran the main stores and the Indians the grocers, greengrocers and small shops. A popular appointment with its agreeable climate the British community enjoyed a quiet and relaxed social life interspersed with pageantry supported by enthusiastic patriotism of special events such as the King's birthday in this outpost.

The Afrikaans speaking community were very devout members of the Dutch reformed Church and to this day there are no pubs, cinemas or

11

shops open on a Sunday.

The South African people were patriotic often with a rugged exterior due to their environment, but kind, generous and hospitable, exhibiting a show of patriotism towards King George V that was in many ways more apparent than in the U.K. During the second world war, they were renowned for their hospitality in entertaining the troops who called into Durban or Capetown en route to the Middle East or India. Their squadrons operated with ours in the desert, and they provided bases for our ships and in all, a valuable contribution to the war effort.

Whilst factions existed between groups in South Africa, there was no violence. I suppose people, particularly those living in remote areas, were more concerned to provide food and the essential needs of their families. These were the days before TV and radio, even newspapers could not be afforded by all. Blacks were separated from whites in every sphere of activity, supported by South Africans, whether they be of British or Afrikaans descent.

The forefathers of my best friend were Boers and had trekked north to the Transvaal in the days when many broke away from the Dutch East India Company. South Africa was in their minds, as much their home and rights of settlement as for the other inhabitants and they learnt to defend themselves against the intrusion of man or animal. Farming was their livelihood. The British had settled in South Africa recognising its strategic importance and the value, particularly of its mineral resources. The South African of British descent, albeit of generations past, considered Britain their real home and lacked the allegiance of the native and Afrikaans inhabitants. Violence in those days was related to Chicago gangsters, the dreamland for those who could afford and have access to the movies. These were the days when Britain was still a powerful nation, with a large Navy, even though still suffering from the effects of the financial crisis and General Strike.

The Commanding Officer of the naval base was Admiral E.R.G.R. Evans, a charismatic character, widely known as 'Evans of the Broke'. During the 1914-1918 war, he rammed a German U Boat and sank it when in command of the destroyer HMS Broke. When he was a Lieutenant, he had served with Captain Scott on his ill fated expedition to the

South Pole.

An uprising occurred in British Bechuanaland on the West Coast of Africa, subsequently to become Namibia. A cruiser was ordered to sail from Simonstown and an armed force of sailors to travel up in an armoured train with howitzers. It was a tremendous drama, the population of Simonstown turned out in force to witness the departure of the train at night. The following day, there was an announcement that the uprising had collapsed, a different story today!

Admiral Evans kept alive the spirit of adventure and the role of the Navy by detaching two sloops to the Southern Ocean to chart the position of Norwegian islands called 'Bouvet Oya'. Apparently they were pretty soulless outposts. A special stamp was surcharged to signify the event.

Shooting was a popular pastime and at Christmas I received an airgun as a present. The firing mechanism was operated by a spring, which when activated, propelled a lead pellet with sufficient velocity to kill a small animal. I was walking through a small forest of trees about 30 feet high and observed a bird with feathers of magnificent contrasting colours sitting high on the branch of a tree offering a challenging target. I loaded the gun, took careful aim, pulled the trigger and there was a 'whoosh' as the pellet left the barrel and a 'bullseye' as the bird tumbled from the tree. It had been winged and writhed desperately on the ground before collapsing lifeless — DEAD. Suddenly I was overwhelmed with a feeling of revulsion and shame. I had caught many fish which had wriggled and squirmed when pulled out of the water, but a sharp blow to the head rapidly put them out of their misery. I would return home proudly with my catch, Why this feeling over a bird? What right had I to destroy this wildlife living in its natural habitat? My shooting skills were developed thereon on a rifle range.

The innocence of youth, being without fear or apprehension was magical at the age of ten. I set off with my colleagues in the 'Boy Cubs' for camp at an idyllic setting in a cove with smooth sands and a shimmering sea. Sleeping on a groundsheet on the hard ground in a tent with the interminable buzzing of insects was to introduce my first taste of homesickness. However hiking, swimming and kindling campfires fuelled our appetites and home was soon forgotten. Mischievousness was to rear its ugly head, for in the evening, a huge stew had been prepared and cooked on a large camp fire. We sat in a circle round the fire, tucking into the stew, hungry from the day's activities in the open air. Unknown to the cub master small slices of bacon had been introduced to the stew. There were two Jewish boys in the group and when they learnt of the so called prank their faces turned green, followed by their being violently ill. Relationships were restored the next day following an inquisition, apologies and hand shaking. An early scar in life of innocence had been experienced.

There was an occasion with my father, when climbing the nearby mountain, having rounded a gorge, we were surrounded by hungry looking baboons, clawing the air and beating their chests, obviously looking for food. It had been known for them to attack human beings and recently they had been heard on the rooftops of homes on the edge of town, at night, scavenging for food. I clutched my father's hand firmly as we stood quietly but silently praying that we wouldn't be the source of their dinner. A huge baboon, the pack leader, let out a whoop and they all moved off dutifully and gracefully to other pastures.

My parents enjoyed a very close relationship which provided me with a very relaxed and happy family life. I respected their trust and enjoyed a freedom of movement beyond comprehension in today's world. My father was highly respected in his profession and as a sportsman. Although young I graduated as the scorer for his cricket team, a momentous boost to my ego. Naval families were a closely knit community in this outpost and enjoyed a wide but simple social life.

I was young, innocent and oblivious to stress, my parents, in my childhood world, were close and always there when I needed them, like a catchpin in my life. Unconsciously I had set them on a pedestal, staunch and solid as a rock.

It was a particularly hot evening and I lay restless, unable to sleep, my bedroom door open to circulate what air existed. We lived in a bungalow and I heard raised voices from the adjacent living room and then my mother sounded as if she was crying. What could this be?

As a child my exterior had become hardened physically but inwardly I was delicate and sensitive to this new experience. My reaction was to jump out of bed and clutching a toy wooden sword rush into the room to

14

confront my father and defend my mother.

Inexplicably, for me and like the snapping of a twig, this unexpected confrontation overcame the tension and they dissolved into laughter and I returned to bed. Perhaps a second notch to experience and innocence!

So many boyhood memories. A particular incident possibly poignant in modern days, was the experience of an innocent gullible small boy, who was to become scared - lost in the magnitude of this ship with its maze of ladders and companionways. What can I do? No means of escape. A glass of lemonade clutched in my hand sitting on the bunk in the cabin of this stranger. 7 o'clock with darkness setting in, my parents will be frantic imagining my drowning in the shark infested waters off the beach. Suddenly, my excitement had somersaulted.

"Be home by 7 p.m." my mother called as I dashed off to the beach to view the arrival of this 8" gun cruiser. A cloudless sky, the sun reflecting the splendour of the light grey painted hull and funnels. The guns and polished brasswork glistening. Signal flags in gay colours fluttering from the yard arm. Sailors in spotless white drill uniforms lining the side. A marine band playing on the quarter deck, the musicians resplendent in their blue uniforms with splendid white helmets adding to the colour and glamour of the occasion.

The largest naval vessel to enter 'False Bay' gently slid alongside the jetty, tugs standing by 'forrad' and 'aft'.

The crowds dispersed. At 10 years of age my life revolved round sport, mountain climbing and a fascination for the mystique and adventure of the Navy. Fishing from the rocks off the beach I watched the sailors stream ashore heading for the pubs and other delights of the port. Three weeks at sea can be a long time.

"Hello son, caught anything?". Looking up to a smiling face, impressive in his uniform and gold braid. He asked my name and said he knew my father. "Come aboard and view the ship while I change before going ashore".

Excitement mounted in anticipation. Thrilled beyond measure as I walked up the gangway and gazed incredulously at all the activity. I became scared and my ardour was dampened as I sat on the bunk in his cabin while he changed. I had hoped to explore the wonders of this mighty

15

ship but instead, was trapped in a maze of steel passageways and ladders, with a man who was a complete stranger. "Please let me go" I explained, "My parents will be desperate". "Don't worry sonny, you show me the way to the town and I will explain all to your father". As we left the ship, dressed only in my shirts and shorts, it was cold and dark as we walked through the dockyard, with dim lights casting lurid shadows on cranes and machinery. He was a kind man and consoling, but it was dark. I was cold, tired and hungry. My heart thumped as visions of my worried parents flashed before my eyes. Clear of the dockyard gates and without a word, I sprinted across the road, lost in the darkness, and raced the mile or so through the town and up the side of the mountain to my home. Dishevelled clutching a few limpid fish suspended from a piece of string, caught in the afternoon.

Panting, not with exhaustion but anxiety, I sped into the house. My mother burst into tears and then sobbed with the emotional fear of what may happen as my father left in a consummate rage, to deal with this impostor.

No more was ever said. Doubtless history will continue repeating the trials of parenthood.

Chapter 3
Career Prospects

Fareham, is a market town nine miles inland from Portsmouth, at the head of the creek forming part of the complicated inland waterway providing the Navy with its historical dockyard and base at Portsea. To return to England at the age of twelve, from South Africa with its open spaces, provided a vivid contrast. The green countryside and scattered villages, fields with the mixed colours of its crops appearing from above like a patchwork quilt. The towns dirty, over populated, with derelict buildings, smoke from chimneys and trains. This was poverty of a different nature. In South Africa while the native population was poor and lived in shacks with no gas or electricity, the balanced climate, and health giving food growing naturally, with wild animals and the sea profuse with fish, produced a different style of poverty. In the early thirties in England, unemployment left pockets of people denied the basic necessities of life resulting in the post war class revolution and union power, but a fairer distribution of wealth.

Life was exciting. A new school, hockey, football and cricket played on tender flat grass pitches. Radio, an incredible innovation enabled me to listen to test match commentaries. On my 13th birthday, I was given a bicycle, providing a new dimension and freedom. Buses, trams, lorries and cars congested the roads in towns but the country lanes provided freedom, natural beauty and the thrill of speed down the many steep hills of Portsdown encircling Portsea harbour. We walked or cycled to school, played football or cricket on the recreation grounds. A fulfilling, healthy outdoor life living on the outskirts of a country town.

The environment has been a compelling influence in my life because my parents had been closely influenced by the Navy, the sea and sport. My ambition was to be a doctor but my father retiring in 1937 at the age of fifty precluded any such desires. There were few grants to university in those days.

The Navy reflected the class distinction of the British citizen evolving as it did from an historic and insular background. My father could not afford to send me to the Naval College at Dartmouth or to a public school to become a commissioned officer.

The opportunities from the lower deck were slim, but my father had achieved this distinction, albeit late in life and by a long and tortuous path.

My mother was proud, with strong maternal instincts, and she was opposed to the prospect of her son becoming a common sailor with 'bell bottom trousers'. 'Fore and Aft' rig consisted of a peaked cap, jacket and trousers, more in line with an officer. An engine room Artificer was the elite of the lower deck, a highly qualified engineer, having served a four year apprenticeship at a Naval engineering training school. Competition in the Home Ports (Chatham, Portsmouth and Devonport) was intense and it meant in those days, sitting a very stiff examination with only a limited number being recruited annually. Schools in the Home ports provided a cramming syllabus. The school I attended concentrated on the then matriculation syllabus, i.e., the arts subjects.

In 1918, the Army Flying Corps and Royal Naval Air Service, were combined into the Royal Air Force, possibly logical in those days. In order to maximise the benefits of this new dimension, it was essential to be thoroughly versed in the naval requirements whatever the role will be, and the operation of aircraft from ships also require the maintenance crews to be integrated within the operation and organisation of the ship. The U.S. Army and Navy had their own air arm, whilst the U.S. Air Force concentrated on the more strategic aspects of bombing and fighter defence of the country.

The Royal Air Force was dedicated to developing all aspects of aviation with first class training for aircrew and aircraft maintenance. Somehow this was maintained, notwithstanding the escalating demands of the war.

The Navy had not fully appreciated the threat of aircraft nor their value to its own naval operations. Appropriations for defence by politicians was always restricted in peacetime.

During the mid thirties, the RAF faced with the threat of a massive Luftwaffe, became preoccupied with intensive activity to build up a strong bomber and fighter force to meet what was clearly going to be predominantly an air war when it came. In 1935, it was appreciated the specialised requirements of naval aviation had been neglected and the return of control to the Navy was to be investigated.

Fortunately for me, before the results of the entry examination were published, an alternative offer was made to train as an Aircraft Artificer apprentice. At the age of 16, this was an attractive and exciting prospect. Aviation - obviously to become the calling for the future - what an alternative to working in the bowels of a ship. I was accepted and my naval career commenced in January 1939.

Portsmouth (Pompey to the sailors) is the largest British naval base and was my home town and where I joined the Navy. A flat featureless island with a natural inland waterway has provided a harbour and base for ships of the Royal Navy over many generations. The town and its environment were totally influenced by the Navy. Industries, business and people all closely affiliated; the dockyard alone employing many thousands of workers. 'Navy Days' were a magnet to sightseers. HMS Victory, Nelson's flagship, an historic symbol. The multitude of pubs a haven for 'Jolly Jack' on his shore runs. Shops in Queen Street, prewar, actually advertised 'condoms' in their windows. Ladies representing the oldest profession, paraded on street corners or outside the pubs. Tattoo shops left their life long mark on many a sailor after a run ashore. Not always a happy or pretty sight on holiday in a swim suit with children or if courting.

Aggie Westons, an indelible home to the sailors before the war, for a meal and a haven of rest after a night ashore. It was akin to the YMCA or Salvation Army hostels but with its own peculiar and special character and rendezvous. The society began in 1876 when Petty Officers from the gunboat, HMS Dryad, asked the well to do Agnes Weston to provide a public house without beer. In order to qualify for its services, it was necessary to sign the pledge not to 'Drink' - a 'Matelots Curse' that would lead to immoral ways and degradation. There were few in those days who maintained the vows for more than a week or so, but all in good spirit. The society built six rests around naval ports caring for the needs of the sailor and his family.

Pride of ship, loyalty, spirit, adventure, comradeship and trust provided a privileged experience to the sailor for the rest of his life. A sustaining influence and contribution when he was to join the mixed ranks of the civilian world. Friday was pay night, off duty watch ashore, sailors crowded the pubs, sang songs and shared jovial banter. Famous names of ships such as Nelson, Rodney, Renown and Hood were displayed on the cap bands encircling the sailors hats. The spirit of healthy rivalry added to the joviality of the pervading atmosphere. Naval patrols were in evidence to deal with any drunks who were out of hand. There was no violence, or drugs in those long lost days. V.D. was a nightmare to a sailor as penicillin was not available until the war. The treatment was horrendous and ineffective.

Willing cooperation was the practice, regulations and discipline serving as a background, strict but rarely abused. Service life and its conditions were hard; low pay, a ship on an overseas commission would be away two and a half years the family remaining behind. It was commonplace for a sailor married with a family not to go ashore during a whole commission. There was an obvious strangeness on return with patience and readjustment necessary.

Portsmouth people were without distinctive attributes or accent, colourless but honest, straightforward, practical and predictable; their heritage and integrity based upon the influence of the Navy and the sea.

Chapter 4
Joining Up

It was a cold grey morning when I reported at the huge and formidable gate of the Royal Navy Barracks, Portsmouth. I joined the other young entrants and we trudged past the enormous parade ground carrying our small cases with the few private possessions that we were allowed, to the new entry building. We were greeted by a Chief Gunners Mate, a frightening figure, bluff and gruff, but his was a kindly smile and manner interspersed with a booming voice. The early days were hard on boys of 16, in many for the first time away from home and the family umbrella. We were issued with a hammock, a locker for our possessions, a knife, fork, spoon and enamel mug, a towel and a blanket. The lavatories, constructed like stables, with the tops and bottoms cut off the doors, to preclude any sharing with a partner. We were escorted by a senior rating for our daily shower. Discipline was tough, breeding some fine sailors to be the backbone in the war to follow. The majority joined as seaman boys at the age of 14, but there was also an entry at 18 for seamen and all specialist rates. Unemployment was still high in the late 1930's and many joined for a job and a roof over their heads. There was a simple entry examination and it was mandatory to be able to read and write.

The service contract was twelve years from the age of 18. Before the war, overseas commissions were for two and a half years. It was commonplace to have a wife in the U.K. and possibly another abroad, hoping they would never meet. The Navy was usually understanding over these matters. It was a bit late for an irate wife when the gangway was inboard and the ship sailed. In those days, Britannia ruled the waves!

The six weeks training period at the barracks comprised lectures on the Navy, its routine, regulations and background, combined with vigorous 'square bashing'. A rifle weighing 10lbs was heavy for a boy of 16, performing parade ground drill, including marching and doubling for an hour. There was no shore leave for the first month, and with no pay to spend in the canteen, we became hungry and homesick. There was a sudden realisation that the Navy owned you and your freedom was lost. The day arrived when we were issued with our uniform. We also had a 'housewife' consisting of wool, thread and needles for darning the clothes. I still treat it as a proud possession. Two thick coarse haired woollen vests and long pants were a 'real laugh' and torturous to the skin, if ever worn! There was a weekly kit inspection with all clothes rolled and the marked name clearly displayed.

Discipline is a controversial subject and difficult for young men to understand but a sense of comradeship had been developed and humour was soon forthcoming. Every night at 9 p.m. in this enormous barrack block with at least 200 on four floors, there was a boatswain pipe 'silence for rounds'. Electric lights were extinguished except for police lights on the walls providing an eerie scene. An officer attired in 'Mess Undress' preceded by a sentry carrying an oil lantern marched down our serried ranks, attired in issued woollen pyjamas, standing to attention by our hammocks. At the time, it seemed bizarre, more akin to a scene from a pantomime. Nevertheless, an essential routine at sea in bygone days ensuring that all hands were present, the mess deck ship shape and secure. Fire was a frightening prospect, but fortunately rare. We smoked surreptitiously in our hammocks. It was an offence under the age of 18, punishable with lashes from the birch in front of the ship's company.

Weekend leave was granted at the end of four weeks requiring a letter of authorisation from a relative. We received our first naval pay at 4 p.m. on the Friday - a total of 7/6d (37^1/2p). I left it on my locker while changing into the uniform for proceeding ashore. When I turned round, it had gone. The Master at Arms, akin to the Police Sergeant, screamed at me for being irresponsible and threatening to put me on a charge and stop my leave. I pleaded diffidently, and he kindly lent me a 1d (^{1}/2p) which enabled me to catch a tram to my aunty who lived in Portsmouth. She lent me the fare to reach my home in Fareham some nine miles away. At 7 a.m. on the following Monday, I reported and returned the 1d. After a further two weeks, we were to travel to RAF Halton, for our apprenticeship training.

During this period, a 'flu' epidemic emerged, the worst since the Great War. It spread like wildfire in the congested and poorly ventilated environment of the barracks and we fell like flies.

Although suffering with a feverish cold, I had to pass the swimming test, an essential requirement for all naval personnel. The requirement was to swim a length of the swimming bath clad in a drill suit, complete with shoes being representative of a situation should it be necessary to abandon ship. I emerged dripping and shivering and proceeded on weekend leave prior to travelling to Halton. My temperature escalated to 103° on the Sunday. A naval ambulance collected me the following day and deposited me in the Naval Hospital at Haslar, near Gosport. The impact of the epidemic necessitated wards to be opened that had been closed since the Great War. They were damp, poorly heated and inadequate, particularly in the heart of winter. I was provided with a nightshirt that ended well above the knees, certainly leaving little for the imagination. The sister, was elderly (possibly 40!) tall, autocratic, dominating. We became inferior, lowly individuals, stripped of all dignity, treated as shirkers. It was mind over matter and within two days, my temperature dropped, and I hoped to be discharged.

Unfortunately, it was not to be, my temperature seesawed from normal in the morning to a 103° at night. After a fortnight it dropped, and there being a shortage of 'up patients', my duty was to cross a courtyard of about 200 yards in the snowy conditions existing, to the galley, to collect the bed patient's meals. Although far from well, I was discharged after three weeks and joined up with my course to commence training as an Aircraft Artificer Apprentice.

It was an odd experience never having travelled on a train in England before. Somehow I traversed London with hammock, kit bag and case.

Prewar, a sailor's pay at the age of 18 averaged 17/6d (87¹/₂) per week, which was in line with the pay of the other services. Food and accommodation was provided, while duty free tobacco and the daily tot of rum were perks for those who thus indulged. After having 'provisioned' for the maintenance of kit and other domestic items, there was little remaining for extravagant living.

In many shore establishments, cinema 'shows' had been introduced with a low cost of admission. They were not, unlike the U.S. Navy, introduced in H.M. Ships till later in the war. Such shows became a vital and important form of relaxation during the war, forming temporarily a means of escape to another world. Also, in shore establishments, there were many who enjoyed a sing song in the canteen where there was usually copious quantities of ale available. Anyone who could thump the keys to enable the audience to render topical songs (crude in particular) became the star!

There was not a pub in Pompey or the home ports that did not 'sport' a piano – a vital investment. Self entertainment provided so much relaxation, happiness and comradeship and it was a sad day when the role of the pub was changed and replaced by taped music, food and the breathalyser. Technology and the motor car drove a wedge into a way of life that provided comradeship to rich, poor and lonely alike. In prewar days, it was the pub and the church that constituted the meeting places in the village, and so it was in the Navy.

Ships on passage could be at sea for weeks with no female company or booze, and with limited space available for recreation. Card games were a highly performed art. A fortnight's pay could easily be lost within a few hours. Ludo was an incredibly popular game played mainly in large ships until after the war. Competitions were staged using large boards.

'Housey Housey' was perhaps the most popular and famous of them all. Post war it was to be taken over, glamorised and commercialised by the civilian population and to be called 'Bingo', a household name in the world of today.

During the early days of the war in the Fleet Club at Alexandria, 1000 or more sailors surrounded with bottles of beer, would avidly listen to the numbers called as they were picked out of a canvas bag and announced with suitable synonyms. The prizes were related to the costs in those days - an evening of innocent entertainment and drama, followed by a sing song, became a night to remember!

Fleet Clubs were popular venues, a rendezvous for sailors ashore, good food with beer reasonably priced.

Jolly Jack has always enjoyed a reputation of being friendly and generous — drunk or sober! Childrens' parties given by the ships company for dependents were always popular events before the war. The parties for charities and Navy days were spectacular events, particularly in large ships with roundabouts. Aunt Sallies, Punch and Judy shows and slides, together with ice cream and sticky cakes.

Chapter 5
RAF Halton

RAF Halton was an Aircraft Apprentice Technical Training establishment with a complement of about 4000 accommodated in four wings located on the side of the Chiltern Hills — a most attractive setting. The officers' Mess was a previous home of the Rothschild family and I believe is still a listed building. The technical training enjoyed a very proud reputation, the beginning of a career for many famous Air Force officers. Roy Whittle who designed and developed the jet engine in 1937 served here as an apprentice in 1923. We were to lead the world in jet aviation; shrinking the world, providing a revolution in speed, safety and economy. The naval detachment under the administrative control of a naval commander, was accommodated in a building within the wing. There were about 30 accommodated in a barrack room and each apprentice being provided with a locker for kit and an iron extendable bedstead. Three horsehair biscuits formed the mattress, hard, bumpy but firm. If the bed was not made up tightly, the biscuits would slip apart, providing gaps and a very uncomfortable night.

A feature of RAF discipline was to maintain highly polished floors. Movement in the room must be made on pads to increase the sheen and avoid dirt from shoes. There was a risk of 'impetigo' from the polish with bare feet should there be a cut or sore in the foot, a very unpleasant contagious skin disease. The treatment in those days was for the head to be shaven and covered with an unsightly coloured lotion.

The RAF, a young service, based its discipline on Army methods. The majority of senior general duty NCOS having transferred when the RAF became a separate service. There was a healthy service rivalry and not to be outdone, we formed our band with trumpets, drums and bagpipes, blown by a real brawny ginger haired 'Jock' to lead us on the march to the workshops. Music was encouraged and it was an inspiring sight at 8 a.m. to witness 4000 apprentices marching to work from 4 separate wings converging to cross a main road to the workshop area.

Sporting and recreational facilities were excellent. It was possible to pursue every imaginable hobby. The athletic track was the finest in the RAF. Ability at sport has always provided a stepping stone to a successful career in any of the services. Whilst I was a promising cricketer, there were many more on the camp more able, but prestige for the Navy detachment provided me a place in the station side. It was the summer of 1940 and the retreat from Dunkirk. The Bedser brothers, identical twins, tall and of fine physique, had returned and were posted to Halton as S.P.'s (special police) normally dreaded but these two with their inspiring personalities, never needed any legal authority, their presence alone was sufficient to maintain the exigencies of RAF discipline. 'Fags' were rapidly extinguished in the 'bogs' (lavatories) when they appeared. The bogs at Halton maintained a special dignity being cleaned by a civilian who circulated with his cleaning equipment in a antiquated Rolls Royce, how and when acquired being a mystery. The Bedser brothers had acquired a place in the Surrey County Cricket side before the war, but it was not until after, that their outstanding ability was realised. Alec was one of England's finest fast medium pace bowlers and subsequently became Chairman of England's Selectors. I was young and at an impressionable age, and they were my heroes. We would play strong local clubs whom they would demolish on their own, the rest of the side providing the fielding. We beat Oxford University by ten wickets. I remember their incredible patience as assiduously at weekly net practice, they would encourage me to improve my batting and discard my many weak shots. Maybe with another year of their tuition, my cricket could have improved. They were great company, treated me as a protégée, feeding me with pints of bitter after the game. I have followed devoutly their activities since those days.

A highlight and stimulating experience was my first flight in an aeroplane, a Tiger DH Moth, a two seat training aircraft used by the RAF for generations. The engine was started by swinging the propeller, a hazardous operation if not correctly performed. It had an open cockpit and communication with the pilot was by Gosport tubing, akin to the voice pipe used in ships for communication from the bridge to the wheelhouse. Whilst noisy and cumbersome on the ground, when airborne there was a sensation of spacelessness and peace. The countryside and towns were reduced to doll's house proportions and the fields with their contrasting colours forming a patchwork quilt. It provided a remarkable feeling of solitude, a transition from the claustrophobia of people, noise and factories. The sudden appreciation

39th Entry 'Navy Air Apprentices'

of space and the potential of this new dimension, this shrinking of the world, bringing people together contrasted with the application for evil to be demonstrated during forthcoming years. As we circled and prepared for landing, my exultation turned to fear, appreciating my training and the frailties of structure and the many moving parts. One failure in this man made machine could sever this illusion. A successful landing a memorable experience for a late teenager. During the first six months priority was devoted to filing a lump of metal to produce a male and female joint to a precision fit. A demoralising experience, particularly in my case when it invariably failed to materialise. Schooling of a technical nature alternated with the practical work. The outbreak of war necessitated the three year course being compressed to slightly under two years, achieved mainly through less sport, leave and leisure time.

The biplane was being replaced by the monoplane, which was faster and carried heavier bomb and weapon loads, made possible largely through the introduction of high powered supercharged radial and in-line engines. Maintenance and assembly became more complicated requiring revised techniques together with sophisticated compressed air for braking and hydraulic systems for undercarriage suspension and retraction. However, biplanes were to remain in service, particularly in the Fleet Air Arm for much of the war. The requirements outstripping the availability and the RAF having the greater priority, it was still necessary, therefore, to be indoctrinated into the arts of rigging, sewing and doping fabric and splicing wire cables for control systems. Wooden wings and fuselages still in service were gradually being replaced by aluminium alloys, light but stronger. This aspect of the training was fascinating and interesting with memories of straight edges, spirit levels and plumb bobs suspended from mainplanes to accurately fix the angles of the lifting and control surfaces. The folding of wings on Fleet Air Arm aircraft was necessary so that they could be taken down on the lifts and stowed in hangars below deck occupying a minimum space. There were many maintenance personnel left with the legacy of their trade, losing a finger while lining up the locking bolts of the folding wing. The assembly and maintenance of aircraft, with their variety of components, all requiring specialised maintenance were gradually replaced by built-in units, reducing time and improving safety. Nevertheless, the advanced techniques were built from the foundation and experience of those old fashioned complicated aircraft.

Time passed quickly, the war created the sense of urgency in the instructional staff and pupils alike. It was a hard but healthy life. 'Reveille' at 5.45 a.m., a duty boy would double to the galley and collect a bucket full of tea. Physical training on the parade ground at 6 a.m. in all weathers. Breakfast at 7 a.m., assembly on the parade ground at 7.45 a.m. and the march to the workshops.

We were aware of the war, the sky lit up at night during the blitz on London in 1940, some 30 miles away. My chum from Scotland was returning from a day out in London on the Sunday when a bomb demolished Baker Street Station. He said it was a terrifying experience and suffered dreams for years to come hearing the screams of those trapped in rubble and the frustrations of those endeavouring to free them. A tremendous spirit existed and people were at work the next morning having been up most of the night with air raids. Pubs and cinemas remained open. When you are young, it never happens to you but to the other 'guy'. There were no mock heroics, life simply adapting to the creature comforts available.

The pressure of work was intensified to complete the course and we passed out in November 1940. The majority of us were dispatched to a naval aircraft repair yard at Donibristle about 20 miles over the Firth of Forth from Edinburgh. An explosion of freedom from 4/-d (20p) per week to 25/-d (£1.25p). Unbelievable to be able to smoke 'Players' openly, after three Woodbines per day surreptitiously, the maximum that funds would permit. It was possible now to drink pints of beer and gorge on egg and chips in the canteen. Whilst rationed in England, eggs were still plentiful in Scotland in 1940. Within three weeks, the majority of us, newly qualified Air Fitters 4th class, were sent on a week's leave, prior to reporting to the Naval Air Station at Lee on Solent, which was also the barracks for FAA personnel. Although not openly stated, we knew we were to be sent overseas.

The war was at a critical state, but being young and ambitious, this sounded exciting, though nevertheless it was worrying for my mother. My father had died in October with cancer, no doubt accelerated by the long hours and responsibility he endured from the day war was declared when he was called back to active service after retirement in 1937 after 34 years service. As a Lieutenant, he was responsible for the total administration of staff and routine of this naval hospital near Bristol, converted from being a mental hospital at the outbreak of war. Perhaps the National Health Service could have learnt some lessons. My father surrendered their rented accommodation upon being called up and suddenly, my mother became a widow, and must vacate the married quarters and become homeless. Because his death could not be directly attributable to the war, her pension was about £2 per week. A common-place reward in those days for widows of service personnel who had served their country as regulars for many years. She returned to Portsmouth,her home town, secured a job and a single room in a residential house where she lived until early 1947, when she was fortunate in renting a house. She was a stout character in adversity, maintaining her pride and self respect with little money. I was the only child and apart from friends, she led a very lonely life. In later years, she was to prove a tower of strength, helping me and my family when my marriage broke up soon after leaving the Navy.

Chapter 6
Convoy

The wind screeched through the halyards and rigging of this ancient coal burning ship, recently converted to a troopship from a meat cargo boat. The intended compliment was 600 but nearer 2000 were embarked before sailing from the Clyde. The demands of war in early 1941 required every available seagoing vessel to act as a troopship to supply the Middle East war zone where the Desert war was intensifying. This ship had a single funnel which frequently belched black smoke showering all above deck with an acrid smelling black soot. The stokers had to "Shovel like mad" to feed the furnaces to provide boiler pressure, so that the ordered speed could be maintained. A curt signal was abruptly sent by the Commodore of the convoy "Stop making smoke", which could indicate a convoy to marauding 'U' boats. Rumours circulated that the 'Deutschland', a pocket battleship, was in the vicinity. Two days out meant that we were in the 'hot spot'.

As the ship lurched, pitched and rolled in company with the other forty ships in the convoy, I reflected on the changes to my life since returning from South Africa only four years previously. School, the Navy with intensive training, and suddenly this heading for the unknown. How different to those carefree days. My first 'Scouts' camp, a trek up to Cape Point the southern most tip of Africa. A breathtaking view with sheer cliffs on either side, gulls screaming overhead. Waves crashing on the rocks below with billowing white and green plumes. The shimmering sea extending endlessly into space providing an intoxicating feeling of freedom. The south easterly wind prevailing in these parts gusted and with a tug, away flew my first Scout's hat, costing all of 'half a crown', a fortune to a boy in those days.

That magnificent country with its mountains, waterfalls, deserts, exotic coloured birds and plants provided endless space. What a complicated and intriguing transition with the return to England. Space was reduced as if to two compartments with contrasts of vivid green countryside, over populated towns with grubby buildings and poorly

31

ventilated homes. Smoke gushed from the tall chimney stacks of factories, railways and buildings, embalming town and countryside with a sticky dust.

A star glittered through the racing clouds on the dark night. Amidst the crashing of waves and spray, a feeling of bewilderment existed with this boundless ocean extending far beyond these silent darkened ships ploughing remorselessly on; stark, silent, each one inhabitated with a similar conglomeration of vibrant life. A moment of revelation.

Time to turn in to a spaceless reality. Imagine the mess deck with a wooden coal chute passing through its middle to the boiler room below. The majority of sailors, this being their first time at sea, slept in hammocks which swayed in unison, with no interspace between them, a sea of other hammocks. This space, blacked out and crowded with sparse ventilation, became claustrophobic with the nausea from the stench of stale smoke, feet, vomit and water from the well deck that permeated through the ill fitting bulkhead hatches.

Youth with its inexhaustible energy, humour, optimism, capacity for endurance and anticipation for the future bonded, in these narrow confines, a comradeship privileged only to those in such circumstances.

Chapter 7
Egypt

At the age of 18, and after three months at sea, apart from a one week break in Durban, I envisaged Egypt a romantic glamorous haven. Disembarkation at Port Said was anticipated with relish after the cramped and squalid conditions of the troopship. We were transported in an Egyptian train converted for troop transport. A bone rattling journey on wooden seats, the boiler heated by wood burning fuel.

A bag meal was issued from the troop ship, containing a corned beef sandwich with stale bread. We were tormented by flies and whenever there was a stop, dirty ragged youths endeavoured to sell hard boiled eggs and dried bread, bottles of lemonade, trinkets and every kind of rubbish. They crawled on the roof and clung to the side of the train. The drink appealed to dry throats in the stifling heat. Doubtless we were saved from dysentery and other horrendous ailments as we were without money. We had not been paid for five weeks since leaving Durban.

The desert seemed endless, a dirty brown, the sand penetrating clothes, eyes, nose and all parts of the body - hardly the romantic illusion of the prewar travel brochures.

Where are we going after three months with only a few days break at Durban in a strange land with dirty sand stretching endlessly and mosquitoes, fleas, bugs and obnoxious smells? England and my widowed mother was becoming a dreamland. War at that moment held no exciting prospects, but youth and comradeship soon dispelled depressions and homesickness. There is always something therapeutic even in a hospital with somebody else always worse off, and so it was then.

Alexandria, situated on a wide sweeping bay, white buildings ringed with palm trees, was a welcome sight as the train finally reached its destination. We completed the journey in a lorry which took us to an airfield in the desert some twenty miles to the west.

The war had reached a crucial phase, Allied forces in retreat in the desert after initial successes against the Italians, together with the fall of Greece and Crete to the Germans.

Discipline in those days tended to be weird. Sailors who had been rescued from their bombed and sunken ships were accommodated in tents in the camp. They had lost many of their chums and also all their clothes and possessions. They were issued with any clothing available but not allowed ashore unless attired in the correct uniform. Alexandria in wartime was hardly akin to the 'Ritz' particularly where sailors were allowed.

It was great to meet up with 'Tunky' an old buddy from my Halton days, he couldn't wait to show me the delights that Egypt had to offer. In those days, at the age of 18, sex was an evasive mystery in which only the brave or foolish engaged. The girls who 'did it' were common to all, the nice girls remained virgins until marriage. A run ashore in Alexandria was an experience of no mean proportions. The Fleet Club, was a rendezvous for sailors where relatively cheap food and beer could be consumed. 'Sister Street' was the brothel area, the tourist trap in those days. My protected life was soon shattered with the squalor and 'goings on'. Maybe my tender youth and innocence and reasonable capacity for drink protected me from sinister consequences. Youthful exuberance and being one of the boys, led to many indiscretions rather than moral degradation. There were two classes of Egyptians in those days. The rich insular minority and the very poor majority, only a step from starvation. Biology is about survival and anybody was fair game.

Chapter 8
Troopship Home

Following the fall of Greece and Crete, the German Luftwaffe held air superiority in this area, and the Navy was unable to operate aircraft carriers effectively in the Eastern Mediterranean. Flying operations to provide reconnaissance, anti submarine patrols, strokes and fighter defence of naval forces was from shore airfields. The Suez Canal area provided the back up bases for the services. We shared a large airfield with the RAF at 'Fayêd' midway between Ismalia and Suez. It was a forlorn and depressing camp in the desert, detached from the active war, no romantics. We dutifully worked long hours in hot and unpleasant conditions to maintain and repair damaged aircraft and assemble those shipped from the U.K. and U.S.A.

Resources were stretched and in addition to the shortage and limited performance of the aircraft available, assembly and maintenance was slow and time consuming. Assembly of biplanes such as the Fairey Swordfish and Albacore were particularly complicated. Frequently delays ensued because of the lack of spare parts or essential items such as split pins, required for locking nuts, that would otherwise work loose with vibration. Safety regulations were temporarily suspended to permit bent wire to be used.

A valued contribution from the U.S.A. during 1941 was the Grumman Martlett, a versatile single seater fighter,fitted with a radial engine. The Spitfire failed to attain its performance in the desert mainly because of the rarefied atmosphere. The Rolls Royce Merlin whilst a high performance engine was susceptible to the sand and special air intake filters were necessary. A bullet through a coolant pipe was 'curtains', a radial would 'splutter and pop' but usually get you home even with a 'cylinder pot' shot away. In those difficult days, each made its contribution.

A psychological break-through occurred in 1941 for the forces in Egypt with the advent of the 'aerograph a single page letter, photographically reduced, providing a corresponding saving in weight and an air mail service to the forces within a few days rather than three months by surface mail. It provided a very successful service and for no apparent reason was discontinued after the war. The war in the desert seesawed akin to a cat and mouse engagement. Rommel mounted a major offensive in August 1942 and the possibility of our being driven out of Egypt appeared a reality. The 'WOGS' (Worthy Oriental Gentlemen) as they were commonly referred, always out to capitalise on a situation reacted with customary greed, chanting, "We want Rommel".

It is doubtful whether they would have been favoured with the protected freedom from the Germans as that afforded by the allied authorities. Wars, age and situations impose a different reality. In retrospect, we viewed them differently then than today with its changed environment. These people were poor, impoverished and uneducated, endeavouring to survive by whatever means they could. We were young and our natural reaction was self preservation from being robbed. Life is not simple!

A plan was rehearsed for the evacuation of Egypt by lorries down the Red Sea to Aden. 'Thank God' it never became necessary. An open truck in the desert heat with inadequate food and water, harassment by aircraft, would have created an atmosphere too horrendous to contemplate.

Rommel was held, defeated at 'Alamein' and the desert war over.

The desert was not romantic as commonly believed, alive with scorpions, fleas, bugs and malaria bearing mosquitoes. Disease was rife particularly dysentery and malaria. Water was rationed and we were very self conscious of hygiene. Sailors somehow always managed to look clean regardless of conditions. A relaxed discipline, mutual respect of the task involved reflected a remarkable feat of understanding and cooperation in an entirely male society with an average age of under 20. One of these was Lanky Smith, as he was called, a relaxed and carefree character over six feet tall, with stooped shoulders, intelligent, with a kindly nature, always out to enjoy life to the full. "Lock up your daughters" was the cry when Smithy's around. There was a major army base camp a few miles away which held a weekly cinema show, Lanky arrived at the cinema one night having consumed a few beers with his chums at the canteen. The beer available was very much of a chemical compound either locally bottled or imported from the U.K., Canada or Australia. It was sufficiently potent if consumed in immoderate quantities. Shortly after being seated, he passed out. An ambulance was called and whisked him off to an army emergency centre. He awoke the following morning to find himself being prepared for an operation to have his appendix removed. He leapt off the trolley in terror, exclaiming "I only have a hangover". He was released and the incident closed.

Sport, particularly football, cricket and hockey was encouraged and although the pitches were rough hard sand packed surfaces, they provided relaxation and the opportunity to meet service colleagues from other camps in the canal zone. Cricket was often played on a tarmac surface with matting for a wicket at temperatures of 110°F and with Indians, Australians and South Africans as opposition, competition was keen.

As a captain of the Air Station cricket and hockey sides I reported weekly to the Physical Training Petty officer. He was tall and well built with a pleasant but non-inspiring personality, responsible for physical training and the sporting activities of the camp. It was a hot evening, the sun a pale orange orb gradually sinking below the horizon of the desert sands, eerie but beautiful. I knocked at his cabin door. He opened it and having welcomed me, took the list and perused it at his desk. Whilst standing diffidently, my gaze observed a picture of his wife and daughter on a locker, and a palliasse in the corner of this featureless but functional cabin. Suddenly, and to my astonishment, he stood up, dropped his shorts and turned exhibiting an enormous erection. In one bound, I went straight through the mosquito netting which formed the window frame and ran like hell to the mess. In future, the list was handed in to the sports office and perhaps by coincidence, shortly after, he was drafted home. The majority of junior ratings were under 19 and considered fair game to the seniors, old men aged 30 to 40. Whilst a fashionable subject and the source of many songs, we took it in our stride; this was my only experience of real harassment. These were difficult days, not easy for vibrant young men without female company. Survival is all about the propagation of the species - 'Freud' - in other words, SEX practised apparently since Adam and Eve. There was no time in those days for 'Sex Discrimination or Harassment Courts', purely rough justice, understanding and tolerance.

Whilst off duty, time could hang heavily with only limited methods of relaxation available. An ancient film was shown weekly in a home made open air cinema. We sat on empty packing cases with a bottle of beer and a supply of cigarettes, hoping that the smoke would ward off the persistent attacking mosquitoes, many of them malaria carrying. Beer was the only alcohol available, but consumed readily. Alcoholics prevail in all societies and Jock was our own special and delightful rogue. He had served for twelve years with the RAF but remained a leading air craftsman during that time because, although an extremely capable and valuable Aircraft Fitter on air frames and engines, periodically would 'go on a bender' which could last up to a week. Early in the war, he transferred to the Fleet Air Arm as a leading Air Fitter. Alcohol was used in aircraft compasses and methylated spirits for coolant systems. It was noticeable that after a shipment arrived, Jock would disappear. Although valued for his technical prowess and endearing as a normally cheerful and genial comrade, the arm of the naval law had to be regularly applied. A wonderful character of a bygone era.

Leave was severely restricted and during the $2^{1}/_{2}$ year period in Egypt, three long weekend leaves were permitted to Cairo, a fascinating city with basic but clean accommodation approved by the authorities. The smart shopping area, akin to the West End, was run by the French. The cinemas were comfortable and popular particularly as they were equipped with bars. The museums and mosques were beautiful and interesting, but the markets, cabarets and bars squalid, and the unwary on his own after a few drinks, was particularly vulnerable from thugs. The superior class hotels and places of entertainment were reserved for officers only. A temporary relaxation of the ban was reimposed following the smashing up of many of them by Australian forces during a drunken spree. Prior to the arrest of King Farouk, and the confinement to his yacht in the Suez Canal, brothels were legal, with red light centres providing protection against V.D. particularly virile at that time. Subsequently, the brothels became out of bounds adding to the mental trauma faced by the British services.

During 1942 and 1943, there was a build up of Canadian and American forces in the U.K. The forgotten services in the Middle East were tortured with 'Dear John' letters, their wives and sweethearts tempted away after a long separation, by these young, wealthy and virile invaders. Surely it was not surprising after the pressures of action and a few drinks that indiscretions occurred. The effect on war-torn young men in the prime of life exposed to such a cruel blow in this 'God forsaken' country provided a serious problem to the authorities. It was like a plague, dissatisfaction and resentment spread in many a burning hatred more profound than that for the enemy. Anglo American relations were severely dented for many years. In normal times, it is difficult to understand how stable, healthy men could become irrational. It is necessary to contemplate the many thousands separated from their homeland which was occupied by equally young virile men, relatively wealthy, separated from the loved ones of their homeland. War is not only about fighting.

Come June 1943 and with the tour of duty complete the unbelievable realisation of a dream; the prospect of returning to the U.K., richer from the comradeship and experiences, but resentful of what was considered then a period of wasted youth. Male company for $2^1/2$ years with the rare coveted glance at a pretty girl in Cairo or a 'tart' on your knee in a bar charging exorbitant amounts for a coloured water drink, who would rapidly disappear if you appeared over zealous.

The along awaited day of embarkation at Suez finally arrived with the 'Ile De France', a prewar passenger liner and now a crowded troopship, blacked out, inadequate ventilation but spirits boosted as each day brought 'Blighty' closer.

A week in Durban and shore leave from noon till midnight. The

South African people never wavering in their hospitality provided an unimaginable relief from strain, tension and repression. Fresh and sumptuous food, wine, beer and lovely girls, wonderful beaches and surf, fragrant flowers, colourful gardens and green pastures providing a feast of fabulous proportions. All the dreams of desire denied for $2^1/_2$ years, like a sponge, the body and mind had become saturated with over absorption. This sudden return to civilisation and friendly English speaking people where alluring pretty girls caused many budding romances to be terminated with tearful farewells.

Silently the large ship left harbour in the dead of night joined by a 'corvette' providing anti-submarine protection, till we were well out in the Indian Ocean and able to plough along independently at about 18 knots, too fast for any 'U Boat', unless directly in our path. Expectations were that we would be home in about three weeks but after rounding the Cape of Good Hope, well to the south, we headed more westerly instead of north. Hopes were dashed followed by gloom and despondency as to what was lurking in the Atlantic following this change of plan.

After about ten days, land appeared. A gaily coloured light aeroplane buzzed the ship and on our port (left hand) side 'Sugar Loaf' mountain appeared with the famous statue of Christ. We steamed into Rio de Janeiro harbour, bathed in sunshine and the beaches appeared packed with people. What excitement; a run ashore in this famous resort, lit up like fairyland at night, no 'blackout', unblemished by war. The anchor was dropped, the chain clanging down the hawse pipe. We were anchored about $^1/_2$ a mile off shore. No shore leave, so near and yet so far, it was like tormenting a hungry dog with a bone that was withdrawn from his reach. There was no information, presumably we refuelled and took on stores and sailed before dawn.

The remaining three weeks dragged. Food was poor, living conditions cramped, the sea rough, the hammocks swung in unison in the interspace with the ships movement.

En route from Suez to Durban, we anchored off Aden for a few hours to take on a number of Asian women. They were being shipped to the U.K. to join their husbands who had been sent home earlier. It was customary for the Army to spend a five year tour of duty in India before the war and consequently many of them married, notwithstanding the fact that they may also have had a wife in the U.K. Because of the war, in many cases, the duty was extended. It was not revealed how much responsibility the authorities would accept when these ladies arrived on their husband's doorstep to be greeted by the other wives.

Youthful excitement mounted as the time narrowed to reaching home, ignoring the threats in our path with the Battle of the Atlantic in a vital phase. A sailor's preoccupation was 'fags', 'women' and 'beer'.

Finally, the day arrived when we steamed up the Clyde. The sun shining on a shimmering sea. The mountains, stark and spectacular sweeping down to the sea, the forests and green adding lustre to their lower reaches. A sunlit spectacular landscape hardly reminiscent of the bleak and dreary day when we left $2^1/2$ years previously.

Troops lined the decks cheering, singing, waving hats as the anchor was dropped and the ship came to rest off Greenock. Disembarkation was swift for fear of air attacks as we were now within range of the Luftwaffe. We boarded a train that was to travel a circuitous route through Scotland and England, touching Wales and finally to Lee on Solent. I was at last reunited with my anxious and joyful mother with three weeks leave to follow.

Chapter 9
Back to Blighty

London was, in my imagination, a mammoth city with enormous stores that I had visited once as a young teenager and later during the war traversed with kit bag and hammock in transit to other parts of the country. My wasted youth must be adjusted and surely London should be the place. The Union Jack Club opposite Waterloo Station was a haven for sailors on leave. Having been provided with accommodation for the night in a cell-like cabin I set off to explore the night life of wartime London. My memory extends to a pub crawl down Oxford Street filled mainly with Canadians, Americans and other foreigners with an absence of British. An attractive lady that I met in a pub escorted me to a tube station guiding me to the platform for the train to Waterloo. Fortunately, I caught the last train and completed the journey hanging desperately to a strap. I awoke the following morning anxiously searching my mind as to the events of the previous night. Whilst not fulfilling my wasted youth with more than a hangover, there came the realisation that in this bombed and war torn city there were still christian people about as well as the unscrupulous. During the war, throughout Britain, this marvellous spirit of comradeship existed particularly with the underprivileged. Money could buy most things, but the average law abiding working class citizen lived within their meagre rations, always producing a hidden gem for a loved one.

My mother was delighted at my return, a glimmer of light at last to enter her dark world. She worked full time at business, travelling to and fro in the blackout with little opportunity for any social life. A combination of lack of money and rented accommodation, necessitated her living in a bed-sitting room in a house rented by two delightfully devout sisters, narrow-minded, poor, but kindly. They gave up a small room enabling me to stay during my leave. It could be difficult, having returned from an evening out which included a few beers, to sit under the stairs reciting prayers during a blitz.

Leave over, and I was sent on a conversion course on aero engines at an RAF training establishment at Hednesford, near Cannock, in the

Midlands. It was an extensive camp located on the top of a hill, which was bleak, barren and uninteresting. Cannock, a small mining town a mile or so down the hill was spiritless and awesome, its buildings black with the residue of the coal dust. Although the location was uninspiring the technical training was excellent. It was a complicated course, being compressed from a year in peacetime to six months. It was essential for those of us who were on a regular engagement to pass to achieve promotion to 'Aircraft Artificer'. We worked hard which was combined with a limited amount of 'play'!

Walsall, was a fair sized town, ten miles to the south, with a disparity of about seven girls, to every man, the majority of able and virile males being away in the services. A dance was held in the town hall regularly every Saturday night. It provided a palatial setting with a 'Jack Payne' or 'Henry Hall' style dance band. Sailors were seldom seen in these parts and were soon in demand. A tour of the pubs followed by a visit to the dance usually resulted in a compelling temptation to miss the last train at 11.30 p.m.

After Egypt and at the 'ripe old age of 20', we figured we had won the war and there were some memorable 'punch ups', with miners on strike, on a Saturday night at pub closing time. There was a particularly memorable Saturday night when after several beers, a sing song, and a chat up with the girls my chum and I were invited to their home for some food. We were young, conditioned 'Never Look a Gift Horse in the Mouth' so we returned with them oblivious at that time of night of what was in store. Their home was in a simple brick built house with a bare concrete floor, bare walls and a large wooden trestle type table laden with food, unobtainable in the shops and requiring a year's accumulation of ration book coupons. There was the Father, in his late fifties, drunk, singing incoherently in the corner with his chum. The lady of the house, middle aged, buxom, her face and expressions radiating cheerfulness, generosity and well being. There were ten daughters ranging in ages from 19 to a squalling baby on the floor. We enjoyed an unbelievable feast and experience. This was a household that prewar existed on the bread line, dependent upon the father, who in those days was a poorly paid miner. In 1943 he enjoyed an improved renumeration with his daughters working in factories involved in war work earning money that contributed to the family budget.

What a transition, these contributions probably totalling £100 per week, a fortune in those days. The outgoings a low prewar rent for the accommodation.

These provided contrasting aspects of the war. The Gods had smiled down at me since a young regular officer in my cricket side in Egypt had recommended me for an interview for the Upper Yardmens' course for a permanent commission. I attended the interview and was recommended for the course in June 1944 following completion of the conversion course at Hednesford. Whilst a commission had always been an underlying and gnawing ambition, the prospect in those days more remote than in peacetime. It was also for my mother that this dream must be realised. She relished the pomp and social world enjoyed by my father in the years before he retired. She found it difficult to contemplate her son spending a career on the lower deck, hardly a Utopia. Her hometown, Portsmouth, was completely influenced by the Navy with industries, business and people all closely affiliated. The dockyard where she had worked during the First World War employed thousands. Her husband, brother and brother-in-law, all intelligent and capable, were nonetheless limited by a system which like weeds entangles and suppresses the realisation of potential abilities. In prewar days, money and prejudice limited the opportunities for young people to be educated and trained, restricting their ambitions and potential value to the community. Whilst engineering was interesting, it had become readily apparent that any talents with which I was endowed, were not in this field, like an investment, secure but less volatile.

As a depth charge disgorges vast quantities of water, so the war upturned prejudices and values. Nevertheless, the Navy like a river, maintained its relentless journey to the sea, steady and unerring, no deviation from the mainstream purpose of maintaining the foundation of established principles. the officers were the "landowners", who must be above reproach. 'God like figures' in a class-dominated society. Nevertheless, they were fundamentally sound, maintaining high moral and fair values which were respected by their subordinates on the lower deck.

To obtain a permanent commission from the lower deck, was a particularly stressful mental and physical experience. Historically, the Navy preferred to select and train officers at Dartmouth from the age of 14 or public school entries at eighteen. Public demand required equal opportunities for promotion from the lower deck, integrated into the officer structure at the junior level. However, the numbers were severely limited and many were failed although within the required exacting standards. Failure, with no second chances, the finality, humiliation, and another ten years to serve, meant the collapse of a fantasy world. Failure brought anguish and torment of nightmarish proportions equal to the severing of the life-line to a drowning man. Success would free unlimited opportunities in ambitions and life style, together with the belief that after the war the Navy would develop more fully the potential of aviation. A permanent commission indeed a 'Glittering Prize'.

My wife was born of a family with strong Catholic beliefs and was firmly influenced by their teaching and practices from an early age. Belief in a firm moral discipline, unbending and unforgiving to those who failed to maintain the vows. Peace of mind and forgiveness never to be regained should they be broken.

The Navy had, and probably still has, this effect. An institution breeding comradeship, trust, high moral values, the superiors akin to the priest — 'Gods' on an unattainable pinnacle. While the lower deck remains brain washed and servile it is forever roused by the sound of the bugle reverberating across the silent water with the ceremony of the lowering of the flag at the setting of the sun.

A permanent commission in the Royal Navy, it was an achievement beyond my 'wildest dreams'. A new dimension, a breakthrough into another world with added and different responsibilities, pride and respect for the high moral integrity required: a privilege to be associated with such values. The Navy breeds professionals, officers and men alike who have a task to perform in a ship and are totally interdependent.

Unfortunately, the business world does not enjoy this support, the structure, particularly of the larger company, depends upon quick returns, putting one over on your customers or workforce. Unfortunately, long term values do not seem to exist, everybody is seeking a better deal.

Technology, the computer and calculator, have converted individuals into robots. In the Navy, it was instilled in training, that the ship and its weapons were for the purpose of finding and sinking the enemy. In the modern business world, the machine runs the man. It was believed that the recovery from an illness depended largely on nursing care. The patient today is a unit on the computer; there is rarely time for individual attention.

Chapter 10
Officer Class

The ruling class in this country evolved from those inheriting the power and wealth of the relatively small number of landowners. Traditions were formed and these, like religion, provided a fine yardstick, in some instances, for services. Whilst a contentious subject, it is a fact that many of our finest officers were from well-to-do families. Freed from the need for money, they performed a valuable vocation and returned to manage the family estate in their vintage years. The state therefore enjoyed a form of quality management on the cheap from these respectable vocations.

As a result of the industrial revolution, a new breed emerged, mainly from the Midlands and North of England; dour, genuine people likewise proud of their heritage. The children of those who were successful and became wealthy were able to join the ranks of this more privileged class.

A junior officer prewar needed private means to provide and maintain the upkeep of his uniform, together with the settlement of his mess bill, which included contributions for the comprehensive entertaining and social commitments that had been evolved. There were post war changes in society which resulted in a more career orientated and efficient officer structure. There was a reduction in the requirements for full dress uniform which helped to redress the costs. When I came to be awarded a permanent commission, having graduated through the Upper Yardman's course, I was granted a single payment allowance for the provision of uniform. Initially the sum provided seemed reasonable as with the war still in progress, swords and mess undress were in suspension. Shortly after being commissioned, I was sent to Trinidad, which necessitated the provision of tropical uniform, and together with other incidentals, the allowance was soon exceeded.

It was a strange system based upon tradition that Messrs. Gieves had a unique monopoly enabling their representative to attend, before our commission was confirmed, and measure us for uniform. There would be no charge if misfortune should befall at the final hurdle, which unfortunately occurred for a very popular colleague. Whilst Gieves stood the loss on his uniform, he equally received no compensation for the shattering effect on his mental system.

It was possible to purchase uniform from other sources at competitive prices but not worth the risk at this sensitive period which could have been considered as a reflection on our lower deck background. Gieves, in all fairness, provided a speedy service, adding the appropriate gold braid stripe upon attaining promotion. Their representatives would come aboard in the main home ports and at Gibraltar and Malta in the Mediterranean. They would agree an interest free credit system providing a monthly allotment was paid to them by the customer's bank. I believe that, certainly until the late 1950's, they would suspend any action over payment for an officer in financial difficulties. Whilst in todays's world this would be considered a club or closed shop, it was nevertheless a comforting service for a young officer.

On the momentous day when commissions were finally confirmed, the uniform suits were delivered. We discarded our serge uniforms and excited, rather like children dressing up for a fancy dress, donned this uniform with its single straight gold braid stripe with its curl at the top. We had achieved an arduous but predetermined ambition, perhaps realising our finest hour. The crossing from the lower deck to that of the officer class wrought a major psychological impact and the moment remains indelible in my mind. Proudly, and suitably adorned, we adjourned to the wardroom for a celebratory drink. Whilst the system was gruelling and tough, we were privileged to be guided by superb course officers.

My commission deserved a celebration. As my girlfriend from boyhood days being recently married, I had no-one to share the celebration, so a night out in London seemed appropriate. As an officer I ought to improve on the Union Jack Club for accommodation. The Strand Palace had been recommended. It was centrally located and not over expensive provided you settled on bed and breakfast with no extras. It had been said that if you left your shoes outside the door for cleaning with one shoe facing one way and the other the other way, female attention would be provided. I was attired in my new uniform and tentatively ventured up to the reception only to be firmly and abruptly advised that all rooms were fully booked. I could try the Savoy over the road for a vacancy. I had withdrawn £20 from my savings for the night out and although in possession of a cheque book, my bank account was only a few pounds in credit. Would I have enough even for the deposit? Nothing ventured, nothing gained, so boldly I crossed the Strand and strode into the Savoy outwardly brazen, but inwardly petrified. A polite, elderly and smartly dressed hall porter checked his lists or whatever documents were hidden behind a glass screen and advised me that there was a single room available on the top floor but without bath. However, the bathroom and 'loo' were only a few steps down the corridor. The cost was something modest, probably about £2. I accepted the terms, ascended grandly in the lift, deposited the carrier bag containing my pyjamas, change of underwear, razor and toothbrush in the bedroom and adjourned to the bar.

There was a young RAF Flight Lieutenant there of about my age, his chest emblazoned with a DFC and bar. We chatted, drank whiskey — not then available in pubs elsewhere — agreeably for about an hour, exchanging experiences with the bar otherwise deserted.

A little while later, I set off in the black out for Soho which I understood then in all innocence was the trendy place to eat. The maximum price that any restaurant could charge during the war was 5/-d per head. there were cover charges, etc. for dancing and any other services provided. It was a seedy restaurant, living as Soho still does on an unsupported reputation.

I found my way to the Piccadilly Hotel where there was a dinner dance for 5/-d with a smart West End band. I teamed up in the bar with a Major and we soon formed company with a couple of attractive WRNS who were also out for an evening's entertainment. It was enjoyable even with my limited dance routine and the performance ended abruptly at 11.00p.m. The Major and I dutifully and decently escorted our girlfriends back on the underground to somewhere like Ruislip. We were awarded a quick kiss as they darted off to report in before midnight when their leave expired. I was then fortunate to catch the last tube back to Piccadilly. The time remaining from then until I returned to the Savoy at about 2.30 a.m. can only be described as hazy. Breakfast was served in the room, an elaborate trolley was wheeled in probably with toast and coffee, the main event being a bath! The water flowed in through taps in the normal manner, but the bath was plugless. I enjoyed the bath but suffered considerable frustration and embarrassment in determining how to empty it. The plug was an early version of the countersunk type in common use today, activated by a lever located between the taps. Fortunately, I had sufficient funds remaining to settle the account, it was an experience never to be repeated.

I walked to Waterloo and fortunately, found my return ticket in an obscure pocket and returned home to my mother in Portsmouth, penniless, having enjoyed a night out and gaining yet another scar of experience.

Chapter 11
Aircrew Training

At long last the ordeal was over and ten days leave provided an opportunity to relax from the physical and mental torment of the past year. Portsmouth had been bombed heavily in the early part of the war and many areas flattened. There were still some good pubs and great company with RAF aircrew from the nearby fighter airfields, and naval personnel on leave from mine sweeping and coastal defence activities. The major naval units were at sea using Scapa Flow, principally, as a safe anchorage from air attacks. Walking home in the blackout about four miles from Southsea to near Cosham was always interesting after consuming several pints of beer. Late 1944 and early 1945 was the era of the 'Doodle Bug' followed by the V2 rockets. The V2 was the most devastating weapon striking without warning. the 'Doodle Bug' in some ways the more fearsome for those in the firing line awaiting the engine to stop, when the bomb would plunge to earth and explode.

My mother and the two old ladies, who provided the accommodation, would sit scared but calm under the stairs. Faith their only protection.

During the leave, I received my first appointment as a commissioned officer to attend a grading course at an RAF training base near Swindon. I had collected the balance of my uniform from Messrs. Gieves during the leave and was now all set, for what I thought as a young man, was to be a new life.

I reported in self consciously at this small RAF training base which had only a small grass airfield, no runways, the grass reasonably short being mid winter. There were about twelve of us on the course all regular officers in our early twenties with varying wartime experiences, the majority having served in small ships providing protection to convoys crossing the Atlantic. The ravages of war had brought home the importance of carrier based aircraft. The war in Europe appeared to be coming to a close and the priority was to defeat the Japanese in the Pacific, where carrier-based operations revolutionised the concept of naval warfare. We were all enthusiastic to become experienced in this theatre recognising the value and importance for the potential role of the Navy in peacetime.

The course involved twelve hours flying in a Tiger Moth, a single engine biplane used by the R.A.F. for initial flight training during the war. A wonderful little aeroplane which can still be seen flying today. Unfortunately, I suffered a monumental cold and perhaps, in retrospect, foolishly declined to report sick. I was anxious not to lose the time anticipating, perhaps rather arrogantly, that with my background of experience with aircraft, that I would be graded to be trained as a pilot. On completion of the course, we were sent on leaving pending the results. Within a week or so, a small O.H.M.S. envelope arrived coldly stating that I was graded to be trained as an observer. My background over the past six years had been involved with aircraft maintenance and the role of an observer was an unknown entity. My life suddenly seemed 'topsy turvy'. As a pilot my experience of aircraft engines should surely have been of benefit, particularly as a test pilot. I had endured the ignominy of learning to be a sailor to obtain a commission and now I must enter yet another world. Perhaps their Lordships, in conjunction with the far sighted civil service administration, had appreciated that this wide ranging background of experience would provide a reward and return for the cost to the public purse of all the training that had been involved to assist me in my later life to run a factory, employ people and contribute, even in a small way, to the economy of the country. Perhaps more simply, it could be fate!

Chapter 12
Naval Observer Training

It transpired that my experiences as an observer were to prove equal to the running of a small manufacturing company as the most enjoyable, motivating and rewarding in my life. In both capacities hopefully I may even, in a modest way, have made some contributions to society.

The initial training for an observer was at HMS St. Vincent near Gosport. Prewar it had been a training establishment for seamen boys who joined the Navy at the age of 14 experiencing a very arduous indoctrination into the Navy. My mother was obviously delighted at the prospect of seeing her son every weekend.

It was a two month course on communications including the ability to transmit coded messages using the Morse code on a key at 20 words per minute. Whilst soon to be replaced by voice transmission using higher frequencies, it provided a useful background perhaps akin in this day and age of learning multiplication tables prior to operating computers.

The wardroom was a grand building built in the 19th century, the walls resplendent with fine oil paintings of naval battle scenes. Highly polished mahogany tables set off an impressive portrait at the head on the wall of King George VI. In the kitchen behind the dining room, notwithstanding all the spit and polish, cockroaches were captured when the Commander had retired and the bar officially closed. They were fed on beer and housed under a jug in the centre of the wardroom. Bets were placed, the starter raised the jug amidst much hilarity and encouragement as they raced across the carpet, the winner being the first to reach the wall.

I shared the course with eleven young naval airmen who, when qualified, would become RNVR officers, specialised as observers. During the war they formed the backbone of the aircrew of the Fleet Air Arm serving with flair, vigour and a great spirit, but not always appreciated by many of the traditionally minded senior officers. In addition, there were two Canadian officers in their early twenties who had served in corvettes with their coastal forces. Two contrasting characters, namely Mickey Coltas, a sub-lieutenant R.C.N., ex lower deck, serious minded, hard working and a plodder. John Robinson was a lieutenant R.C.N.V.R., a relaxed type with an innocent and whimsical smile, intelligent and well educated. He had left university to join the Navy. His father was serving as a Canadian Ambassador in the U.S.A. John was a wicked but delightful character, serious in the professional aspects, but a rebel in all other aspects. "Lock up your daughters" when John was about. He had a delightful worldly confidence for a young man and could bluff his way out of most situations. We had enjoyed a salubrious evening touring the pubs of old Portsmouth. He missed the last ferry to Gosport and with his natural panache, strolled into H.M.S. Vernon, a formal naval establishment near the ferry, found an empty cabin and turned in for the night. As he was leaving the following morning, the Padre entered, having been out for the evening, to find this strange dishevelled officer about to vacate his cabin.

He failed to appreciate the innocent side of the proceedings nor accept John's abject and rather confused apologies and instead followed a rather tortuous inquisition. As he was a Canadian RNVR officer, the matter was eventually shelved. However, if instead it had been a junior regular officer, the matter would have been treated more seriously. No doubt the angels will seek some retribution from the Air Command in the sky. It has always been an addict in the Navy, it is not what you do, but for being caught.

A week prior to the end of the course, the war with Germany ended. The reaction of the majority was simply an expression of relief, an opportunity to celebrate, and the alcohol circulated to relax the mental system confused with a diversity of memories.

The observer flying training was conducted at a naval airstation in Trinidad, West Indies. The journey was remarkable, taking about six weeks in all. We sailed from Liverpool in a troopship that took about ten days to reach Halifax, Nova Scotia. We then endured an interesting but uncomfortable journey by steam train that belched a filthy black smoke into the carriages. It was June and the weather was very hot which necessitated having the windows open. The route was along the St. Lawrence to Montreal. We were only there a few hours before joining a train that took us to New York where we were accommodated in a hotel for a week awaiting onward travel. John met up with his girlfriend, who had become pregnant following their farewell when he left for observer training in the U.K. He was fortunate, since being a senator's daughter, she had access to the facilities of early days of pregnancy testing. The result was positive and she was able to have the pregnancy discreetly terminated. Hopefully he didn't leave any of his friends in the U.K. in a similar condition, it is doubtful whether they would have been able to share similar privileges. Mickey Coltas and I enjoyed the bars and the sights of New York albeit in a modest way with the limited funds we had available. Time to move on and we joined up with our naval airmen course mates who had been billeted in a USN naval barracks near New York. We joined a scheduled train at Pennslyvania station that had two carriages isolated for troops. The journey, including unscheduled stops, lasted about four days. It was hot and uncomfortable with only bag meals for food which made it difficult to appreciate some of the magnificent scenery as the train wended its way through the southern states finally crossing the mighty Mississippi and ending its journey at New Orleans. Opportunities when young must never be missed and although tired, we managed to tour the seedy clubs as they were in those days. Unfortunately these brief impressions did not encourage me to return there, notwithstanding the post war colourful advertising materials. We embarked the following morning in a small coaster type vessel, broad in the beam and with a shallow draught, probably a banana carrying boat, which had been converted during the war to carry troops for US forces. It rolled like a barrel in the swells as we crossed the Gulf of Mexico. There was no dining room and meals were served American style with the food all mixed on a tray which we perched on the ship's rail overlooking the sea. It was very hot and humid with the majority of passengers ill with the rolling motion of the ship combined with a nauseating diesel oil smell and acrid smoke from the ship's funnel. There were no decks to make it possible to obtain fresh air and exercise. We were all certainly relieved when the ship finally docked at Trinidad.

At long last, the flying training to become an observer commenced in July introducing yet another era into my naval career.

David and I teamed up in Trinidad in 1945 sharing the same Observer flying course. The climate was unpleasant, hot and humid. The routine debilitating; flying from 5.00 a.m. to midday with lectures or night flying in the evening. Saturday night was for relaxation, with rum at 6/-d per bottle an attractive contributing feature. Port-of-Spain, the local town, had little to offer. We could be members, under sufferance, of a local night club. The controlling middle class of the town, Creole by extraction, an insular, unfriendly and standoffish society, resented the British and the servicemen in particular.

Awaking on a typical Sunday morning in an alcoholic haze, and gazing up through my mosquito net I observed an enormous black spider. David on the other side of the cabin had also noticed this furry monster. Simultaneously, we realised that this was no apparition but alive and real. Petrified, ignoring pride, we fled in our briefs to find our locally born cabin steward. He took one look and with a nonchalant air, declared "No problem 'baas', only a tarantula, I soon deal with" and the beast was demolished.

The war ended following the nuclear bombing of Hiroshima and Nagasaki. VJ day in Trinidad perhaps can only be described as a frightening dream, the twenty four hours that followed remain a blank, no doubt the rum must have had some effect. Training was shortly to be terminated and the air station closed. David and I being regular officers were to return to the UK to complete our training. We were to join a ship that was on passage from South America to the UK, but had broken down in Rio-de-Janeiro with boiler problems. An end of the war celebration ball was to be held in the wardroom so we volunteered to assist with the decorations. We caught the camp bus into Port-of-Spain early one morning, purchased the necessary decorations and with an hour or so to spare, paid a visit to the factory where Angostura bitters were produced. Colic had been a common and debilitating illness prevalent in Trinidad. Dr Siegert produced bitters from aromatic herbs at Angostura, Venezuela in 1824. Because of its delightful flavour and aroma, it became extremely popular for use in soups, salads, cooking, soft drinks and alcoholic beverages. Angostura bitters have been produced in Trinidad certainly all this century. A pink gin has been synonymous with wardrooms in the Navy for generations. It became world famous after the war, particularly for cocktails. In a bar it is commonplace to find the standard bottle with the yellow cap and body wrapped in the distinctive white paper, the small print describing in different languages, the origin and ingredients of these bitters usually with a vivid mauve stain discolouring the text, where the drips ran down, whilst distilling the drops through the narrow aperture at the top of the bottle. Following the interesting tour where the process was described, we adjourned to their bar to sample examples of their tantalising invigorating and inebriating concoctions.

The sun was high in the tropical sky at 1.00 p.m. when we boarded the bus to return to the camp. As we entered through the camp gates, a lorry with some of our course colleagues complete with kit, drove out. When we dismounted with our purchases for the wardroom ball, still aglow with an alcoholic haze which tended to promote a light headedness in the midday sun, we were confronted with an irate course officer exclaiming that we had missed the ship, which, unknown to us, had repaired its boilers and jetted up at an unbelievable speed from Rio.

The war was over and the exacting rigours of the peacetime Navy had returned. Meekly, we explained our activities during the forenoon conveniently overlooking the visit to the Angostura factory. Fortunately, the 'bark was worse than the bite' and we were firmly instructed to report to the other side of the airfield at 6.00 a.m. for a flight to Miami for onward transportation to New York. We dutifully packed our kit ready to be loaded onto the utilicon in the morning and adjourned to the bar to conform to the routine of having a farewell drink with our fellow officers. The war was over, spirits were high, and one drink led to another.

We retired in convivial spirits and thanks to some ethereal influence awoke to find that my bed had collapsed and that my head was throbbing. I woke David, dragged myself up, scurried to the 'loo' followed with a splash for a wash, donned my uniform and bleary eyed, we boarded the utilicon (vehicle like a jeep) with our kit and were driven to join our flight in a Liberator to Miami.

Upon arrival we were advised that the aircraft had developed a fault and that there would be a delay. A few hours later we were transferred to a 'Dakota', a twin engined workhorse, that had performed so valiantly during the war transporting troops and equipment. The aircraft had not been equipped to carry passengers so we were seated on a canvas bench type seat running down the side of the aircraft. Notwithstanding the discomfort, it would have failed the safety rules of today.

Setbacks in those days all combined to provide an ingredient and spice for living. We set down for refuelling after about a four hour flight, in Puerto Rica, an American Island base in the Caribbean. There was sufficient time for a sandwich before continuing the flight to Kingston, Jamaica. We were the only aircraft on this spacious airfield and as we taxied to the control tower, were greeted with ladies wearing colourful dresses who administered ice cold rum cocktails, a certainly welcome and appreciated gesture. Tourism was already being promoted for Jamaica. Seen from the airfield, the harbour provided a colourful and scenic background. We were then driven to a hotel situated in a quiet and secluded spot outside the town where we were to be accommodated for two nights before continuing the journey. There was little glamour or romance to be observed in the town where the people lived very basically in huts along the main streets. Port-of-Spain was opulent compared to this town. Apparently, conditions were improved up country where there were the sugar plantations. It is not surprising that so many West Indians emigrated to the UK.

The journey continued with a memorable flight to Nassau in the Bahamas. The still clear waters reflecting the colours from the prolific banks of vegetation found in these waters fed by the Gulf Stream the scene for the fascinating stories of the sea by Ernest Hemingway.

The island was barren and derelict - obviously due to the war and the loss of tourism. We stayed in a hotel where the gardens were overgrown, the paintwork was flaking and the inside derelict. The RAF kindly allowed us to enjoy the facilities of their officers' club which had a bar and a swimming pool. David and I were the only ones to partake of these facilities. The following morning, we took off for Miami, Florida, less than an hour's flight. We were then under the auspices of the US Navy who issued us with a railway warrant to travel by train to New York the following day. We checked our bags in at the railway hotel, our main kit had been left in Trinidad, to be forwarded to the UK by sea in due course.

We were determined to explore Miami and were fortunate in meeting up with a US Naval officer and his wife who invited us to their home for a meal and drinks. They directed us to Miami Beach, which was the tourist centre for entertainment and the beach the principle attraction. Although not a night to be remembered, we toured the resort returning to collect our bags from the hotel in the morning. They were sympathetic and understanding - we were all British - the war was over, and they made no charge for the room. Feeling jaded, we made our way to the platform to catch the train and to my horror and disbelief, saw two enormous crabs with psychedelic colours on their backs. "Christ", was I suffering from D.T.'s? Admittedly, we had been living it up and perhaps overindulging. I looked at David and he looked at me and we sped at high speed across the track and boarded the train. They were apparently land crabs, common in that part of the world. We slept soundly on a bunk akin to those in the third class sleepers (if you could obtain one) that plyed north on the LMS and LNER. However, there was an observation car with revolving seats enabling us to enjoy the fantastic scenery of the southern states.

We arrived in New York, tired, hot and dirty, without money or clean clothes. The British authorities in New York provided us with a reservation in an hotel the cost covering the room with bed and breakfast. Breakfast was in reality a thermos flask of coffee together with a doughnut shoved through a flap in the bedroom door. The humidity in New York in August is some of the worst I have experienced. It was worsened because our white tropical uniform was dirty and we must wear our heavy blue uniform suits.

Chapter 13
A Week in New York

The Americans in addition to being very hospitable, were very public spirited and self conscious about us having suffered the major brunt of the war. There had not been a bomb dropped on mainland America and they were most anxious and fascinated to hear or read about the blitz. They were apprehensive over Trueman as President and Winston Churchill was their hero. As we must wear uniform, we became a magnet for the curiosity of the genuinely interested, the mainly inquisitive and a section of the business community who would rub in their contribution with lend lease.

At the conclusion of the war all equipment supplied must be returned or ditched. It was heartbreaking to push modern and still much needed aircraft over the ships side rather than the cost and complication of returning them to the Americans. The futility of political deals for, in less than five years, we were to be their ally again during the Korean war.

British servicemen were offered generous encouragement to enjoy the abundance of entertainment available in New York. We reported to the Commodore Hotel and were provided with a pass enabling access at reduced prices to hotels, bars, theatres and night clubs. We made a visit to the English speaking Union Club our first port of call. It was a club for British officers in transit in New York and proved to be an oasis enabling us to cool off, relax and enjoy cheap but excellent meals. It was run by lady volunteers, principally mothers and daughters. We were befriended by a very pleasant middle aged lady with her attractive daughter and girlfriend who invited us to visit their home in Long Island. We promised to 'phone as soon as we could ascertain the date of sailing for the U.K. An opportunity to escape from New York was appealing, particularly with the prospect to discard our hot uniform and change into a pair of shorts if only for a day. We were given instructions the following day to join the Queen Elizabeth I within a week when she was sailing, still as a troopship, to the U.K.

David awoke in the morning with a head infection and reported to the U.S. Naval medical base, who diagnosed it as 'impetigo'. They shaved off his hair and anointed his scalp with a revolting mauve unction. He not only felt uncomfortable, but extremely embarrassed standing out like a beacon in uniform and with a shaven head. The combination of our financial problems, the heat and his malaise, meant that we had to operate by night. We would emerge from the hotel around 5 p.m. and find a quiet bar where we could listen to Chopin Polonaise on the juke box and drink '10 cent' beer. We attended on another evening a superior show at Radio City with the free pass obtained from the Commodore Hotel. Fortunes improved when David met an old friend serving at a naval facility near New York. He was invited to dinner and stay the night. A major bonus was being able to cash a cheque which revived our very low resources. I arranged to visit the American ladies in Long Island.

The journey was in a commuter style train from Pennsylvania Station, initially pretty depressing and sordid as it rattled its way past the tenements of the Bronx, the smoke billowing from tall chimneys, acrid smelling, depositing a mantle of black dust where it settled. The depressing suburbs gradually merged into green and pleasant country, a shimmering sea and golden beaches completing the skyline. The train shuddered to a halt with a jerk and a friendly passenger advised that this was my destination. I descended onto a deserted platform in that rural retreat for the wealthy. The locals were profuse in providing directions to my friend's home and fascinated with this strange uniformed officer. "Say, you guys have sure had it rough, those V2 rockets must have been something; we sure admire 'Winnie' a real bulldog - how come you have voted him out?"

The walk was peaceful and cool beneath the canopy of tall resplendent trees reflecting patterns of light from the sun's rays. I found their house nestled amongst the trees and coloured foliage set on a rise overlooking a tranquil sea, the waves gently lapping on the shore. An enormous Cadillac sat in the drive beneath the colonnades of this grand and eloquent colonial style home. Apprehensively and nervously, I tugged at a wrought iron rod, aside the weathered pine door, reminiscent of that at coaching inns. A clamour of bells reverberated, dogs rushed out barking, tails wagging as the door was opened and 'Gayle' appeared resplendent in a cool, colourful but simple dress, her long fair hair falling gracefully over her shoulders enhancing her slim and attractive figure. She greeted me with

61

a whimsical smile and an extended hand. Joined by her sister and younger brother, we relaxed on the verandah with a welcome cold drink, followed by a swim in the inviting sea. I was favoured with generous hospitality including a fabulous meal of southern fried chicken, corn and home grown vegetables, followed by fruit pies doused with cream which I had not seen or tasted since before the war. Gayle's parents, obviously opulent but modest and disarming, were to spend the evening out with friends playing bridge. They suggested that we take a walk through the woods to the father's club. We spent an enjoyable hour or so in conversation. The girls were drinking coca cola or an equivalent soft drink and the brother and I cold beer which seemed pretty innocuous. As we set off through the woods to their home, I suddenly realised that he was stumbling in his words and walk. I took his arm and steadied his pace as we wended our way in the dark through the forest of trees back to their home. Fortunately his parents had not returned and we settled him down and to our relief, he slipped into a deep sleep.

I felt very responsible, being relatively a senior citizen, to these lovely people, the girls nineteen and the brother sixteen. Fortunately, I still remained in high esteem. The value of relationships of different generations within our own nation and those of others had not been appreciated. In those days it was the elders and those in positions of responsibility who tended to preach, perhaps even today we still love to hear our own voices. It was simply then a feeling of not having let the side down. Later in my business life I appreciated the psychology of selling, to explain to a client why he should buy your product, in other words, using your own ego to flatter his. It is still sad, with the opportunities of today's world, technology and communications, the jet age enabling working people to travel and experience the problems and ways of other people in the world, that lack of trust and dissatisfaction still occurs.

As I returned to New York the following day, I realised that these people had left an indelible mark in my memory and although sad at the parting, my life had been embellished by the experience.

The remaining few days were a jumble of nocturnal activities. We made use of the pass and paid a visit to the Plaza Hotel, where 'Hildegarde', a popular night club singer, was the entertainer. We were plied with drinks and awarded a kiss, good PR for the Americans and a fun evening for us. I met up with a newspaper reporter who had covered the 'Coronation' in London before the war. He insisted that I view his 8mm filming of the event. We returned to his ornate flat nearby. I felt apprehensive regarding his intentions as it was the early hours of the morning. The photography and presentation was superb and I escaped without embarrassment retaining a clean slate.

The following night, in view of our improved finances, we ventured further afield and explored Greenwich Village, the nearest equivalent, I suppose, to Soho. We vaguely remembered the next morning that we danced on a table in uniform at a Greek wedding. It is doubtful that their Lordships would have approved of this behaviour. Memories become indelible in the mind and must reflect in all walks of life of a better understanding between peoples in the world. Maybe our entente cordial in this convivial environment may have made some contribution however small to international relations.

The penultimate day in New York and I was offered two tickets for a dance on the roof garden of the Waldorf Astoria. I 'phoned Gayle and she was delighted to join me and be able to stay overnight with her aunt. A fabulous atmosphere, a warm and intoxicating air as we danced gazing at the fabulous skyline of illuminated skyscrapers, certainly a unique experience. I had 2 dollars (10/-d) remaining which stretched to a beer and a soft drink for Gayle who was a teetotaller. We were young and it was a moonlight night as we walked to the flat where her aunt lived. Distance was no problem under those circumstances. A young, vivacious and lovely girl. It was a wrench to say farewell.

There was a sequel, as recently, my wife, who had been 'clearing a cabinet', unearthed a crumpled green letter, the address and post mark faded and illegible. "Who is this from?" she inquired, the handwriting evidently that of a girl. "How should I know, where has it come from?". Upon closer scrutiny, there was a college address with a faint date of 1946, obviously a student, with a scrawly hand, expressing naturally her feelings having recently started at college and being surrounded by books and females. The philosophy was fascinating and mysterious, echoing the conversation with my wife from the previous evening. In her letter she elucidated that literary talents and education, whilst extremely beneficial, could never replace seeing the world and how it lives, the experience broadening the mind and creating a deeper impression far more than obtainable from reading. Surely it is only through the material things that we can read and appreciate the spiritual side. Maybe being young she used flattery, as the scorpion with the sting in its tail, disguising the envy of my drifting life at that time with the Navy, to her imagined dreary slog at college. An interesting thought for a teenager. A faint signature 'Gayle'. A letter buried, traversing a lifetime.

Chapter 14
Scotland 1946

David and I boarded the Queen Elizabeth the following morning with the equivalent of a farthing. Fortunately, after much persuasion, we were able to cash a cheque enabling us to travel home from Southampton on arrival. The conditions on board were far from luxurious. About twelve to a small cabin, sharing a small basin with only cold water for washing, which was only available for about half an hour in the morning and evening. However, we were still young and heading from home with the prospect of a fortnight's leave.

The mighty Queen Elizabeth docked at Southampton in the morning and the many thousands of us including some civilians, were disembarked on to the jetty to await the unloading of our luggage. There were trains for those travelling to London who were fortunate enough to retrieve their baggage. There were no refreshment facilities and we were tired, irritable and hungry. Eventually, at about 7 p.m. as dusk descended, we recovered our baggage and reported to Customs for clearance. We were cleared without any delay, but a fellow lady passenger (she was English but had been married to an American officer, killed during the Pacific war) who was returning to visit her parents, was being subjected to a thorough investigation by the Customs authorities who were convinced that she possessed hidden jewellery. They damaged her baggage and were generally aggressive and uncouth. Our appeals to them were of no avail and the poor lady was left in tears. Was this for what we had fought the war? Welcome home! The war over and Churchill voted out. Bureaucracy rapidly asserting itself. At the expense of missing our trains, we assisted the destitute lady, lashed up her damaged luggage and managed after much difficulty, to procure a taxi to take her to a hotel in Southampton. We were fortunate and caught the last train from the docks.

I was granted two week's leave which provided a pleasant respite and enabled me to devote some attention to my mother, who had borne the drudgery and loneliness of working under the difficult conditions of wartime, returning to a single room at night with very few opportunities to brighten her existence. The life for a widow in her forties, still in the prime of life, can be pretty awesome, in any era, always feeling the odd one out at any social function. It was particularly hard on my mother as she had always enjoyed life, had travelled, was an outgoing person and then suddenly found herself, isolated. Although it was still early days, we investigated the possibility of renting a flat or house. In early 1946 everybody else, young and old, were pursuing a similar course. She registered with agents and fortunately, a year later, was able to rent a small but pleasant terraced house with friendly and christian neighbours.

The opportunity in those days was very restricted to purchase the freehold of a property. The down payment and mortgage repayments precluded any such prospect for a single person. The affluent days were far off when, with both husband and wife working, it was possible to purchase the freehold.

With leave over, three of us were to resume training at Rattray Head, an air station 50 miles north of Aberdeen. It was a remote part of the coast. Accommodation was in 'Nissan' huts, heated by coke fires, that emitted a foul and acrid penetrating smell. Relaxation was confined to drinking, walking and sport. Everything was run down and, with the war now over, we became an unwanted breed.

Similarly the course was disorganised, but we worked hard, a career at stake in a peacetime Navy. We qualified within six months and sent on leave pending an appointment. Finally, we were authorised and proud to wear our Observer Wings.

The Observer was required prewar in a specialised role for reconnaissance to provide navigation and radio communication when operating at long distances from a ship in the open ocean. Radio telephony was limited to short distances so communication was maintained by Morse code and there being few navigational aids available, accurate navigation was essential. It was not conceived that naval aircraft could sink a warship, but that the naval battle must be finalised with gunfire.

The role of the aircraft in the ensuing battle was to spot the fall of shot. During the war with the introduction of radar, improved communications and other electronic equipment, naval aircraft were employed efficiently in more sophisticated roles, necessitating the Observer to become more versatile acting at times as an airborne information centre.

Whilst operating from the backseat and not enjoying the glamour of the pilot, he was primarily the navigator and radar operator who practised his skills on a chart board about 2 feet square with an enormous metal rule that could be used to draw lines on an azimuth. Brass dividers with 3" steel points were used for measuring distance and a circular slide rule about 9" in diameter as a calculator.

This cumbersome, archaic and ancient equipment was housed in a green canvas bag suspended from a cord. Boarding an aircraft with this equipment at night in a high wind on a carriers flight deck into the narrow confines of the cockpit was somewhat of a nightmare. The kit was certainly still being used into the turn of the 1950's. Accurate navigation was necessary in an aircraft operating from an aircraft carrier in an ocean miles from shore on three or four hour patrols. There were few navigational aids and radio telephony limited to within about fifty miles. In view of the additional risk factor, their 'Lordships' bestowed upon us the additional princely sum of 3/-d (15p) per day, taxable, providing 2 pints of beer. A counterpart in the US Navy was paid and additional half of his base rate pay. We flew because of the desire and not for the money! There was no insurance cover available until about 1949. The impact of this came as a reality when a colleague was killed in his mid twenties leaving a wife and child. Marriage allowance was not paid till the age of 25 and therefore no pension payable to his wife.

Leave soon became boring with the inactivity and the detachment from friends of common interests. After three weeks, a small envelope arrived in the post. It was notification of an appointment to a carrier in the Far East. That David was to receive similar news provided a worthy cause to meet up for a celebration. My enthusiasm was short lived as a week prior to embarkation, a further small envelope arrived with the brief, but shattering words, "A reappointment will follow". David set off and I was sent on a boring three week administrative course. Encouraging news followed for I was to join a new squadron to be formed in Ireland following a course at Rattray on new equipment recently introduced to the Navy.

News came from David, together with a pewter tankard complete with dragons. It had a glass bottom which unfortunately was cracked. My mother ever superstitious, warned that this was a bad omen.

On my final day of leave, the prospects for the future seemed encouraging. I was reading the paper after breakfast and noticed a small column tucked away in an obscure position. 'Naval plane crashes off Hong Kong during night flying exercises, crew killed'. A line followed, 'the Observer, Lieutenant Mayne performed valiant service during the war in small ships'. With my mind numbed by the shock I gazed at the tankard on the shelf.

David, a solitary minded individual, joined the Navy at Dartmouth as a cadet aged fourteen. He was not typical of the normal career type officer. The regimented routine stifled his individuality and this was not a happy era. He recognised that the future should lie in naval aviation and he volunteered for flying training.

We had complimented each other, he was quiet and intelligent whilst I was extrovert and flamboyant, our contrasting temperaments providing a close, respectful and relaxing relationship. Friendships are cemented by experiences, these we had certainly packed in during the preceding year. The melody of Chopin Polonaise, played on the Juke box in a bar in New York at 4 a.m. symbolised a sad but memorable memory. I set forth for Scotland the next day endeavouring to imagine the future lying ahead. The night train for Aberdeen left Kings Cross at 7.30 p.m. and it was customary to meet up at the bar beforehand. I strolled in and sat in the same seat as previously, not many weeks ago. The same wooden clock was ticking away, its large hands moving irritatingly in steps. I greeted the same barmaid and unconsciously ordered two pints expecting David to arrive shortly. Confounded, bemused, I downed them both and joined the train as in a trance. At 7.30 p.m. the whistle blew, the train shuddered and jolted as it moved out on its long journey north. As if in farewell, the smoke belched from its funnel rebounding from the dirty glass roof of the station. I drifted into a fitful sleep with the motion of the train, dreaming of bygone days, of David with his angelic face, devoted to his widowed mother who was fortunately innocent of his devious activities such as when we danced on the table at a Greek wedding in Greenwich Village in New York.

Ironically I was to be accommodated in the same cabin on the same camp at Rattray. Life was dismal, an air of gloom pervaded as the air station was to close. A farewell party was arranged for the last night. During the proceedings, I dislocated and fractured the bones in my ankle and ended up in hospital. Perhaps my mother's omen was vindicated!

Chapter 15
Call of Duty 1946

The daily events in life became history as the streams become tributaries and finally form the river that flows to the sea, often following a devious path. The cancellation of my appointment to a carrier in the Far East was at that time a blow, to be followed by the loss of my chum. However, I was young, ambitious and enthusiastic and anxious to join my first squadron as an observer. My ankle injury came as a bitter blow and difficult to comprehend at the time. The experiences of life are akin to the nourishment to the body, building the infrastructure providing the vital ingredients of wisdom, tolerance and judgment so essential for leadership in the years to follow.

I had completed a course and on the following day was due to start a fortnight's leave before joining the squadron. The air station was closed and a party had been arranged to finish up the mess stock of beer. As a junior officer, attendance was a prerequisite as also it was to engage in playing a wild horseplay type of game called 'High Cockalorum' played by the children in a school playground. We divided into two teams, ours formed a line with the leader at the head with his hands placed against the wall, the remainder with heads down clutching the waist of the man in front. The other side ran and leapfrogged, as far ahead as possible, over the bodies and on to their backs. The object was for those under to hold the line hoping that those on top would fall off before the line collapsed with the weight. My ankle stayed put but my leg and body twisted, a crack, and hence the injury! My C.O. conscious of my career, reported the accident to the sick bay explaining that I had slipped in the dark mounting the steps to the wardroom. Unfortunately, it was the Senior Medical Officer who answered the telephone and considered it a tall story but promised to send a 'utilicon' when it became available. The soporific effect of the alcohol reduced the pain and I continued with further mess games at the party. In due course the utilicon arrived and the two mile journey in this vehicle with a hard suspension over a bumpy road was not only painful but certainly not conducive to good 'first aid' practice with an injury soon to be realised as serious. It was midnight and I was installed in a bed in the dark in an open ward. I slept until the intensifying pain was felt and the effect of the alcohol wore off and it became necessary to alleviate the call of nature. I returned to fitful sleep.

In the morning, the ankle was X-rayed and after what seemed an interminable period, the Senior Medical Officer explained that the injury was sufficiently serious to require the attention of an orthopaedic surgeon if I was to walk properly again. "Oh god, what have I done?". The sudden impact and realisation of my predicament, my career at stake, all because of a few beers and a foolish game. The operation was to be conducted at a military hospital near Brechin on the edge of the highlands. There was no ambulance available for the journey of about seventy miles. A WRNS, accompanied by a colleague, was to drive me in a saloon car. My leg was bound and being long, must be bent to enable me to be accommodated in the rear seat. We set off and after leaving Aberdeen, took the wrong road and ended up on the edge of the cliffs overlooking the North sea. Two hours of discomfort and pain had elapsed since leaving the air station. Fortunately, we had a map and I navigated, under difficulty, from the rear seat. We finally arrived at 6 p.m., a 3 hour journey that took 6 hours. The hospital staff were displeased as I was due in the operating theatre at 5 p.m. Fortunately, a successful operation was performed and I awoke about 10 p.m., with my leg in plaster up to my knee joint and informed I would be in bed for three weeks and in plaster for seven. A severe ward sister enquired as to the cause of my injury and was far from sympathetic when I explained what had happened. Apparently, the previous occupant of my bed had been Fleet Air Arm, had played the same game, and was in hospital for over two months having dislocated his hip joint. I was soon to be shocked out of my self pity. The occupants of the ward were of varying ages, backgrounds and disabilities, the majority acquired during the war. The work performed in this hospital was astonishing, many of the patients suffering with horrific wounds acquired in Europe in the final months of the war. A magical spirit permeated throughout the hospital staff and patients, spirit and hope being the salient features. Physiotherapy was in its early days and a most endearing blind man assisted many orthopaedic cases back to mobility and recovery.

War is not for the faint hearted. It is a brutal and unforgiving process by either side. There was a delightful old Scottish sea captain in his sixties who had plied the China Seas scraping a living from his coaster. He was interned by the Japanese immediately after the outbreak of war. The conditions in Japanese P.O.W. camps have been well publicised and described but this elderly man, a non combatant, suffered indescribable tortures and violations, particularly as he was married to a Japanese lady. She had been imprisoned separately and tortured with the belief that she must have disclosed secrets to the enemy. They had been married for many years and she had maintained their simple home in China for when he returned from his sea journeys. She was a delightful lady and visited her husband daily. He suffered from an enormously distended stomach, mainly acquired as a result of malnutrition. The effects of the torture that she had endured were apparent but she shielded them with a delicacy and gentleness peculiar to the East.

At long last, the day arrived when I was allowed out of bed. I was permitted to travel into Brechin, the nearest small town two or three miles away, and to return on the last bus at 8 p.m. It was a glorious day in September, the country beautiful being on the edge of the highlands. I enjoyed tea in a local cafe and met a friend from the ward, a commando in the Black Watch, with one leg plastered up to his hip, which he had broken when parachuted into France during the war. He asked me to join him for a drink in a local pub with a friend he had met. We were then invited back to his camp for a 'wee dram'. The return to the hospital some hours later in a taxi was rather hazy. We dismounted in the darkness at the gates. He leant against a tree while I procured a wheel chair. Suddenly, the moon emerged from behind a cloud silhouetting me as I wheeled it across the drive. Voices and the scurry of the feet of the nursing staff emerging, hurrying to the dining hall for their midnight meal. Desperately, I joined my friend behind the tree who managed somehow to board the wheel chair. When all was quiet, painfully and apprehensively, I wheeled him into the hospital and along the long corridor to our ward. I pushed the wheel chair out of sight and commenced undressing in the dimly lit ward. Footsteps approached, leather heels echoing with a high pitched sound as they clicked on the stone floor. We struggled into our beds, drawing the bed clothes level with our chins. A fierce, tall, scowling night sister gazed down the dimly lit ward. As all appeared quiet, she retreated, and with relief, we fell asleep.

The relief was to be short lived as at 6 a.m. the irate sister rushed in, blinding us with the lighting of all the ward lights and without more ado, she pulled back the bedclothes of my chum and then mine to the muffled guffaws of the other patients, providing a fillip to their recovery. We were exposed ignominiously fully clothed, akin to naughty boys caught scrumping. Then followed a tirade of unrepeatable words and threats, but she had a kind heart, fortunately, and a 'bark' worse than her 'bite'. We were left with sore heads and very painful plastered limbs.

Beds were at a premium and as the repair of my ankle was purely a matter of time, I was sent on leave with instructions to report to Haslar Hospital at the end of the month, it being the nearest naval hospital to my home. Fortunately, my healing was good and within the month as the X-ray was satisfactory, the plaster was removed and I was discharged for a further fortnight's leave. Haslar was unable to offer any physiotherapy and the advice was to exercise my limbs. I purchased a second hand bicycle and cycled about five miles to the sea where I swam in the cold October water. The muscles soon built up and at last, I was able to join my Squadron in Ireland.

Chapter 16
'Watchkeeping'

Training, although sometimes tedious, was essential, particularly in naval aviation with the sophisticated equipment requiring skilled and trained operators. Finally, I received an appointment to an operational squadron based in Northern Ireland. It was vital to identify the potential threats of future conflicts. Submarines in the First World War and more particularly the Second, threatened the nation's livelihood.

Londonderry during the war had been a base for the escorts that protected the Atlantic convoys. A natural harbour for small ships and submarines with established airfields provided an ideal setting for training and research into anti-submarine warfare. The fast but silent nuclear submarine like the stealthy tiger stalking its prey was the particular threat.

The overnight crossing from Glasgow to Londonderry in early 1946 was a memorable experience. The Scots with their capacity for whisky epitomised a night anaesthetised from the stormy seas.

The initial training was "aircrew familiarisation" in a training squadron of all aspects to prepare us for forming and working up a first line squadron. There was a comprehensive anti-submarine joint services course based at Londonderry. Owing to a delay of a least six months in the formation of the squadron, I was fortunate to be able to gain six months seatime experience in the flotilla. It was necessary for promotion to be proficient in the activities of a seaman officer including watchkeeping at sea. This appointment was to prove particularly valuable in the future when operating with the surface ships in the anti-submarine role, particularly as our captain had served actively in this role during the war. Success of anti-submarine warfare depends on teamwork between surface ships and the air including an understanding of the operation of submarines, only possible by physical participation. Involvement and the understanding and appreciation of the other man's job provides a comradeship and bond akin to a successful marriage, perhaps the ultimate fulfilment in life.

After a week or so at sea with no alcohol or women, men reacted in a perfectly normal animal-like way when the ship docked and they were released ashore. The majority would have a meal, fish or egg and chips, hit the pub/bar when it opened and end up at a dance (providing they were still upright) to find a girl. Whilst many were a trifle unsteady they were usually pleasant and harmless and handled quite easily by the girls who they often met subsequently in a more sober environment. Naval ports in particular, were prepared for this invasion with strict patrols. Local police were often able to exercise power not normally available and they were inflexible. Woe betide the Jolly Jack who got drunk even though basically harmless. The standard practice was for them to be put in the local police station all of which had a cell with a sloping cemented floor. There were no toilets and in the morning, their first task was to clean it. Invariably, the ship or establishment was notified and they were discharged to be dealt with on return accordingly. If there was a civil offence involved, then they were kept in the local prison until they came up at the magistrates court. In a small ship a drunk could be a hazard and as there was no cell, he was locked in the lavatory. If he had been allowed to sleep in his hammock, there was a risk of falling out during the night in the dark on to the steel deck. To be officer of the day on the first night back after a week or so at sea, was usually an unenviable duty.

A highlight of the six months spent in the flotilla was the review of the fleet in the Clyde by King George VI in the summer of 1946. At the end of the in 1945, the Navy had grown to a size greater than at any period in its long history. It included 15 battleships, 54 aircraft carriers, 63 cruisers, 257 destroyers, 137 submarines, 542 sloops, frigates and corvettes. Additionally, there were minesweepers, motor torpedo boats and miscellaneous craft. The Clyde provided a memorable and spectacular setting for the assembly of a representative proportion of this formidable force. It was a wartime fleet to be remorselessly reduced as peacetime progressed. The Clyde was an historic port of the U.K. and an assembly point for the convoys of the war. The shipyards such as John Brown's building the mighty Queens.

The mountains to the north rose from Loch Lomond and the Gare Loch with the forests adding to the lustre and contrast to a blue sky and shimmering sea. The scenery in those parts was quite spectacular. Ships, yachts and fishing craft plying the waterways adding colour and completing a picture of life and activity.

Maybe it is the idiosyncrasies of the British that collectively provide an interesting nation. A collection of small islands with its remarkable influence throughout the world and yet when the nation requires unity, the Scots, Welsh and Irish all plead for independence. When these people of different creeds are brought together, such as on a ship, they are united in a common bond of comradeship and understanding.

Throughout the world it was common to be able to buy a drink in a bar at most times of the day and night throughout the week. In Scotland, Northern Ireland and most parts of Wales, alcohol was not sold on the Sabbath. It was possible in Scotland if regarded as a traveller. It was customary, together with friends, to catch a bus to a village a few miles up the road, where there was a hotel with a bar, and to drink merrily the whole afternoon. On return in the evening, we would wave at the travellers on the reverse process from our village. Whenever a time restriction is applied there is always over indulgence. The forbidden always being more appealing.

The Clyde review provided trade for the local inhabitants with sailors coming ashore in droves, the landing point being at Greenock. Saturday and Sunday were the only days when leave was granted from midday. The unfortunate duty watch on Saturday could only spend their turn ashore on the Sunday walking round the country side. The more adventuresome who travelled further afield, may have proved more fortunate if accepted as travellers. There was tremendous discontent by both locals and the shore going sailors.

The seaway was a busy highway for pleasure craft with sightseers able to view these mighty ships that had served so valiantly for the nation during the war. There was considerable social activity between ships, including an impressive concert party by the ships company in a battleship attended by His Majesty, visiting dignitaries and officers resplendent in their mess dress uniform. A ship's concert epitomised the comradeship of sailors, with the light hearted banter, sketches, sing-songs in the confines of the ship — a big happy family.

Officers enjoyed the privilege of being able to drink in their wardroom mess. In small ships, the bar was normally closed while at sea. It provided an excellent medium for entertainment impressing foreign dignitaries in particular. The Navy was a tremendous representative for Britain. There was always an atmosphere unparalleled in entertainment ashore. Civilians found a romantic experience boarding an HM ship, the friendly assistance of the sailors, the passageways, the enclosed and unique but comfortable environment of the wardroom with a warm genuine and persistent service and hospitality. The negotiation of gangways and ladders particularly boarding a bobbing ship's boat in the dark to return ashore could be difficult. Drinks were always generous in their measure helped by being duty free in sea going vessels. The Navy was proud of its hospitality and contrary to widespread belief, not subsidised, except in very special circumstances, by the state. The cost although shared by all officers on a stripe basis, was nevertheless, often hard on a junior officer particularly if married. In addition to supporting his wife, he had his mess bill which included laundry messing and entertainment.

Chapter 17
A Requiem to the Ritual of the Rum Issue

As an island nation our heritage has been related to the sea. The life of a sailor in the Royal Navy in the days of sail was hard, monotonous, living conditions and food were foul, scurvy and other diseases commonplace. Climbing the rigging in a 'Force 6 Gale' hardly conducive to the weak at heart. Pressgangs recruited down and outs, drunks and those lacking in intelligence. Discipline was harsh but individuals locked together in the narrow confines of a ship developed a comradeship and the fine traditions of the Navy transpired albeit in a devious way.

Routine and discipline are essential in maintaining a ship of war at sea. Whilst routine tends tends to stultify initiative it was necessary for every sailor to be able to react individually in an emergency. Survival must be an ingredient of comradeship. Privileges and traditions develop forming a vital and necessary aspect of life.

Until 1740 a sailor could elect to draw an issue of 4 pints of beer, twice daily, alternatively 2 pints of wine or $^{1}/_{2}$ pint of rum or brandy daily. Storage of beer was bulky and water became brackish. The daily issue of rum was introduced which became a cherished ritual peculiar entirely to the Navy. The victualling yards located at the main ports were responsible for provisioning a high grade white rum imported from the West Indies. In order for it to be identified an additive was incorporated providing the current dark brown rum as it became known.

'UP Spirits' at noon became the most popular pipe of the day. The sale of alcohol was not permitted in any form to sailors on the lower deck and the rum issue was the only source at sea, which in distant days could be for a year or more particularly when ports of call were without bars. Officers were not included in the issue except on the special occasion of 'Splice the Mainbrace'. They were privileged to be able to purchase drinks from their 'Wardroom bar', this privilege though was very honourably observed at sea.

The regulations for the control of the rum issue was rigid and comprehensive. A tot was $^{1}/_{8}$ of a pint (equivalent to about 4 measures in an English pub) issued daily to all men over the age of 18 or 3d (old money) per day in lieu for those electing not to draw it. When introduced the money had some appeal but post war became ludicrous with inflation. Although contrary to regulations many 'Old Salts' would perform tasks out of all proportions for a tot, even to the extent of keeping a watch.

The performance of the rum issue in a small ship, would be considered bizarre in todays world. As 'Officer of the Day' in a destroyer he was presented in the morning with the stores record list for the day of crew eligible to draw their tot. The rum was stored in small barrels in a compartment at the after end of the ship, a hazardous occupation in a rough sea of bringing it up on to the upper deck and transporting it to the forrad part of the ship where it was issued. The rum was measured out in a range of highly polished copper measures from a quart to a gill. The Chief and Petty Officers were privileged to draw theirs neat, but not permitted to bottle and store it. Serious punishment was awarded to anybody caught taking it ashore. The balance of the issue was then mixed in a large oak cask with three parts water to one of rum. The cask was encircled with highly polished brass hoops top and bottom and the front emblazoned with large polished brass letters 'GOD BLESS THE KING' or Queen as appropriate. A representative from each mess would be measured out the appropriate number of tots. the tot was supposed to be consumed at the issue, although a blind eye would be turned to those who were to be on watch in the afternoon and drank it in the evening. In a hot climate the issue was made at 6 p.m. It was customary for each member to give a 'Birthday Boy' sippers (not gulpers). The less hardened drinkers could be paralytic in the afternoon, particularly if it was hot and exposed to the sun, even more so on a shore base when followed with beer.

On completion of the issue the Officer of the Day must witness that any residue from the cask be deposited down the suppers (drains). There were likely stories of them being tapped, the liquid recovered and distributed for favourable rewards. Incredible and amusing tales circulated of the ingenuity of 'Jolly Jack' cheating the system. The priority in bygone days was 'Rum, Bum and Baccy'. Alcohol was soporific in the narrow confines of a ship, supplemented poor food and in its effect similar to smoking.

A special issue of rum could be made during 'Action Stations' or following the order 'Splice the Mainbrace', granted on a special occasion such as a visit to the Fleet by Royalty, the Coronation, birth of an heir to the throne, VE and VJ Days. The officers were included on these occasions.

In 1970 the Government of the day discontinued the privilege. The fleet went into mourning at the cessation of this most jealously guarded and sacred privilege.

We are all motivated by incentives, bonuses, awards and appraisals. Whilst contentious and bizarre are we better for the removal of these long standing rituals which provided a discipline, comradeship and way of life akin to the bond of a child with its Mother?

Are we becoming stereotyped, cold and detached in this modern world steadily being dominated by the bureaucracy of technology?

Chapter 18
815 Squadron

The six months in the flotilla operating out of Londonderry, soon passed. Londonderry is approached from the sea through a narrow passage with Moville (Irish Free State) on the right hand side and Northern Ireland on the left opening out into Loch Foyle about five miles wide and ten long which is picturesque, and a haven for wildlife. The final passage of about five miles is up the winding narrow River Foyle to Londonderry which is an historic walled town.

Shirt manufacturing was not prospering in early 1947 which was the main source of employment. The town on the north side of the Foyle ringed around within a mile or so of the border with the Free State, was ill defined but carefree and relaxed in those days. Betting was a disease involving rich and poor clergy and atheist. Parallel to the main shopping street there were innumerable grotto-type betting shops. It was customary for sailors on shore leave on a Saturday, the pubs being open from 9 a.m. to 9 p.m., to sit and drink in the bars combined with betting. It was a ghost town on Sunday everywhere shut including pubs.

There was a single track railway that ran to Buncrana a small town in the Free State located on the shore of the spectacular and beautiful Loch Swilly. The small steam trains that puffed and rattled along the single track line were packed with service men and women with a sprinkling of local people on a Sunday day out, all bent on consuming local Guinness and steaks.

The shops did a roaring trade in silk stockings, jewellery and materials for suits and dresses all of which were still rationed or unavailable at home. The return journey in the evening was usually an hilarious affair. Drinks, sing songs and at the border, the Customs. Jewellery was a popular present being cheap and easily hidden, silk wrapped in layers round the bodies of WRNS doubling their girth.

A local from Londonderry had purchased a suit in Buncrana, and as the train approached the station at the border, tossed his old one out of the window. He then donned his newly purchased suit. Meanwhile, the shopkeeper with a view to maintaining trust and good faith, had alerted the customs, who on arrival at the border post, duly compounded it. The wretched man completed the journey covered in newspaper. The services were probably only popular because of the money they spent in this drab, bleak underprivileged part of the world. The Irish in those days from either side of the border, whilst living in the past, were broadly friendly, kind and helpful with infectious characteristics. As in all remote parts, a kindly and generous assistance was available to a brother in need.

My six months spell in the flotilla was to end. It had helped to develop my appreciation of the comradeship enjoyed in a close community, the smooth running of the ship depending upon every member of the crew performing his allotted task frequently overlapping as the occasion arose. Trust and respect between fellow man perhaps the most fulfilling and inspirational experience. Unfortunately in today's 'Hi Tech' and materialistic world, it has become an unknown feature.

YOU MUST REMEMBER THIS

(To the tune of the same name from the Humphrey Bogart and Lauren Bacall film, "Casablanca")

You must remember this — a Barra's poor as piss,
On that you can rely;
No matter what their Lordships say,
It still can't fly.

And when you press the tit, it belches fire and shit,
Right in your fucking eye;
No matter what their Lordships say,
It still can't fly.

Long extended mainplanes, set high above the crate,
High strutted tailplane — very out-of-date,
Woman has man, and the Navy has this Fate
That no-one can deny.

81

It's still a Fairy story,
A dice with death or glory,
A case of do or die:
The Fleet will always welcome Barras,
When they can fly.

PASSING BY

(Tune: "Passing By")

There is an aircraft that's brand new,
Called the Barracuda Two,
I did but see one passing by,
But yet I'll fly her till I die.

Vanishing wheels and but one plank,
Fuselage borrowed from a tank,
God only knows how it can fly,
But yet I'll fly one till I die.

D.R. Compass gives you track,
Going out — not coming back,
Pilots who prang them make me cry,
But yet I'll fly them till I die.

I returned to RNAS Eglinton in August 1947 with further anti-submarine warfare training preparatory to forming up 815 squadron on 1st December 1947, the first specialised anti-submarine warfare front line squadron since the war. Our Commanding Officer was Ken Pattisson, an experienced pilot, intelligent and dedicated to the task in hand. He was also a keen yachtsman and the father of nine children. His son Rodney became an Olympic champion in the dinghy class. We were a 12 aircraft squadron with the Fairy Barracuda, designed as a strike and reconnaissance aircraft powered by a Rolls Royce Merlin. The crew consisted of the pilot,

82

observer and aircrewman. Teamwork was essential, the pilot in addition to flying the plane, was the principal lookout. A periscope in a rough sea was a very small object to identify. The observer was responsible for the navigation and maintaining the search pattern, together with search on the radar; and communication with other ships and aircraft involved in the operation. The crewman was a further lookout and maintained watch on a lower frequency using the Morse code necessitating a trailing aerial which was a length of wire with lead weights. Highly dangerous if not wound in before landing. In the event of a submarine contact, he must launch the special underwater listening equipment to a complicated laying pattern initiated by the observer.

The crewmen who had previously been air gunners and radio operators were eventually to be trained as observers with the introduction of modern aircraft which discarded the need for an air gunner and radio operator transmitting the morse code by key. We were in the transitional period, the importance of naval aviation required restructuring with new equipment and aircraft. The back bone during the war had been RNVR and many of them were required to serve on extended service and eventually many on a permanent basis. There were few experienced regular officers and it was not till the 1950's that there were commanding officers of carriers wearing wings.

These were happy days, we worked hard and played hard adjusting to the gradual changing process of peace. The Irish were friendly, the pubs fun and the availability of foods ashore, such as steaks, a novelty, still being rationed on the mainland. We were a close knit community generating our own entertainment. Accommodation for the officers and ships company was sparse in leaking Nissan huts erected hurriedly during the war. They were dirty and unhealthy, heated by a coke fire in the middle of the hut.

During this period many of us met our wives to be. We all dreamed of settling down to what we remembered in our youth as the stable times. Whilst matured in years, ahead of our age in terms of professional ability and responsibility, we were immature in terms of social relationships. Marriage was instinctively the logical sequence, somehow it would work out without any appreciation of what was involved. Girls were another sex but respected. However, the biological differences were never appreciated or understood by the male chauvinists. The permissive society did not exist, marriages were for life and unfortunately a balance of the narrow mindedness of that generation has not been balanced with the permissive attitude of the 1960's.

Although marriage allowance was not payable until an officer was 25, I was that age and was the only bachelor in the squadron.

WRNS and V.A.D.S. (nurses attached to the services) performed a valuable contribution during the war and were an integral part of the air station complement. In addition to their professional qualifications they provided a stabilising feminine influence in this outpost. Relationships were usually established at the camp weekly dance. Dates were arranged for a Saturday and we would all join up on the camp bus for the run into Londonderry, the nearest town for an afternoon and evening out. It was an enjoyable and exciting time and I became engaged on the 21st Birthday of my future wife. It was romantic, we fell in love and within a few months were married. I enjoyed the company of her parents greatly who lived in Lockerbie, Scotland. I learnt to appreciate the comradeship and integrity of the Scots, generous, simple, hard working country folk. The countryside was delightful, green fields, rolling hills, fast running rivers providing a fishermans delight. Our holidays there were always a pleasure.

Married quarters were introduced in early 1948 and our accommodation was in a dilapidated building with a bedroom, a minute room combining the function of a dining room and sitting room. The kitchen had been converted from an outhouse that had housed a single lavatory. Relations were harmonious and although the site was isolated by some miles to the main camp, there were always friends who could be called on close at hand.

The main transportation in those days was by bicycle. Later on a few indulged in owning dilapidated and unreliable old motor cars. My pilot had an American Model T Ford, a magnificent upright looking vehicle built in 1920. There was a dual fuel system that enabled switching from one system to the other. The use of paraffin was apparently illegal but widely used because of petrol rationing. The black market in petrol was rife so neither presented a major problem.

84

The main exercise area for ships, aircraft and submarines was the North West Approaches, the shipping route round the northern part of Ireland and the western coast of Scotland, studded with the barren, but spectacular islands such as Islay, Jura and Mull. The weather and mountains provided a major hazard for low flying aircraft. The prevailing weather was from the west providing fog and low cloud; a nightmare for an unwary aircraft. Thanks mainly to the conscientious and responsible maintenance crews, failures of electronics, power plants or airframes were rare. Piston engines were very complex compared with the modern jet engine, hydraulic and compressed air systems were not as advanced and working conditions not conducive to the nature of the work involved.

Air Sea Rescue was a vital organisation to every aircraft carrier and air station. A Sea Otter, which was an antiquated amphibian biplane capable of 100 knots was always on standby and ships and submarines available in emergency. John Skinner, a reliable and experienced pilot, with his crew, were on exercise in early February. He reported engine failure and force-landed in the sea off Islay. He made a successful ditching in a rough sea and fortunately, the crew all managed to board the aircraft dinghy. A search by all available aircraft was instituted and within an hour, the dinghy was sighted. The Sea Otter, with a single radial engine perched above the fuselage more akin to Disney World, with the crew a pilot and observer with space to accommodate three, lying flat in the fuselage. The engine power limited its ability to take off in high wind and heavy sea. The pilot whilst appreciating the risk involved landed in the rough sea, realising that he may be unable to take off again, particularly with the additional load. He executed an excellent landing and the appreciative survivors clambered aboard. Weather conditions worsened but fortunately during this time, a frigate arrived and rescued the crew. The Sea Otter was abandoned and eventually cracked up on the shore of Islay breaking up on the rocks. the aircraft had fulfilled its function with the survivors rescued, even though its loss was costly and depressing.

Meanwhile, all aircraft of the search were recalled to base. We climbed from circling the scene of activities with a feeling of relief that it wasn't us. The weather was deteriorating and the prospect particularly inviting that within the hour we would be enjoying a beer and lunch in the wardroom at Eglinton. A cough and splutter as the engine cut. The pilot ordered "standby to ditch" and we sent out a 'Mayday Signal' together with our position. On such an occasion you hope that there is a 'God' as you prepare for the ditching and evacuation of the aircraft. The hungry sea appeared to be rushing up when suddenly there was a splutter followed by a roar as the Rolls Royce Merlin fired and developed power and we climbed unbelievably to safety. Our pilot, Bradbury, a close friend, a stoic individual, had remained cool and professional throughout. He was not happy that we should risk crossing sixty miles of rough sea with a 'dodgy' engine, so we landed at Islay only a few minutes flying time away. The airfield was laid out with a single strip runway, managed by a civilian air traffic controller. The main activity was the twice weekly mail plane on its circular route of the islands from Glasgow. We spent a relaxed but inebriated evening being the sole guests in the local hotel. Following a high tea of local fish, scones and other fare, we imbibed locally distilled malt whisky.

An early shake with transport to the airfield at 7 a.m. to receive an ambulance plane from Glasgow. This was February 1949 the early days of the Health scheme. A middle aged woman on the island was stricken with an acute appendicitis. She was flown to Glasgow and within the hour, was on the operating table, a life saved to return to a happy and grateful family. Prior to the health service with no hospital or surgeon on the island and without resources for private operations, she would probably have died. A wonderful institution, so abused on all sides over the years and woefully in such a state of disarray today.

We waved to the ambulance plane as it left on its mercy mission and shortly after a maintenance crew was flown out. Our aircraft was checked and the 'gremlin' had disappeared and we returned to base as heroes with our picture in the Scottish Daily Express, how or why, only the media could explain.

Life is all about people and comradeship and certainly in 815 Squadron there was no shortage of either. Many achieved success. My pilot, Chico Roberts, during the first year, made Rear Admiral; Rob Greenshields, a good friend, made Captain and Den Deakin, godfather to my eldest son, disregarded by their Lordships for a permanent commission, became 'Senior Pilot' of Quantas.

There were sad parts too. Soon after I left the squadron for a year's exchange with the U.S. Navy my great friend, pilot and comrade in many exploits was seriously injured, and fortunate to survive, but grounded from flying. It was on return from a night sortie, when he left the aircraft to cross the perimeter track to the dispersal,shielding his face from the wind and rain, that he was knocked over by the bus that had arrived to take the aircrew back to the camp. Flying was a major part of his life, a stoic type, and after a course, he became an 'Air Direction Officer'.

Further sad news was to follow. Periodically, aircrew must practise survival should they ditch or descend into the sea by parachute. It was treated as a day out for the 'boys' being held in a hotel with a swimming pool, some thirty miles along the coast. It was customary after the ordeal to retire to a local hostelry (Inn in Ireland) and consume the local 'Guinness' before returning in the bus to Eglinton. About halfway along the coast, a stop was made to answer the call of nature. It was necessary to climb up a steep cliff from the road, and apparently David Wynne Roberts, the C.O., slipped and collapsed. After what must have been a frightening drive back to the camp, and whilst on the operating table, he died, apparently from a burst bladder.

A sad end for such a young, ambitious and gifted officer. He had become C.O. of the squadron in April 1949, and was a natural and enthusiastic leader and competent pilot who rapidly motivated our activities. He was a devout supporter of the Fleet Air Arm, newly formed at the outbreak of war, with inadequate and obsolete aircraft, which flourished thanks in particular to the RNVR and special service officers such as himself who helped to create an unique sensitivity and pride. They certainly stimulated a change of thinking in a Navy buried in tradition and resentful of change. After the war, many stayed on with a four year extended service commission becoming R.N.(A). In 1949 their Lordships issued an Admiralty Fleet Order that the 'A' symbol be removed. David had arranged a memorable party as a requiem to the cessation of the wearing of this distinction. Woe betide any officer who removed it prematurely! The Captain and Commander were the only non 'A' officers invited. At the midnight hour, suitably refreshed with alcoholic stimulant, we all somberely filed past a draped coffin in the wardroom, chanting the 'A25', with a bottle of Guinness upright in the starboard hand and the 'A' deposited into the coffin with the port. I believe there was a signal made to all air stations and carriers coordinating the ceremony. It was observed on the following morning that a pair of 'WRNS bloomers' had been hoisted close up the yardarm of the Wardroom flagpost. Perhaps bizarre in this modern world where we have become a number on a computer screen.

The A25 Song
(Tune: Villikins and his Dinah)

If the Fleet Air Arm has a hymn, although that is not quite the correct term, this is it: sung in the Wardrooms of every carrier and naval air station all over the world over the years in many varying forms; but always with the chorus playing tribute to the ability to sign the Accident Report Form A25. The original Song Book had 13 verses; now, very appropriately, 25 have been found, including the original version written in Cabin 75, in the Arab Quarter of HMS Formidable 1942/43 by David A.Wright of 893 Squadron and Derek Stevenson. Since then, deserved popularity and constant repetition has resulted in scores of small variations in the lines, some changing of the original (particularly verse 3, first line), as well as many additions, right up to the 1970's with Phantoms and Buccaneers. Apparently a separate 'Rotary Wing' version exists. The version printed below includes much of the original (some verses of which did not become as popular as others) and the best that could be done was to arrive at a full, acceptable, and reasonably well-known form of words.

1.   I'll sing you a song about sailors who fly,
     A Formidable Fleet Air Arm pilot am I
     I've seized up 'em all — Merlins, Cyclones and Taurus
     And many's the time that I've chanted this chorus.....

Chorus (between each verse)

**Cracking show, I'm alive,
But I've still got to render my A25.**

2. They say in the Air Force a landing's okay,
    If the pilot gets out and can still walk away,
    But in the Fleet Air Arm the prospects are grim
    If the batsman says cut and the bastard spins in!

3. I fly for a living, and not just for fun,
    I'm not awfully anxious to hack down the Hun,
    And as for deck-landings at night in the dark,
    As I told Wings this morning, 'Fuck that for a lark'.

4. Tail up down the flight deck to do an umbrella
    I remember to late to fine pitch the propeller,
    So I stamp on the wheel brakes and then get the shits,
    As the whole bloody issue goes arse over tits.

5. When the batsman gives 'Lower' I always go higher,
    I drift off to starboard and prang my Seafire,
    The boys in the Goofers all think that I'm green,
    But I get my commission from Supermarine.

**815 Squadron
A Quiet night at sea**

Chapter 19
USA Duty

David the C.O., realising that my time in the squadron was drawing to a close and that my experience could be of benefit, recommended me for exchange duty in an anti-submarine squadron with the U.S. Navy for a year. Fortunately I fulfilled the requirements required in rank, seniority and experience in anti-submarine warfare. The news seemed unbelievable, what a break, America, the land of plenty modern aircraft and equipment, an adventure into the unknown, the first 'Observer Exchange Officer'. It was permissible to take a family, transportation paid for by the Government.

We were to sail within two weeks, in naval terms, 'a pierhead jump'. Formalities were complicated, my son only eight weeks old and registered in Belfast, the Cunard Line restricted the travel of babies to under three months. Innoculations, vaccinations etc. all to be finalised. A visit to the Admiralty and thanks to the incredible cooperation of their civil servants, we embarked in the Queen Elizabeth I from Southampton, my Mother waving nobly from the quayside. Unbelievable luxury after wartime days, food and accommodation paid for by their Lordships. Because of the tight currency restrictions, we were only permitted to leave the country with £5 per head, pretty meagre to cover a five day crossing including a baby. Nevertheless, an unbelievable experience after austere Britain, five glorious days, superb service, fabulous food and company shared with wife and son. There were three other officers for exchange duty with day and night fighter speciality. Ray Lygo, an outstanding pilot who subsequently became an Admiral and was Knighted. He followed his naval career by becoming Chief Executive in British Aerospace. Nick Goodhart an outstanding glider pilot and engineer officer also became an Admiral. He invented the mirror deck landing system which was adopted by the U.S. Navy.

The skyline of Manhattan provided a spectacular impression as we sailed up the Hudson river viewing the Statue of Liberty with the mighty skyscrapers dominating the background, still unique to New York in those days.

We were dispatched from the British Joint Services Mission in Washington to our respective units within the U.S. Navy. Ray Lygo and I were given orders to report to staff headquarters Atlantic (COM AIR LANT) Fleet, Norfolk, Virginia. The heat in early August was humid and stifling and the journey by paddle steamer down the Potomac and Chesapeake Bay, instead of being romantic was stressful. The heat, change of routine with feeding made it very debilitating to my son still under three months old. We landed at Norfolk, Virginia in the morning and checked into a hotel room, hot and tired, my wife and son particularly distressed. I dug out a creased white drill suit, smartened myself up and caught a tram to the naval air base some ten miles away.

The size of this base was 'mind boggling', the air base probably larger than Heathrow as it was in those days. Illusions of grandeur soon diminished as we sat as it seemed for hours in a soulless office ignored by all. Suddenly, a tall well built Lieutenant Commander appeared who I recognised as the C.O. of the PV2-—Neptune aircraft, a new plane fitted with sophisticated electronic equipment. He had visited us in Northern Ireland last year on a supposed flag waving mission. I learnt in later years that the US Navy were endeavouring to sell it to the RAF Coastal Command but apparently without success. I rose and introduced myself and he recognised me immediately, wheels were soon turned. When his Captain appeared he soon dispensed with the formalities, Fred inquired where we were staying and as soon as he appreciated that my wife and baby were alone, he 'phoned his wife who drove over and collected them. Ray Lygo was then a bachelor and moved into the bachelor officer quarters on the base until he left to join a squadron in Jacksonville, Florida.

Chapter 20
Fred & Dottie

Fred was like many young men in the war, suddenly torn away from their dear ones. He was the son of a Commander in the US Navy based in Florida where he spent his final years at school. He was a great sportsman excelling at boxing and American football. He gained a scholarship to university because of his prowess at football from which he suffered serious injuries to his chest and legs resulting in disability in later life.

The war clouds were gathering when he graduated from university. He applied to join the U.S. Air Force but was rejected because of his physical disabilities. The U.S. Navy, however, were desperate for pilots foreseeing the possibility of war, and he was accepted for flying training. Fred was a newly qualified pilot stationed at the main naval base at San Diego when war broke out in the Pacific. It was here that he met Dottie, a graduate at the University of California, a very intelligent, talented and attractive young lady. A whirlwind romance, typical of those times and within two days of meeting, they were married. As with so many newly weds in those days, the euphoria was terminated as suddenly as it had erupted for within a fortnight, Fred was given orders to join a PBY (Catalina) Squadron in the West Pacific. Dottie meanwhile graduated and found a job.

The PBY was a twin engined amphibian (capable of landing on land or sea) obsolescent with a maximum speed of 190 mph entirely unsuitable for operating against Japanese task forces with fighter protection such as the Kawasaki (Swallow) capable of flying at 368 mph. The Americans possessed experienced and ingenious aviators who appreciated that the PBY was versatile and ideal for operating amongst the Solomon Islands. The Japanese moved troops and supplies in merchant ships with destroyer escort at night. The PBY was painted black as camouflage and would attack low down at night using the islands and darkness as cover. They inflicted considerable damage providing a valuable contribution to the war effort. They were known as the

'Black Cats' and feared by the Japanese.

Because of their versatility as an amphibian, they were also used for Air Sea Rescue and covert operations landing intelligence personnel to cooperate with the friendly native islanders supportive to the allied cause by reporting enemy movements.

Fred was on patrol and observed what appeared to be ditched aircrew waving from their dinghy. He was unable to raise his base regarding the sighting and for permission to make a rescue attempt. The weather conditions were unsuitable for a normal landing, but Fred ditched bombs and superfluous weight and displaying great airmanship, landed and rescued the crew. Take off was extremely hazardous being exposed to the fire of the Japanese and the difficult sea conditions. He returned to base and received a citation and 'Air Force Cross' by a senior Air Force Officer for his courage and resolution. Apparently, one member of the crew was a senior Intelligence Officer who had been working in the islands, and was being hounded by the Japanese and had lost the means of radio communication. Fred was fortunate and warded off a court martial by his Commanding Officer for exposing his crew and aircraft to unnecessary risk without first obtaining permission. The ways of authority, even in war, can be puzzling.

Fred returned to his bride and they produced two lovely daughters and a son, all extremely successful. He continued a successful career in the Navy. Aviation was his true love, flying all types, including the Constellation prior to retirement around 1960.

We maintain a close relationship, visiting each other's homes and enjoying the fascinating experience of meeting each other's middle aged children and their families. Perhaps it might be considered arrogant in today's world for naval aviators to find and enjoy a common frequency tuned into by their civilian counterparts.

Fred. a pugnacious, determined and dedicated personality, concerned with the affairs of his country and the world. Physically and mentally strong, a rare personality in the world of today. Dorothy (Dottie) his wife, a most attractive and endearing lady, intelligent, discerning and patient. She has been a rock and provided a stabilising influence releasing Fred to be able to realise his attributes naturally.

Fred Gage

Love and partnership in marriage enable a success in life that might otherwise have been repressed. Friends unite and this book is about people and comradeship. Our relationship with Fred and Dottie will remain as a tattoo throughout our life.

An interpretation of life in the carrier U.S.N. 'Mindoro', an escort carrier, by a colleague who was in the squadron VC23.

FIRST EPISTLE FOR THE NIGHT CARRIER PILOT
or
"You speak, Joe"

1.   Harken all ye fledglins who wouldst fain operate the great iron bird through darkest night, from the tilting airdrome of ye Fallen Angel MINDORO; for it requireth technique which cometh to no man naturally, and is acquired only by great diligence and perseverance; throughout ye endless hours flown on "Ye Clearance Operationale", countless let-downs via ye GCA at the witching hour of midnite, and an all abiding faith in the Father Almighty and Wild Bill Privett.

2.   Listen ye to the Centurian, for he speaketh from vast wisdom and great knowledge. He hath experienced ye tightened grommet many times whilst being catapulted on a one-finger turn-up into the pit of blackness that yawns onward from Fly One; pedals at ye sign of the come-on; and myriad are the numbers of liberty launches he has piloted through dark and stormy seas, whilst friends cavort gaily in ye cabarets. And take heed that by these presents ye shall know that he is a wiser and sadder man than thou.

3.   Heedeth ye not he who speaketh of the romance and glamour of the high seas. Be ye not swayed when he extelleth the sting of salt spray upon thy lips and the roll of the stout deck beneath thy feet,and the exotic people of foreign lands beyond the horizon.

4.   For the salt spray wideth up in the joe, and the roll of the stout deck putteth thee on ye binnacle list with a wretching of the belly, and he who enticeth thee will wave thee goodbye from the shore, and consider the foolish plight o'er a cool glass at ye local bar.

5.   He wouldst fain take thee from thy loved ones and cast thee amongst the riff-raff of all nations who will approach thee with extended palm, (or offer to exchange thy money for ye local worthless script).

6.   Turneth ye a deaf ear to all these things for he speaketh as a man with holes in his head and quoteth from "Our Navy" and wouldst fain have it in you rather than him.

7.   But then thy time cometh to go, as it must to all producers, go ye forth bravely, heed ye all the words of wisdom, and treat ye well the main propulsion assistant, lest he blow tubes in thy face at the cut.

8.   Saluteth grandly ye Officer of the Deck, lest he inspect thy suitcase as thou smuggleth thy weeds ashore in foreign lands, gripeth not at the unfairness of the mess share, and criticise ye not those who weareth the black shoe, for at the mercy of Bupers, ye may some day be one of them, and be forced to weareth ye bridge coat at starboard aft. helping aboard ye drunken sailor.

9.   Dreameth ye not whilst in thy hammock of thy loved ones, for verily I say unto you, thou wilst be bitterly awakened by ye strident tones of ye general alarm, known also as "Ye Officers Reveille" and be forced to climb ladders to the cold and forbidding roof of ye airdrome for quarters.

10.   Delayeth not at the signal to man thy blue winged monster and beware thy saddist at Fly One, regard him with exceeding wariness. For while he bringeth ye up to the spot, and smileth confidently, he concealeth a serpent in his breast and plotteth all manner of evil against thee.

11.   He smileth not for thee, but smirketh thy youth and helpfulness and gleaneth greatly at his power over thee, all the while appearing like a green monster in the glow of thy starboard wingtip lamp.

12.   Heed ye his signals promptly, else he windeth thee off whilst thou art checking thy mags or whilst the number one elevator goeth down, for he is a man of great imagination and enjoyeth a jest mightily.

13.   Know ye well the officer called "Landing Signal" for he is short on brains and poorly coordinated. Though he smileth at thee and feign friendship, he looketh only for the ride to ye beach, and hath been heard to murmur "Bust your Ass" as ye pilots take ye cut.

14.   He has eyes with which to see, but they are weak and he distinguisheth day from night only with exceeding difficulty.

15.   He waveth off ye helicopter saying "Land ye not on a pass which is so long in the groove.

16.   But angereth him not lest he bringeth thee in low and slow and spinneth thee into the potato locker, laughing all the while at thy stupidity.

17.   Cursed be he who lingereth in the arresting gear for he causeth his wingman to be waved off on a "Roger" pass and the new man to become long in the groove.

18.   He is thrice dammed and all people even unto the Air Boss shall revile him and use strong language on his behalf, for he is indeed a plumber and a plague upon the Squadron.

19.   Render unto Caesar that which is Caesars. As the two-finger turnup is the signal to fly, so is the cut the signal to land.

20.   Therefore I say unto you, "Holdeth ye not after the cut for whosoever floateth into the barriers soweth great anguish in the breast of the maintenance officer and causeth a blue cloud to form at the bridge, and meaneth five days in hack upon return from ye Sea.

21.   The wise pilot engageth an early wire smartly but the fool shall dwell in his quarters forever.

22.   Hell hath no fury like a Catapult Officer scorned, for whosoever arouseth his wrath receiveth a cold shot and the next of kin knoweth great anguish and collect 10 G's.

23.   Beware ye of ye Old Man on the bridge, and regardeth him highly for he is all-powerful. When he approacheth, linger ye not in Flight Deck Control, for he falleth like a Whirlwind upon the idle, and launcheth his anger upon the idle, and launcheth his anger upon the junior grade Lieutenant without compassion.

24.   Adventure will be thine in strange, intriguing lands, but heed ye well thy boat schedule, lest thou be set upon by temptation and lust, for it is truly known that ye warm sack is a better bargain at 200 lire than ye cold bumboat at 500.

25.   Let local vintage tempt ye not, lest thy stomach revolt, ye head explode and ye grommet work double time, for it is truly said that ye native drink is often ye American poison.

26.   Spendeth not thy hard-earned cash for the baubles and trinkets offered thee, for verily they are made in the U.S.A. and anyway, they canst be bought with weeds.

27.   Scorneth not the urchin of the street, for it is said in the Scripture "God Bless him, it may be your own".

28.   Heedeth well these words, for they are the bitter fruit of those who go before you, guard thy virtue jealously, lest thou curseth thyself and fear to pass the load Heavenward when lost and spinning on instruments.

29.   Know then, should ye choose to follow these sage words, ye shall live to retire on thirty, and so shall your words benefit those who follow you. For in the realm of the night carrier pilot, many are called, but few are chosen, so harken ye to join the chosen few.

Chapter 21
VC23 USN

My duty was with an anti-submarine squadron based at Norfolk, Virginia, USA.

Fred and his wife, Dottie, were wonderful and assisted in finding an apartment. We learnt to our horror that 'furnished' didn't include kitchen utensils, bed clothes, cutlery, etc. On our stretched income, a capital item was impossible. Fred and his captain came to the rescue again with sufficient items for immediate needs. In fairness to our authorities, we were the first exchange officers to be able to take wives and children, nevertheless, pretty indifferent liaison. The US Navy though supplied free and excellent medical attention to their families for which fortunately we qualified. Whilst in the UK, babies were still fed on National dried milk, in the U.S.A., they were more advanced on formulas and very soon our son was provided with a suitable one. It was a turning point; he thrived, gained weight and I believe this provided the foundation for him to become strong and successful in life. We were to suffer a further setback, for within a few weeks of our arrival in the 'States', the £1 sterling was devalued from 4.00 to 2.80 dollars. It was the impact of reading it in the paper and being so isolated that was so disturbing. We depended upon communication by post from our mission in Washington entirely for our finances. Fortunately, our hardship prospects were short lived, the differential was compensated adequately and we fared extremely well, to the extent that we were able to save some money which was to prove a salvation on our return home.

My early days in VC23 proved bewildering. Their administration being quite different and an observer officer not forming part of their aircrew complement. The pilot performed the navigation and an enlisted man (a rating in our Navy) operated the electronic equipment. Although intelligent, and qualified, not being officers, they lacked the status and influence to develop fully the equipment from the tactical concepts. The aircraft were TBM's (Avengers) an adequate platform for the carrier based anti-submarine role. There was equipment installed that had not been used.

The C.O. (Wild Bill Privett) - a wonderful man, quiet with a Texan drawl, a tall, confident and relaxed individual and very shortly I appreciated that he was dynamic and extremely qualified, a professional aviator, a natural leader with an intelligent appreciation of the tactical requirements. The course fortunately was at Norfolk, the staff excellent, knowledgeable and cooperative. The three weeks course proved to be a major influencing factor in my enjoyment and contribution in this squadron to which I was attached for nine months.

I was soon accepted particularly when it was appreciated that I could contribute as a member of the aircrew team. Flying was treated as a way of life, similar to driving a car. The experience in the Pacific war operating large numbers of aircraft from carriers assisted in providing this professionalism. They were also fortunate in having sturdy, reliable and high performance aircraft. The scale of operations were to a totally different dimension compared to our declining Fleet Air Arm with a different concept of aircraft carrier design and operations.

The U.S.A. occupies a vast land mass from the high altitudes of the cold north to the desert and swamps of the south, Florida being only slightly north of the Tropic of Cancer. A young nation comprised of dissident Indians, Negroes of slave origin, the bulk of immigrants from Europe providing a very diverse population many with criminal backgrounds and those disenchanted with living conditions and unemployment all of varying intelligence and education. During the 20th century, intermarriage developed a population with varying attitudes, religions, principles and beliefs. I have always found them serious, enthusiastic, dynamic, hard working and generous.

Whilst devoid of class, they respect success, no doubt a legacy of their spirit with which they moved west with their families against all odds, an unbelievable achievement. The Americans are extremely hospitable people, natural and matter of fact, genuine but without drama. At sea, the wardroom would invariably be crowded with off duty officers all diligently working on projects or correspondence course for promotion, resettlement, etc. They were most interested in our history, country, way of life and Royal family. The American legal system had been based upon ours, similarly their naval customs and administration. Undoubtedly exchange schemes with the services and colleges with younger people integrating directly into their society provided a broader understanding. They set the U.K. on a pedestal, as they do their parents, who must do no wrong. Unfortunately, it is not a perfect world, survival encourages jealousy and distrust within families, countries, nations and continents. The wayward path of parents reflected in their children. We were periodically embarked on a CVE the U.S.S. Mindora, a small aircraft carrier with a wooden deck that carried our 12 Avengers. These ships were built rapidly and cheaply during World War 2 for convoy escort duty.

During my tour of duty, we exercised in the Davis Strait, Atlantic and Caribbean, totalling probably three months and during this time,flying was continuous 24 hours a day, aircrew averaging a day and night trip each of 4 hour duration. It had been a ritual in previous years for units of the fleet, during a break in the exercise pattern, to call at Havana, Cuba. This was a highlight for the USN sailor, a lively port, cheap booze and pretty girls. V.D. was rife and particularly virulent and in view of pressure from the Roman Catholic judiciary, we were denied the visit. Instead, we anchored with our escorts off a small Caribbean Island for a day's rest from the activities. We played volleyball and other physical activities. During the cinema show in the evening, an emergency crew was assembled to fly a sailor with acute appendicitis to US naval base at Guantanamo Bay at the eastern end of Cuba. I eagerly volunteered to act as the radar operator to guide us to the base. As soon as we had landed, the patient was collected from the aircraft by ambulance. We scurried to reach the bar in the Wardroom before it closed at 11 p.m. We certainly made the most of the half hour remaining and then enjoyed a sound night's sleep in a proper bed. Ships of the US Navy have been dry since the days of prohibition. It was to my astonishment on the following morning that I discovered that surreptitious arrangements had been made to load cases of whisky in the bomb bay of the aircraft. We picked up an arrester wire with less deceleration than I had experienced ever before. The aircraft was parked aft and in the briefest time, the cases were unloaded down the catwalks out of sight of the bridge into various officer's cabins.

By midnight, there were many intoxicated officers with only a residue of coca cola bottles as evidence of the proceedings. The Roman Catholic priest, a popular character of Irish descent, downed his last dram five minutes before midnight, the following day being the Sabbath. Visions of a court martial loomed as I turned in with an alcoholic haze; an RN exchange officer, disgracing the flag, moral integrity, etc.etc. Doubtless a blind eye had been turned on the proceedings - certainly appreciated by all. At 4 a.m. the following morning, a pipe rang out, range four aircraft, aircrew muster in the briefing room, back to business.

Bill Privett conscious of providing me with the opportunity of varied experience during the exchange scheme, recommended I be transferred to a special composite squadron which was evaluating the latest equipment in Key West Florida. I was most reluctant to leave VC23 where I had made many friends and attained a peak of satisfaction by assisting in the flying operations. I had also attained considerable knowledge and experience in carrier flying and the latest aspects of US Navy operations in the anti-submarine role. Farewell to Norfolk and our friends the Gages.

Chapter 22
Key West Florida

Key West, the southern most point of the U.S.A., a small key jutting into the Caribbean - the Gulf of Mexico on one hand and the Atlantic on the other. Originally as an army base there had been a single track railway destroyed by a hurricane. The US Navy appreciating its strategic value built a road prior to World War 2, named the Overseas Highway. We travelled with our son and luggage by Greyhound coach on this highway from Miami, Florida. It is a remarkable engineering structure linking the keys, providing an ocean drive of panoramic beauty, the Atlantic Ocean meeting with the Gulf of Mexico. Below in the clear blue waters an abundance of fish with brilliant colours darting between the rocks, barracudas and sharks, a galaxy of underwater wildlife prompting memories of the classic stories of Ernest Hemingway. The scenery is idyllic until devasted by the ravages of nature in the form of hurricanes, most common in late August and September.

Key West, had been a naval base since World War I. It was still relatively unknown and undeveloped. President Roosevelt found it a quiet and relaxing retreat during the war. There was a strong Cuban influence, the island being only 80 miles to the south. The Gulf Stream attracted the wealthy sportsmen in their luxury cabin cruisers trolling for the super size fish that abounded in these waters. Tourism was growing with hotels, restaurants and night clubs being built. The beaches were poor and unsuitable for children and sea swimming dangerous. It was early days for development by the large hotel groups. The naval air station was located at 'Boca Chica' a key four miles to the north. I was appointed to a composite squadron of 100 or more aircraft all of various types designated for special research projects for anti-submarine warfare. The scale of the operation was beyond my comprehension. The officers were specially selected for their various qualifications and experience. I was assigned to a project based on my experience in VC23. The work was most fascinating and challenging both the ground and air research certainly the most interesting in my career. Whilst the comprehensive reports I submitted received little impact in our Navy, I understood later that some of my recommendations were adopted by the US Navy; perhaps in a way a back hand reward. There was a tremendous spirit of enthusiasm and once it was appreciated that I was able to contribute, I became part of the team, enjoyed generous hospitality and lasting friendships. I even graduated to play baseball for our flight. During a three week fleet exercise in June 1950, the war broke out in Korea. The Americans were enamoured at how quickly we rallied to their side, appreciating the British as the allies that could be trusted. There was a large call up of Naval reserve aviators, some having only resettled in a civilian job for a year or so. It was to continue till 1953. Whilst tight security restrictions were incorporated in the fleet and naval bases, there was no restriction on my activities. I was encouraged, greatly respecting their trust and proud as a lone Englishman in this large aircraft carrier to be able to support our traditions and virtues, an exciting period.

My exchange tour had been extended at the request of the U.S. authorities to avoid a break of continuity in the research project. In view of the obvious success, an old friend, who had served with me in 815, was appointed to relieve me on exchange duty. Before joining the squadron at Key West, he was to enjoy three months experience at San Diego which was the base for their Pacific fleet.

Before returning to the UK, I spent a week in Washington completing reports for our Naval staff at the Joint Services Mission. It became apparent to me in those early post war days with the shortsightedness of the Government that valuable business opportunities were being missed. The Americans respect competition, value a wide market and like to be sold products on merit. Our representatives and products would have been well received if they had been properly presented. European competitors soon caught onto this market and we lost valuable opportunities in those early days. Unknowingly, the seeds of business were growing in my mind. The service with the USN had been exhilirating and was to have a profound effect on my thinking. My illusions for the future were, however, soon to be dampened.

Chapter 23
The Mighty Queens

The passage home in the Queen Mary, the elder sister to the Queen Elizabeth, was somehow symbolic. These magnificent liners, the pride of Briain, their quality and service unsurpassed by any other luxury liner. The Queen Mary won the 'Blue Riband' before the war, for the fastest crossing of the Atlantic in under five days. These ships served the country so nobly during the war acting as a shuttle transporting troops from America to the U.K. They carried on average about 12,000 each and on one occasion, a record of 16,500 in the Queen Elizabeth. The speed at which they steamed was never disclosed but certainly in excess of 30 knots (34 mph). Because of these high speeds, they could travel unescorted. A 'U' boat, unless directly ahead, would be unable to close within range to fire torpedoes. Air attack, however, was a threat when within range of German aircraft. Naval escort with anti-aircraft gunfire protection was provided until within range of fighter cover from the U.K.

During a crossing in 1942, the Queen Mary was steaming for the U.K. on a zig zag course to confuse 'U' boats. The Curacoa, a light cruiser with a complement of 250 officers and 313 ratings was on station ahead to provide air defence. She was also maintaining a zig zag course. Although the true facts were never disclosed, the zig zags coincided and this enormous ship over 950 feet long, gross tonnage 80,000 carrying 15,000 troops sliced clean through the Curacoa at night on the 2nd October. There were apparently only 26 survivors. The Queen Mary steamed on because of the threat of 'U' boats, suffering only a dent in her bow. Apparently the passengers below decks were undisturbed and unaware of the event. It was a problem that did not fall easily within the 'Rules of the Road' at sea and was the subject of much controversy. The Queen Mary was exonerated from blame. A sad and terrible tragedy adding to the score sheet of the consequences of war.

The advent of 'shrinking the world' with jet air travel signified the end of these magnificent ocean liners. The Queen Mary is now a museum piece at Long Beach, California, and the Queen Elizabeth ended up in the 'knackers' yard. Falling orders and competition resulted in the closure of John Brown's Shipyard on the Clyde. They had built so many of these proud ships — 'the end of an era', 'the sea our heritage' tobe replaced by so called financial services!

Chapter 24
RNAS St. Merryn, Cornwall

There was always a magical and exciting feeling when returning home from a tour abroad. It also meant so much to my mother who led such an insular life. Her grandson, a tiny baby when we left and now aged 15 months, sturdy and active, already taking his first steps.

I welcomed the prospect of two week's leave providing the opportunity for me to sort out my next appointment. It would seem logical that the Navy would wish to benefit from my experience with the US Navy. I reported to Admiralty during the leave and was informed that my next appointment would be as an instructor at the Observer Training School at St. Merryn near Padstow in Cornwall. Whilst the appointment's officer expressed surprise at what appeared as an oversight, he explained that it was irreversible. Regular officers who had served during the war and obtained flying experience were still not sufficiently senior to have influence on policy. My dream world collapsed. I was to teach basic navigation and tactics — little had changed from prewar. I was without experience in teaching and it was six months later before I was sent on a course of instructional technique.

The early days were very difficult, my boss, no doubt sensing my disillusionment, adopted a lofty and stern attitude and was far from encouraging. The Cornish were withdrawn and resentful of the invasion by the Navy of their privacy in this delightful, still unspoilt part of Cornwall.

Tourism was on the increase and flats or houses were rented out to tourists at a substantial price for a fixed period in the summer. Service personnel in those days were moderately paid and those married with families found accommodation very difficult to obtain when moving every $2^1/4$ years at the change of appointment. It was possible to rent adequate accommodation in Cornwall at a reasonable price for nine months of the year, but the problem was the remaining three months. We were shuttled around four times in two years involving finally the sharing of a small house with another naval family, the rent escalating from £3 per week in the winter to £100 per week for three of the summer months. Greed is an ingredient of life that has existed and no doubt always will.

Life is like a seesaw, up and down, which no doubt, and to some extent, provides a motivating factor. I settled down gradually to the role of being a school master, and within a year, a new C.O. was appointed, 'a breath of fresh air', initiating a revision to the curriculum. The Australian and Canadian Navies used our facilities for training their observers and I was privileged to be the Course Officer for 8 Canadian Midshipmen. They were delightful and enthusiastic young men. At the age of 28 I felt like a father even though I was only ten years their senior. The war packed in such considerable events providing a maturity in some respects out of all proportions to the years involved. The spirit in the Fleet Air Arm was fantastic, maybe chauvinistic, insular, but providing a comradeship sadly never to be repeated.

The squadron providing the aircraft and pilots for the training of these observer pupils were previous RNVR pilots serving on an extended service commission. The training role lacked the glamour of the carrier based front line squadrons, but nevertheless, vital to maintaining continuity of the operational role that naval aviation could provide.

The attribute of leadership is rare and often disguised and not necessarily requiring superior intelligence. Woods (commonly referred to as Woody) was of this category, physically a fine strapping young man, skiing champion of the Canadian Navy, natural, never overbearing and yet with his calm and charming manner was respected by his colleagues. Although not particularly intelligent, in today's jargon, having a low I.Q., he realised his limitations and worked hard. I appreciated his qualities and provided every encouragement possible to overcome these shortcomings. He spent his last Sunday with us on the beach. My son, who was two year's old, grew endeared to him through his attention.

During the first three months of the course, navigation flying exercises were only carried out by day. Night flying training was then introduced once a week subject to suitable weather conditions. It was a fine clear evening and the route of the first leg was planned along the edge of the north coast of Cornwall and Devon. The crews were briefed on the exercise followed by the Meteorological officer regarding the likely weather to be experienced. The training aircraft was the Firefly, a two seater monoplane strike and reconnaissance type aircraft powered with a Rolls Royce Merlin engine. Six aircraft were to be engaged on the exercise and they took off in succession into the night sky.

I settled down in the operations room maintaining a running plot, as they reported their positions, checking also that it conformed to the exercise planned. They climbed to their exercise height and set off on the first leg. The operations room was businesslike with the background noise of aircraft reporting and the subdued voice of the plotter as the messages were acknowledged. Suddenly, like a clap of thunder, an urgent voice broke through the ether "Mayday, Mayday, Mayday, engine failure am crash landing near Ilfracombe". The atmosphere became electrified, the other aircraft were instructed to report any visual sighting and the police and ambulance authorities in the area alerted. Flames were observed by one of our aircraft on a cliff close to Ilfracombe. We held bated breath. Could he have made a successful landing at night, he would have had more chance over the sea? The fire brigade and ambulance arrived on the scene within a quarter of an hour or so and our worst fears were realised, the crew had perished. The remaining aircraft were recalled to base. The pilot, a Lieutenant, a Scotsman, whose parents lived in an adjacent village to Lockerbie - the home town of my wife. He was twenty five and engaged to be married in the Spring. The observer pupil was 'Woody'. The engine and cockpits and most of the fuselage was burnt to cinders and the cause of the accident never ascertained. There were no takers that night for the night flying supper that had been prepared. A few repaired to the bar with the remainder retiring in solemn calm to their cabins.

It was as though a pall of smoke had descended with everybody being temporarily obliterated by the enormity of the event; the pilots, maintenance crew and fellow pupils all feeling a responsibility. This was the first tragic accident during my appointment and fortunately the last.

Two talented young men cut off in the prime of life. Wood's mother, a widow, was overwhelmed and was flown out from Canada to the service and burial in the local church in the village of St. Merryn, a quiet and peaceful recluse in this remote area of Cornwall. Woody had loved the

111

rugged cliffs, the coves, sandy beaches and crashing surf. A contrasting climate, wild winds, sea mist akin to a peasouper fog, with the sea in all its moods and guises dominating the scene.

My wife and I called at the house of the distraught parents of the pilot. They lived in a small, simple cottage with a charm created by its natural environment. We were served with tea and scones by these dignified people as they inquired about his life and friends in Cornwall. He had attended the local school and joined the Navy when he was 18, trained as an Airman to become a pilot. He and his colleagues formed the backbone of the Fleet Air Arm. He was accepted for an extended four year service commission after the war and in 1950, was transferred to the permanent list. These proud people displayed no bitterness as they were left with their own cherished memories.

The seven remaining pupils, young and resilient, became more closely bonded as the course continued in a more serious and dedicated manner. 'A scar in Life for Ever'. They presented me with a silver cigarette box as a token of their appreciation at the end of the course. Although I ceased smoking many years ago, it occupies a prime position in the study.

My second son was born in July 1951 and from thereon, the memories of St. Merryn were happy ones only marred by the sad loss of our King who had served us so well even though suffering with ill health.

It was a pleasant routine, as apart from once a week night flying and the occasional turn as a duty officer, I was home soon after 5 p.m. We enjoyed walking along the cliffs, swimming in the bay and socialising in the many lively and friendly pubs; sport was an important part of the curriculum in which I revelled. We possessed an old car enabling us to enjoy the stimulating scenery. The drive from Padstow to Newquay could be hair raising like a 'Big Dipper', with splendid views from the top of cliffs sweeping down to the rocks below. The coast road twisted and turned with hair raising bends, and we prayed not to meet another vehicle ascending. The road would open out into a picture postcard bay with roaring surf and fine clean sand.

The Cornish people were remote, honest and hard working, living from the land and the sea; a natural and healthy life.

RCN COURSE MATES

Woody-

113

The promise of an appointment to the squadron with special early warning radar was realised. Training was to be in America and with little notice, my family remained in Cornwall. As it was still summer, we were fortunate in being able to move into cheaper accommodation.

St. Merryn remains a corner in my heart with the mixed memories of my family, Woody, some super companions and an excellent environment, but it was time to move on.

Chapter 25
AEW Training 1952

It formed part of the agreement under the Marshall Aid Plan for the supply of these complex aircraft that a proportion of the aircrew must be trained by the U.S. Navy in America. There were four of us selected for this particular course, two pilots and two observers. Bill Sabey, the senior officer, was a pilot of considerable experience qualifying before the war as a rating pilot. During 1942 when Malta was under severe air attack by Italian and German aircraft, major efforts were necessary to supply them with Spitfires to provide air defence. Bill acted as a guide shepherding reinforcements into Malta that were flown off from a carrier before it was in range of air attack. On a particular occasion in order to ensure their safe arrival in Malta and without sufficient fuel to be able to return to his carrier, he was forced to ditch in the sea: fortunately, he was picked up. As he was a rating, he was awarded the D.S.M., whereas as an officer, it would have been a D.S.C., strange why it is necessary to differentiate awards for an act of heroism.

It was recognised by their Lordships that there were only a relatively small number of rating pilots and observers remaining and it could not be sustained in a squadron that they should be subservient to a newly qualified and inexperienced Sub-Lieutenant R.N.V.R. The stringent method of selection of regular service ratings to a permanent commission through the Upper Yardman's course, was temporarily modified to enable these misfits to be commissioned. Bill was a fine and loyal officer, a great friend, lean and strong, smooth and attractive to the ladies, a great sportsman and socialiser. Men with these attributes have always been in short supply.

Biff Nash was the other pilot, the antithesis of Bill, a burly sheep dog like personality, sincere, deep thinking and intelligent. He likewise gained his commission through the Upper Yardman's course. He joined the Navy as a boy seaman and became a Telegraphist Air Gunner early on in the war. He was a finely built man being over 6 feet tall, strong and with a fine physique; could be described as a 'man's man', a fine pilot and a good friend, he enjoyed a tremendous capacity for food and alcohol and was great company when on a night out with the boys. A 'Jekyll and Hyde' character, a paragon of virtue at home with his family. He was completely dominated by his wife who, although dwarf like by comparison in size, she managed him with a 'rod of iron'.

Steve Holroyd was my comrade as an Observer, a commissioned officer having risen up from the ranks. He had joined the Navy as a seaman boy at the age of fourteen. Training was tough for boys in those days. At 6 a.m. they had to scan, barefooted in the heart of winter, a 120 foot tall mast, the replica of that in a sailing ship but located on the edge of the parade ground.

He qualified as a wireless telegraphist, a specialist rating, operating a Morse key at high speed of up to 40 words per minute when Morse was the principle method of communication with the fleet. During the war he transferred to the Fleet Air Arm as a telegraphist Air Gunner when communication in reconnaissance and strike aircraft was by Morse on medium frequencies. The TAG also acted as the rear gunner in aircraft such as the Swordfish. Steve had finally qualified as an observer during the war, providing a wealth of skill and experience particularly in communications. He was disgruntled with the appointment being faced with the prospect of further separation from his family having only recently completed over two years abroad. He had limited prospects in the Navy and hoped for a training position nearer his home in Southampton where his family had settled. Nevertheless, he completed a quartet of married men, experienced and dedicated, but also intent to benefit from the opportunities that may arise. America was still considered an 'Eutopia' which only the privileged were able to visit.

The crossing of the Atlantic was again in the Queen Elizabeth I, but this time on a sadder note, with the wife and family waving goodbye from the quayside at Southampton. The giant liner eased out into the Solent the decks lined with waving passengers repeated by those ashore. A mighty blast on the ships siren, the tugs cast off and voyage commenced. We were again restricted to being only able to take out £5 in sterling. There was much gaiety aboard with mainly Americans of all ages, returning home after their holiday of a lifetime. Service life was not easy for a married man: money a constant headache with the equivalent of two homes to maintain. Temptations were often difficult to resist particularly with an unhappy marriage.

The first half of the training was mainly technical and carried out at the Naval Air Station, which was three miles from Norfolk, Virginia. This was an enormous base dwarfing the nearest equivalent in the U.K. The routine was agreeable flying or lectures commencing at 6 a.m., conducive to the climate, which was very hot in August and September. We normally finished at 1 p.m., leaving the remainder of the day free. Our American colleagues were most hospitable inviting us to join them at the local beaches in the afternoon. Accommodation and food for officers living on the camp was first class. Naval bases provided facilities for recreation including tennis courts and a swimming pool. Additionally there was a club managed by a civilian consortium providing a restaurant and bar for entertaining friends from outside the camp. Some were quite luxurious with a candlelit style night club, a dance floor and a live band. Prices were monitored by the Captain of the base enabling officers of all ranks to enjoy a high standard of entertainment at a relatively low price.

I enjoyed the friendship of many Americans, admittedly those with mainly naval affiliations and found them of high moral integrity accepting people for their value and ability rather than their background. It is intriguing how moral values are influenced in history by the changes in environment. In the 1950's the Americans were recognised as the permissive society probably because of the freedom and independence provided by their affluent society.

A friend, who was an US Navy pilot in the squadron, offered me a lift to Washington DC enabling me to to spend a weekend with my friends the Gages who lived in a town nearby. During the journey he created the impression of one devoted to his family. I inquired about his proposed activity for the weekend and was shattered when he disclosed it was to be spent with his girlfriend.

In the 1960's, the pendulum swung, the Americans returning if anything to more stable moral values whilst suddenly those of the British burst forth into more bizarre proportions. The era of the "Beatles', the pill, sex becoming a free for all, the traditional married family becoming classified as "square".

History usually repeats itself, being part of a biological cycle. A stable relationship normally flourishes if the sex is satisfactory, combined with the need for trust, self respect a vital factor of security for which we all strive. The improvement of living standards, education, higher wages, married couples both working, the relaxation of discipline in dress, litter laws, manners, respect for others, moral attitudes and the divorce laws have all contributed to complicating the balance of the way of life.

The U.S.A. provides a fascinating example of a complex body of people of different colours and creeds living together in a united community. Undoubtedly the factor of survival, together with an adventurous spirit and freedom and opportunities for all, resulted in them becoming a mighty and successful nation with the responsibility for stabilising world affairs. In 1950 they still preserved a simple and fundamental approach to life.

In a small carrier with a complement of about 250 there would be church services on a Sunday for three denominations of religions all of which were well attended. In the Royal Navy attendance at church service had been compulsory until after the war when it became voluntary. It would be unusual to find more than half a dozen ratings attending a service. The officers all dutifully attended to maintain the example they should provide and perhaps be within the eye of the Captain. Society would appear to support the attitudes that are suitable and reject those that are alien. Perhaps our forefathers were fortunate in having a faith. Modern thinking in society tends to reject religion. Perhaps we are inclined to ignore the ten commandments which provide a sound basis for the preservation of a pattern for living.

Whilst sex and violence provoke the attention of all members of society, male and female of all colours and creeds, I have not emphasised those aspects of any indiscretions which play only a minor role in my experiences and could easily become distorted out of their true proportion. My belief gained through experience is that leadership necessitates integrity, high moral value and practices. We surely look to our leaders for example and set them on a pedestal. Similarly, the family which is the foundation of society requires this trust and security if it is to flourish.

The second half of the familiarisation course was held at their 'Garden

Style' air station, Quonset Point, Rhode Island. It was flat and ideally located for a naval aviation support base, the grounds were beautifully laid out and quite magnificent in the Fall (autumn), the Maple leaf trees providing a particular splendour. There was a nine hole golf course on the base and an excellent club providing evening entertainment, albeit on a smaller and simpler scale than at Norfolk, but nevertheless tasteful and with a close relationship. We were a close knit foursome, worked hard enjoying the course and at weekends, relaxed enjoying the local amenities. Obviously, there were temptations, the local girls well versed in the ways of the virile young men available at the base.

The Korean war made heavy demands on American reserve forces, creating a hardship to many who were called back for service having just settled into a civilian occupation, became married and started a family. There was a particular friend who insisted that we use his home as a base for a weekend in an idyllic small township near Cape Cod. Until the call-up he had been the headmaster of the local school. We were welcomed with a warmth and hospitality as though we were long lost friends who had returned to the fold. The majority of the inhabitants on this coast were of Scots, English and Dutch descent, devout people, the majority of Presbyterian faith. Whilst of varying financial backgrounds they were integrated as a family, sharing many common social activities. We spent two weekends with these delightful people who were hungry for information regarding what to many was still the 'old country'. The weekend was for parties, each family taking a turn of holding it in their home, when they would provide the food, sumptuous still by our standards at home. Everybody attending would bring their own bottle according to their individual taste. A particular lunchtime get together stands out in my memory. A Scotsman by birth and heritage having lived there for thirty of his forty years, although a bachelor and scraping a living out of fishing, provided a 'clam chowder' cooked on a wood fire under the trees on a sunny autumn morning. The colours of the leaves provided an unbelievable splendour to the occasion. A meal of flavour to become a treasured memory.

The Fall (autumn) provides as beautiful a display on the Eastern seaboard as only nature can. The different hues from the variety of trees and vegetation, particularly from the splendid maples all at different stages of natures cycle, produce a magnificent spectacle of colour. On Saturday and Sunday mornings in order to provide a flexibility for off duty activities, a 'brunch' was served between 9 and 10 a.m. I became involved in polite conversation with an American officer with whom I was sharing a table during the meal. He inquired regarding my interest in American football and typical of their hospitality asked whether I would like to join him to watch a game between the universities of Harvard and Yale. I accepted enthusiastically and we set off at about 11 a.m. on the 200 mile journey to the ground through magnificent countryside.

We arrived just in time for the game which I found utterly bewildering. It was a spectacle of noise and colour with marching bands, cheerleaders, who were attractive young girls with lovely legs and wearing short skirts.

The game over, we completed the return journey in time for 'chow' (the evening meal) served between 6 and 7 p.m.

The course was nearly complete and the days approaching for our return to the U.K. Fred invited me to Washington for a farewell weekend. Hitchhiking a flight was an accepted custom for the military in those days. An American colleague who was to spend the weekend with his crew on flight training offered me 'a ride' with take off at 6 p.m. The weather was completely clamped with dense fog when I checked in at the airfield at 5 p.m. It was decided to cancel the flight and try again in the morning assembling at 6 a.m. It had been a busy week and customary on a Friday to meet up at the bar in the club for 'happy hour'. Between 5.30 and 7 p.m. the drinks were half price. I invited the crew of the flight along and introduced them to my colleagues. A riotous evening ensued with a taxi down to what we innocently thought was the equivalent of the local pub. It was a club with an ornate bar, a juke box and dance floor located about three miles from the camp and a rendezvous for the local ladies of the oldest profession. We socialised feeling that we were doing our duty as good British officers in a foreign land. There were stony looks from the women when we elected to leave alone about midnight and return to the camp. It was not easy the following morning at 5 a.m. to crawl out of bed, feeling far the worse for wear, and to report to the airfield to join the flight. A strong black coffee helped revival and we took off on a clear sunny morning for Washington.

I spent a relaxing weekend with Fred and Dottie. When I explained about the cancellation of the flight and the night at the club there was a frosty silence from Dottie particularly about dancing with girls. When later I asked Fred, he explained that the club had a very bad reputation some years previously when he had been attached there. She obviously appreciated the temptations and it remains one of my standing jokes when I am with them.

On Sunday I asked Fred for a lift to Washington to catch the train to Providence, Rhode Island, the nearest point to the air station. He would not hear of me travelling the long and expensive journey by train. He 'phoned up the local naval air station for a flight plan in a 'Beechcraft' a twin engined two seater training aircraft explaining that he needed to fly at weekends to keep up his flying hours, as his job kept him deskbound during the week. It was a superb two hour flight and a lovely afternoon over sprawling green countryside. Fred landed and declined my invitation to dinner and after a coffee and checking the weather, returned to Washington, by which time it was dark. Wonderful people, genuine hospitality with no fuss.

The course concluded with a farewell party to our many American friends, an experience to be remembered. Tinned fruit and meat were still unavailable at home and one of my friends provided me with a superb tin trunk that I filled during a visit to their PX stores. All US Navy bases had such a store, operating under a franchise with the price of goods strictly controlled and considerably lower than those from the local civilian stores. It was the equivalent of a supermarket today selling a wide range of goods including electronic equipment, cameras, clothes and food.

The US Navy were, and I believe still are, very caring towards their personnel. Free medical treatment has always been available to their families. It is simple psychology that a man will perform his duties more productively and efficiently with the knowledge that his family is under care. It is not always apparent to civilians that naval personnel (US and British) move around every two years or so often in remote parts and frequently parted whilst the husband is at sea. I understand that more consideration and facilities are available to dependents in 1995.

121

CANDIDATES AT THE COMMODORE

NOVEMBER 1952

Commodore Chat
Candidates at the Commodore
November 1952

122

Chapter 26
849 Squadron

Life is a journey never straightforward or without turmoil. The post arrived just before we departed for the rail journey to New York where we were to embark in the 'Mauretania' the following day. A letter from my wife with the news that she may be pregnant with our third child. However, the doctor had second thoughts suggesting that it may be a growth. Whilst our parting had not been happy, she was the mother of our children, and here I was three thousand miles away, detached and unable to provide any constructive assistance in a mental turmoil. But at least she was with my mother who could look after the children.

It was voting day for a new president on the day of our arrival in New York. We were accommodated in the Commodore Hotel which was where President elect General Eisenhower had his headquarters. Biff Nash, an ever thrusting type, wormed his way into the proceedings, claiming to be a UK press representative for the Navy News, the name for a fictitious paper that he had fantasised. The bluff proved successful and he attended the party in company with General Eisenhower and his entourage. At midnight, the results were declared and the jubilation followed the announcement of his election as President.

We sailed on a drab morning at the end of October 1952, the passengers mostly travelling on business, a contrast to the holiday atmosphere of the tourist on the passage out in the Queen Elizabeth. The Mauretania, a smaller and older passenger ship of the Cunard line, comfortable with excellent food and service. The passage was to take a week compared with the Queens which crossed in five days. Each day seemed interminable and I found no appeal for the ship's entertainment, in fact it was difficult to settle to anything, being cut off from the outside world. The day finally dawned when we docked at Southampton, a small figure was waving and as we drew alongside the jetty, their was happiness in her face, my depression lifted like the light of the sun transforming night into day. We were soon to disembark, a farewell to my colleagues, and down the gangplank to the arms of my wife and the welcome news that I was to be a father for the third time. Perhaps the doctor who diagnosed the growth needed a revision course on pregnancy.

There was a week of leave to find accommodation and move the family to the Helston area of south west Cornwall. Accommodation was to be more of a headache than round St. Merryn. We lived in two cottages during the next six months neither of which had running water, gas or electricity. Heating was by paraffin stove, cooking by a primus stove and lighting by oil lamps. Sewerage was non existent, the lavatory a bucket in a shed up the garden. Fortunately, because we had two young children and my wife was in an advanced state of pregnancy, we were fortunate to be able to move into one of the early completed married quarters within six months. It was difficult in those days to fulfil maximum dedication to a naval career and raise a family.

My service for the following two years was to be with 849 Squadron based at Culdrose in Cornwall. The C.O. was Lieutenant Commander John Treacher, a charming man, charismatic and obviously wisely and specially selected for implementing this new and vital concept of the operations of high power radar in a carrier aircraft.

He was to become Admiral Sir John Treacher KCB following a successful and illustrious career.

In the Pacific war, low flying Japanese Kamikaze aircraft had inflicted a heavy toll on task groups and convoys, including the radar pickets and at the same time proving the inadequacy of the Fleet's radar to detect low-flying aircraft. A radar set was designed in America and installed initially in the TBM Avenger that could detect a ship at 200 miles, a small to medium size aircraft under good conditions at about 30 miles. The AEW aircraft patrolled ahead of the fleet thereby extending the early warning coverage and enabling combat air patrol aircraft to be vectored out by the AEW aircraft to intercept the enemy aircraft before it was in range to launch its missiles. Unfortunately, the AEW squadron had been disbanded before the Falklands War, their presence might have saved the loss of ships and destroyers sunk by low flying Argentine aircraft using 'Entourade' missiles.

A further application was in anti-submarine warfare. The Germans had developed a 'schnorkel' which enabled a submarine to proceed under diesel power and charge its batteries without being exposed on the surface. The schnorkel reduced considerably the range that they could be detected visually or by radar. The APs 20 radar could detect a schnorkel under reasonable weather conditions at about 20 miles, providing a considerable contribution to anti-submarine protection to a fleet in convoy.

The equipment was later to be installed in the AD4W skyraider aircraft, a very versatile aircraft employed in many roles particularly as an attack aircraft. It continued to provide a useful role for many years including Vietnam. It was produced by the Douglas Aircraft Company in America as a low wing single engined monoplane, the AEW version, AD4W powered by a Wright Double Cyclone engine driving a four bladed propeller and developing 3,300 h.p. to take off. A crew of three was carried, a pilot and two observers seated side by side in the rear compartment.

A total of 20 aircraft were supplied under the Mutual Defence Aid Pact. The first four were delivered in November 1951 and the remainder followed during 1953. On 7th July, 1952, 849 was formed as a front line squadron. The squadron was to be divided into 4 flights, together with a headquarter flight with its primary role to be that of training replacement AEW operators and pilots and also providing aircraft for exercises and trials as required.

We became 'B flight' with Bill Sabey as our C.O. We worked hard during the next few months to improve our techniques and develop the potential of the aircraft and equipment. We were favoured with a first class crowd of fellows who comprised the maintenance crews, although relatively young, they were experienced and enthusiastic. The introduction of sophisticated radar and electronic equipment stretched the resources of suitably qualified personnel. We were fortunate in having a number of intelligent ratings on national service. The majority had some experience of electronic equipment in the civilian world, they were keen to develop their knowledge and on leaving the service, provided a background for the development of the new technological age of radio and television. Fortunately, the equipment was new and well designed and required a minimum of maintenance. The Navy, including the Fleet Air Arm, had always recognised the importance of maintenance and recruited quality personnel. This was a particularly valuable feature during the war when we were required to operate with inferior and obsolete aircraft and equipment with the inevitable shortage of spares. The post war Fleet Air Arm was complimented with some fine intelligent balanced and experienced aviators and maintenance personnel capable of absorbing and developing the revolutionary changes in jet aircraft, weaponry and electronic equipment that was evolving.

We were something new, attracted attention, and soon became much in demand. Lord Louis Mountbatten, C in C Mediterranean appreciated this innovation and in June 1953, we were detached to operate from Malta, providing an opportunity to work with the fleet and develop the finer techniques and potential of their equipment.

Lord Louis paid us a visit within a day or so of our arrival. He was advised on the capabilities of the aircraft and its equipment and given a demonstration flight. Bill Sabey was the pilot and apparently soon after take off, to his horror, the engine cut, but fortunately after nail biting seconds and a juggle with switches and controls, it restarted. Lord Louis was fortunately oblivious of the event. He was very well informed on electronic equipment having been a signal's officer in his earlier days and soon appreciated the technicalities and potential of the equipment.

The Mediterranean can be very hot in summer and operating at relatively low altitudes with this equipment which emanated a great deal of residual heat, could be pretty debilitating. The age of transistors and printed circuitry was still a decade or more away from service use. Whilst even an intelligent individual will not accept a reduction in performance, his ego personifying the challenge that his performance will not deteriorate even when hot, tired and under stress. Studies in more recent years have provided statistics of the reduction of time related performance in all spheres of activities particularly those requiring intense concentration and when operating at altitudes such as in an aircraft. Ships and aircraft in those days were not air conditioned.

The routine was very pleasant flying from about 6 a.m. till 1.30 p.m. followed by lunch and in the afternoon, sport or swimming off the rocks. During the week it was early to bed and early to rise. The weekends were normally free and little time was wasted, playing sport, sailing, socialising or touring the island, which usually included visiting the numerous hostelries on the Friday and Saturday nights. Beer was of a lager type, Maltese wine reasonable at 1/3d (6p) per bottle.

Malta is a small island approximately 15 miles long and 10 miles wide straddling the Pantellarea straits about 50 miles south of Sicily and 150 miles from the North African coast,midway between the Straits of Gibraltar to the West and Alexandria to the East. It was a vital base strategically placed for the British and attracted considerable attention during the war from the Italians followed by even more devastating air attacks from the Germans. The island survived the onslaught and was awarded the George Cross which included a considerable sum of money towards the reconstruction of bombed buildings.

The Maltese were devout Roman Catholics producing large families and were generally very poor. As in many islands of the Mediterranean it only rains during the winter and with high temperatures in the summer, there is always a drought with limited water available to supply the needs of the population. It was significant when we flew in there was a green patch like an oasis in the middle of the island. This was the property of the exclusive Marsa Club comprising cricket, polo and tennis facilities. Whilst the supply of water was strictly controlled in the island, the sacred cricket ground was excluded. I must confess to having enjoyed playing there some most satisfying and enjoyable matches.

It appeared to many of us in those days that the contribution towards reconstruction in the island was concentrated mainly on the Churches. They would regularly hold festivals involving the most extravagant and spectacular firework displays.

Chapter 27
H.M.S. Eagle

Whilst the detachment in Malta had provided valuable experience, the majority of us were married with families, and looked forward to returning home. My daughter had been born in the May and my wife suffered a difficult time with a new born baby and two young boys to look after particularly being located so distant from help from either of our parents.

We were in a front line squadron and within a month of arriving home were to be detached to HMS Eagle in January 1954, a fleet carrier, that was to work up from Gibraltar with its newly formed air groups including two squadrons of jet fighters. Whilst a blow to the families, this was naval life. There was a social change in the country, service families were recognised more as an important entity and there were now married quarters alleviating many of the problems that had previously existed. Bill Sabey was to take up a training appointment having had a long run of front line duties. I was fortunate to have the opportunity of taking over as C.O. of the flight, a much valued privilege and my only command and claim to fame in my naval career.

We joined HMS Eagle in the channel, the maintenance crew and spares joining her at Devonport the previous day.

Eagle, a sister ship with the Ark Royal, were the largest aircraft carriers to be in service with the Navy carrying between 60 to 100 fighter and strike jet aircraft. They were 803 feet long, displacing 36,800 tons and fitted with the modern launching catapults, latest aircraft handling equipment, high powered radar and two hangars for aircraft storage and maintenance. Sophisticated damage control resulted in the ship being like a rabbit warren very difficult to negotiate a route below decks until completely familiarised, often a nightmare to muster aircrew in the briefing room in the island at short notice. There were other modern innovations such as an air conditioned mess deck although the ship's company still slept in hammocks. There was centralised messing with meals being taken in large dining halls, a considerable improvement. The food was considered better than that served to officers in the wardroom where it had to be transported from the galley located in a deck on another level. Because of the large complement, fresh water was strictly rationed when at sea. The water in the bathrooms was only available at night for half an hour - bad luck if you were delayed in landing from a flight.

We soon formed a happy relationship with colleagues from the other squadrons, a few gins in the wardroom soon developed comradeship and understanding. During our cruise the ship carried a squadron of TBM (Avenger), our AD4W conventional aircraft using petrol as a fuel (AVGAS) and a squadron of Attackers and SeaHawks, jet fighters using paraffin (kerosene). AVGAS was obviously hideously explosive and a fire hazard of nightmarish proportions from both an aircraft and ship aspect in addition to the space required to carry two types of fuel. We were to work up in our various roles requiring understanding of each others's capabilities and team work where we were to cooperate in Airborne Early Warning and Anti-submarine warfare projects. Why cannot this spirit and cooperation operate within the nation's industry?

I believe it to be leadership, the survival instinct in the civilian world is in the accumulation of money. Private enterprise motivates the competitive instinct and the greed. Workers historically have been oppressed and abused by the large corporations, the unions by laziness and bureaucracy, cooperation, trust and leadership is not understood within their itinerary. A naval officer generally has performed all the functions expected of his men rarely experienced in large companies. We were fortunate in having an inspiring leader in our Captain Holland Martin, although not an aviator, undoubtedly his previous service in small ships assisted him to weld a spirit of respect, pride and willing cooperation into this multifarious ship's company in this soulless metal hulk.

A pride, spirit and comradeship grew unbelievable within a few weeks.

He was to become Vice Admiral Sir Holland Martin C.B.D.S.O., D.S.C., and remains in my memory with respect as a notable leader. We were to work up and operate out of Gibraltar where there is normally a pleasant climate in January and February, and particularly good conditions for flying. We would sail early on a Monday and return to Gibraltar around

6 p.m. on a Friday. Gibraltar was still a good run ashore, cheap booze and entertainment. Saturday morning was devoted to the maintenance of aircraft, completing reports on the week's activities, and preparation for the following week. There would normally be sport in the afternoon, which you either played or were obliged to support. Sailing was a popular pastime with the ship's dinghy available at weekends. It was not my favoured sport, probably psychological with a complex developed as an Upper yardman who was the only course member not brought up in boats and it was a prerequisite to be able to sail a boat to qualify amongst other things for a commission.

After a hectic week with flying exercises by night and day, we berthed on a Saturday afternoon. the most important event upon arrival in harbour was the circulation of the mail. Silence would reign on the mess decks, officers would retire to their cabins to indulge in the privacy of reading the news from their loved ones. Unfortunately, there was also the 'nasties' — bad news, unexpected bills and other problems.

In the evening, numerous drinks, a meal and a run ashore with the boys on the town. Sunday morning was to follow with a unpleasant awakening, a drumming head with the frightening thoughts of 'Divisions' on the 'Flight Deck', followed by Church service. which now being voluntary, was attended only by dutiful officers. A grizzly memory filtered through the alcoholic haze that in the afternoon, I had agreed to sail the ship's dinghy round Gibraltar with an enthusiastic and ambitious young RAF officer on an exchange duty in my flight.

'HELL' — hope the weather clamps, sailing was not my idea of how to spend the afternoon. We adjourned to the wardroom for much needed coffee after Church.

The wind was rising and the forecast bad. My young protégés ambition was not to be thwarted. Professing his experience with dinghy sailing and my reputation at stake we embarked on this ill conceived nightmare trip. The harbour was massed with ships at anchor of all types, shapes and sizes. The rock of Gibraltar towering some 2000 feet deflects the wind in varying directions over this exposed harbour. We must have easily broken all dinghy records careering round the harbour missing ships by hair's breadth. The sea grew angrier and we decided to 'call it a day' and homed into the calm of the lee of the carrier. Peace, calm and still water. Pride and reputation had been sustained as we commenced lowering the sail preparatory to tying up alongside the jetty. Suddenly, unannounced, a gust of wind deflected from the flight deck of the carrier, hit the lowering sail, and over we went into this murky, icy cold water of early February. We righted the boat, dived and recovered the drifting oars, baled madly to keep the boat afloat. Two miserably wet and cold creatures, water dripping from the hair and clinging to the sodden clothes provided an amusing event to the audience of cheering sailors proceeding ashore in the ship's pinnace. Their siren signalled a cheery and sarcastic blast. Fortunately, a boat from a Dutch carrier berthed astern, appeared and cast us a line and towed us ignominiously to the jetty. Hardly a scene from 'Yachting World'.

ENTENTE CORDIALE

I was to be regularly reminded of this humiliating episode during the forthcoming months of the cruise. Sailing was erased from my retinue of activities.

Apparently relations with the French Navy were still sensitive after the war. In early July 1940 after the fall of France, the UK took preventative methods against French naval forces to avoid them falling into German hands. The French fleet was attacked and neutralised at Oran in Algeria. A very depressing episode shelling and killing many of our recent allies.

We were the first Royal Naval vessel to visit the port since the war. We berthed alongside at the naval harbour of Mers El Kebir near Oran, the shell holes in the harbour walls still plainly visible.

The French Navy, however, proved very hospitable with organised trips into Oran for sightseeing and to enjoy the nightlife including a superb opera at their principal theatre. The highlight was a trip of about 50 miles across the desert to Sidi Bel Abbes, the headquarters of the French Foreign Legion. It proved to be a most fascinating experience, these tough soldiers of varying nationalities drawn together mainly to escape from the misfortunes of life. Our guide was a Sergeant, an Englishman who had been a Wing Commander in the RAF during the war. He had returned home to find his home bombed and wife and children killed. At this time, the French were heavily involved with the war in Indo China, suffering heavy casualties to be repeated in only a few more years with the Americans in Vietnam, as it became known. The Foreign Legion were losing 30 officers a day at that time, their inscriptions recorded on the wall of their sacred and attractive chapel. Notwithstanding the bravery of the French, in particular the Foreign Legionnaires, they were defeated at the battle of Dien Bien Phu in 1954.

We were royally entertained in all respects with a Legionnaire orchestra entertaining us during lunch combined with copicious quantities of wine. The return journey to the ship was convivial and hazy to say the least. A superb weekend and we sailed on the Monday refreshed with a notable experience.

We sailed from Gibraltar in March for exercises with the fleet followed by a visit to Toulon as part of a NATO goodwill commitment.

Eagle was the largest ship to berth alongside in their naval dockyard. It involved a very difficult operation dependent on the right state of the tide, a nightmare for the Captain and navigating officer to avoid going aground. The mud was 'churned up' as the screws were used ahead and astern to complete the final docking. This proved an impressive beginning to the visit with this superb carrier occupying a dominant position at their naval base.

The Navy was renowned for its hospitality and proficiency for entertaining foreign dignitaries. A drinks party was held in the hangar deck for selected NATO officials, the stewards were not averse to lacing the drinks creating an admirable atmosphere for the Royal Marines to celebrate the ceremony of 'Beating the Retreat' on a floodlit flight deck on a beautiful clear moonlight evening. The inspiring music embellished with two Scot's bagpipers from a regiment in Gibraltar adding sentiment to the occasion with their wailing pipes echoing across the still waters of the harbour. There were many tearful spectators moved with this emotional ceremony enhanced by the benefit of alcohol. It was always said that the Royal Marines achieved more entente cordial in an hour's ceremony than from a multitude of politicians!

The following day we sailed on the next leg of showing the flag for Naples. Flying, following the previous night's entertaining, was discreetly confined to navigation exercises which also gave us the opportunity to view some of the splendid coastline of southern France and northern Italy. On the following morning comprehensive exercises had been programmed with a take off at 7 a.m. At 7.50 a.m. all aircraft were recalled.

It had been reported that radio contact had been lost with a civilian aircraft that had taken off from Rome proceeding south. We were ordered to steam south at maximum speed. The powerful engines responded, the ship vibrating, as it ploughed purposefully through the tranquil seas on this lovely morning.

A yellow object was sighted in the sea off Stromboli by a civil aircraft. We were about 200 miles to the north and our aircraft with crew was launched at 3 p.m. to search the area with our radar.

News filtered through that it may be the wreckage from a 'Comet' that had taken off from Rome with 80 passengers bound for Johannesburg.

133

It was a fine clear morning as it had headed south climbing to its operating altitude of 30,000 feet. Silence, about 120 miles south of Rome radio contact had been lost and all aircraft and ships in that area of the Mediterranean were alerted.

Flying south to the area, my crewman, Jock Ewing, and I with eyes glued to the screen, contemplated what we could expect. Our pilot kept in radio touch with the ship and maintained a visual search. A blue shimmering sea, a cloudless sky, how could such a catastrophe occur in this tranquil scene?

Nevil Shute, a forward thinking man served in the R.A.F. and was a qualified aeronautical engineer. He became a popular author after the war with an easy style. His books on aviation were particularly interesting and gripping. High altitude flying was a recent innovation and its associated problems not fully appreciated. He predicted that structural stress in jet aircraft would have catastrophic effects.

The De Havilland Comet was the first fully jet propelled passenger carrying aircraft. It completed extensive trails successfully and commenced commercial flying in the then BOAC in 1952. During 1953 a mysterious crash occurred at Karachi Airport involving many fatal casualties. Notwithstanding a thorough investigation, no cause was revealed.

1953 was the year of the Coronation. Queen Elizabeth was on the throne, a new Elizabethan era dawning. Whittle had invented the jet engine, the Hawker Hunter had established an air speed record and we were leading the world with jet air travel.

Now, in our search for the Comet, we arrived at the scene to be greeted with a devastating spectacle. The aircraft must have disintegrated at altitude and the passengers and debris rained down to the sea, gradually to emerge to the surface.

The weather was calm and the sea still as our large carrier gently steamed in the area as darkness descended. Boats were lowered, their oars muffled, manned mostly by young midshipmen still in their 'teens'. They worked all night in the eerie darkness, illuminated by the ship's searchlights, to recover bodies and debris. A sickening and nauseating experience in this floating graveyard.

There was only a mournful gloom, no flags, bands or boatswain pipes as we somberely but gracefully entered the harbour in the picturesque bay of Naples with the mighty volcano Vesuvius towering in the background.

As the ship was secured and the gangways lowered, there followed an invasion by the world's press reporters, who scrambled, pushed and shoved, jabbering in incomprehensible tongues to obtain pictures of clothes and relics and for any stories of the events.

Investigations again were of no avail with no logical or factual cause for the disaster. There was to be a further Comet disaster later in the year, the aircraft crashing into the sea shortly after take off from Rome Airport with no survivors.

Lord Louis Mountbatten was still Commander in Chief Mediterranean and recognised the vital importance of these disasters to civil aviation and the country's prosperity. He despatched tugs to the scene and with the latest underwater photographic equipment, divers assiduously gathered every fragment of the plane from the seabed. The aircraft was somehow rebuilt at R.A.E. Farnborough, and under simulated conditions on a test bed, was run until it shattered. The failure was attributed to a structural fault in the design of the cabin windows and the fuselage, as had been predicted by Nevil Shute in his book. The fault was remedied and the Comet reintroduced to passenger service and in 1959 provided a transatlantic passenger service to America.

Naples proved an anti-climax, no doubt following the events of the disaster. We were involved with entertaining NATO dignitaries providing a similar repeat to Toulon. Whilst located on a magnificent bay with undoubtedly some fine buildings, the area near the dockyard where I walked was the scene of some extreme poverty with children, bare footed, begging in the streets. There was an excursion laid on from the ship to Pompeii, which was certainly a most fascinating and interesting experience.

We resumed the programme of the cruise to join up and exercise with the Mediterranean fleet based at Malta. Grand Harbour is an imposing sight when approached from the sea with its fine forts and battlements, dhaisos bobbing across the harbour and the attractive town of Valetta overlooking the harbour reflecting the ancient history of the island. It was still winter and the island was green, transformed from the burnt up brown as it appeared when we were there in the summer some months previously.

Towards the end of April, the Royal Yacht Britannia, newly commissioned and on her maiden voyage, arrived at Grand Harbour with Prince Charles and Princess Anne on board to join up with their parents at Tobruk on the completion of their visit to Australia following the occasion of their Coronation. They acted normally like any other young children of that age, fascinated with the visit to the ship, clambered round the aircraft and particularly enjoyed being driven round the flight deck on the tractor used for towing aircraft. The Navy has always enjoyed a reputation for its instinctive and natural way of entertaining children. The sea in its various moods provides a bonding and levelling effect encouraging the spirit of comradeship and teamwork on the crew. The visit was obviously hugely enjoyed by the ship's company. Royalty has this magic in boosting morale.

The Americans in particular have always been envious. Royalty acts as a figurehead, a pinnacle, still existing whilst religions fade as they become a convenience, without faith or dedication. How can you remain a Catholic if you take the 'pill' or use a 'condom'? Saddam Hussein hardly seems a good advert for Muslim nor Buddhists in Sri Lanka burning Hindus on bicycles. Maybe the world should pause and contemplate before allowing itself to be totally dominated by technology. Bureaucracy greatly assisted by the computer, has become a creeping catalysis embracing our lives in all its aspects. Man could easily become a slave to the power that he has created.

The fleet sailed on the 1st of May, the ship all recently painted with the light grey of the Mediterranean fleet, the brass work on the guns glistening to provide a welcome to Her Majesty and the Duke of Edinburgh in the Royal Yacht that only Lord Louis Mountbatten and the Navy could provide.

We were flown off at first light on the 2nd of May to fix accurately the position of the Royal Yacht on her passage from Tobruk. Position and timing was essential to enable a complicated and spectacular steam past by the ships of the fleet. We quickly established the position although not permitted too close for a visual sighting in case the noise would disturb Her Majesty's slumbers.

The fleet navigating officer, a senior member of the Admiral's staff, disputed the bearing we had provided. We were still 'new boys' in the eyes of the surface Navy, considered imposters by some of the hierarchy. A reputation and possibly a career at stake! The navigation equipment in a ship portrays true courses and bearings. Aircraft compasses are magnetic and must be corrected for the variation of the magnetic to the true. We sneaked in low and as close as possible which we trusted would still be out of audio range and rechecked the position and bearing of the fleet from the Royal Yacht. Fortunately, as the sun rose, the haze dispersed and we were able to confirm a visual sighting at about 8 miles. Whilst there were no bouquets on our return, the Captain was pleased and relieved. After a quick breakfast, all hands were required to prepare aircraft for the fly past in the afternoon.

The steam past, an awe inspiring sight, the ships steaming at 30 knots, ensigns steaming tautly and proudly, the sun shining from the clear sky onto a shimmering sea, reflecting the graceful lines of the ships. The ships' companies lined their ship's sides and as they drew adjacent to the Royal Yacht steaming past in line astern, the order was given for "Off Caps" and three cheers for Her Majesty "Hip Hip Hooray" echoed across the water from the ratings and "Hip Hip Hoorah" from the officers, supposedly a distinction of their authority.

The Queen and Duke were clearly visible waving from the bridge of the Royal Yacht as the ships ploughed past engines throbbing, bow waves hissing, the water churned into a whirling crescendo between the ships. The Royal Marine band resplendent in their blue uniform and white helmets, played 'God Save the Queen' from the flight deck of the carrier. On completion, the ships reformed to provide an impressive escort to the Yacht as she entered Grand Harbour. A 21 gun salute boomed out across the harbour, the shore lined with waving and cheering crowds. The first visit by royalty since the war to this war torn historic island.

On return to Malta, we were honoured with a visit by Her Majesty and the Duke of Edinburgh. She had expressed a wish to visit the ship that she had previously launched. It was a blustery day as she took the march past of the ship's company on the Flight Deck. It was an impressive occasion, a tonic to morale and a memory for all involved. The Heads of Department of the ship together with the Commanding Officers of the squadron were all presented to the Queen. Although thoroughly briefed, nevertheless, I was still nervous at the moment of shaking her hand, hoping not to trip over my sword or create some other horrendous disaster. We then adjourned to the Admiral's cabin where the Queen was presented with an engraved momento produced by members of the ship's company. A slight but dignified lady, demur and sincere, providing a warmth with her gratitude of appreciation.

The Royal visit terminated our cruise and we set sail for the U.K. This enormous steel hulk with a crew the size of a small town, happy and efficient, welded into a formidable force with the aircraft, its weapons being capable of dealing with a variety of situations. A floating aerodrome, a will of the wisp, capable of moving its position 300 miles or so overnight to strike at will.

The visit of the Royal Yacht to Gibraltar en route to the UK had soured relations with the Spanish. We anchored off Gibraltar. There was no shore leave, alcoholic runs over the border and bull fights at La Linea were suspended for many years. The Rock of Gibraltar in the 1990's still as solid as ever, still British, a duty free haven for tourists, a magnet for supermarket shoppers. The days of happy sailors drinking their way down the main street with its innumerable lively and noisy bars and cabarets blaring out topical Spanish music, all a fading memory.

849 'B' FLIGHT

139

HMS EAGLE - FLOODLIT 'GRAND HARBOUR'

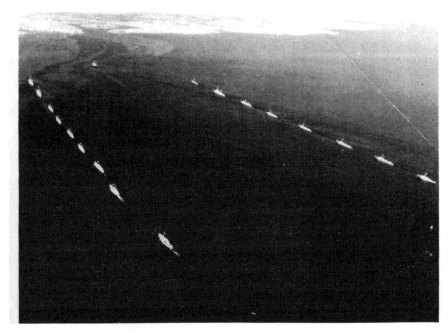

ENTRY TO GRAND HARBOUR

140

849 FLY PAST (A & B FLIGHT)

ROYAL YACHT - STEAM PAST

QUEEN VISITS HMS EAGLE

**PRINCESS ANNE AT THE
HELICOPTER CONTROLS**

**PRINCE CHARLES ON THE FLIGHT DECK
APRIL 1954**

Chapter 28
Fish Head Training

Home again, reunion with the family and the realisation that I was becoming a stranger, particularly to my eldest son, who by then was five year's old.

Career was all important and for promotion I needed further proficiency in the working of a sea going ship and to obtain a certification of seamanship. I was appointed to H.M.S. Aisne, a destroyer operating with the home fleet from Scotland joining her at the end of August with the understanding that it would be for six months. We were required to move out of the married quarters on the change of appointment with only a weekend available between my leaving the squadron and travelling to Scotland to join the ship. We motored down to Portsmouth in our 1940 Ford 10 with three young children and our goods and chattels to stay with my mother. Fortunately, we found a flat that we could rent for three months, it was very small but a makeshift in view of the situation.

Upon joining H.M.S. Aisne at Invergordon, the Captain was displeased that my appointment had been curtailed from six months to slightly over two because I was required for an appointment at Admiralty. When he realised that this was without my knowledge, he provided me with every assistance to obtain the experience to enable me to obtain the qualification of becoming a fully qualified executive officer. They were a fine bunch of officers providing me with every assistance. It was a fascinating experience being involved in a NATO exercise operating in the Norwegian sea. Following a work up with other ships of the flotilla, enabling me to brush up on my watchkeeping, we rendezvoused with the fleet at Scapa Flow and then proceeded to Vestfjord. The role of the destroyer was to simulate escorting a convoy down the canals connecting the fiords to Tromso in the north. The enemy was represented by a cruiser with aircraft support to hazard the operation. The weather was superb with clear blue skies by day and the northern lights at night. The scenery was spectacular sailing up the canals with towering snow capped mountains on either side opening out into vast fjords. The system of pilotage was unique, simple and safe, essential for the safe passage of the ships navigating these waterways.

Upon completion of the exercise, the ships diversified to meet their future commitments. We crossed the Norwegian Sea and sailed through the Pentland Firth, located between John O'Groats and the Orkney Islands about 15 miles apart with some small islands in between.

This area is renowned for the race of the sea which particularly in bad weather, makes it very dangerous for shipping, many ships large and small have been lost throughout the years. We were on passage to Plymouth for a refit and to give leave to the ship's company. I left the ship at Newport, South Wales, where we called for a flag showing visit. The town was being modernised, the council offices having recently been completed. The Mayor provided a reception which all officers had to attend. We returned the hospitality which happened to fall on my last night in the ship occasioned also by my being officer of the day. We invited the Mayor and councillors to a 'Cocktail Party' ostensibly from 6 to 8 p.m. They duly arrived and to our surprise, complete with wives or girlfriends. They were 'hearty Welsh' and consumed vast quantities of alcohol. At 8.30 p.m. there was no sign of movement. I discreetly inquired if we should order taxis and explained that the stewards must finish in order to have their evening meal. They all firmly believed that as taxpayers they should enjoy their fill, this being a ship of Her Majesty's Navy. I explained ineffectively that whilst the drinks were duty free, the ship enjoyed no entertainment allowance and the cost was shared between the wardroom officers on a stripe basis. A sub-Lieutenant would pay 1 share, a Lieutenant 2 and a Lieutenant Commander $2^{1}/_{2}$, being the highest ranking officer on board. The Captain was excluded not being a member of the Mess. Mess bills could be a hardship particularly when the ship made a number of courtesy visits particularly for junior officers married with families. They all finally left rather the worse for wear around 9.30 p.m.

The following morning, with my duty complete, I bade farewell after breakfast to the Captain and my brother officers. A short, enjoyable and rewarding stay, next to the Fleet Air Arm, small ships with their efficiency but relaxed discipline, closeness and lack of red tape were always most appealing. A mixture of sadness at leaving my friends with whom I had shared exploits at sea, sport, runs ashore and in the wardroom, and yet with the excitement always experienced when returning to the family.

The train journey from Newport to Portsmouth seemed interminable, a local stopping train wended its way through the lovely autumn countryside of Wales and South Western England.

Chapter 29
Admiralty Duty

After a few days leave with the family, I became involved in a completely new experience; service at Admiralty, London, the Navy's head office. Since we worked with civil servants, we were obliged to wear suits and being naval officers must wear a bowler or Anthony Eden style headdress. My boys thought this hilarious and within a week my 'smart' Anthony Eden 'trilby' had been squashed and used as a rugby ball. In company with my colleagues, it would only ornament our heads as we entered the illustrious establishment. It proved to be a very interesting appointment serving under the Director of Radio Equipmet, prior to the terminology of electronics. My boss was a Captain RN., an observer, an excellent man who warned it would take me six months to understand the system and be able to contribute. Basically our responsibility was to ensure that the equipment pulsed (radar) or non pulsed (radio) on order for forthcoming aircraft, met the naval staff requirements. There was a healthy competition with the surface Navy, the civil servants, obscure in the background, controlling the purse strings.

The surface Navy (including submarines) were fortunate in being able to arrange their own contracts direct with the shipbuilder. Not so the RAF or FAA, we must deal through the Ministry of Supply which was set up during the war by Winston Churchill under the control of Lord Beaverbrook to ensure that equipment for the services was available when required. Bureaucracy was to entangle the system in peacetime like an octopus spreading its tentacles.

When a requirement arose, which in many cases was common to the RAF and FAA, there was a research project set up to evaluate that the equipment wouldmeet the required standards. A specification was drawn up and manufacturing companies invited to tender for the contract. The successful firm was anxious to set up production and commence manufacture so as to obtain a turnround of the investment. The Ministry of Supply would set up committees and act as the middle man, delays would inevitably occur and frustrate the whole programme. I vowed that as and when I left the Navy, I would not join the civil service.

The work was challenging and interesting, the majority of the projects with which I was involved were conducted at R.A.E. Farnborough. The scientists with whom I had to cooperate were dedicated to their work and not interested in attending lengthy meetings in London which they generally left to me. It was a fascinating period. Jet aircraft were becoming more powerful and flying higher and it became essential that communication equipment must be installed in a smaller space, be lighter and more reliable. Transistors and printed circuits were on the drawing boards but the Navy was still reluctant, principally for reasons of maintenance, to convert to a revolutionary and unproven system. Reflecting on those days with the modern technology of the 1990's is akin to a comparison with the 'Ark'.

The routine at Admiralty was so different to that of a ship or air station. Travelling to and fro by train in the rush hour was certainly no picnic. We would normally arrive in the office at 9.30 a.m. and leave at 6.30 p.m., avoiding the peak times for travel. On a typical winter's evening in 1955 clutching a book in one hand to read on the train and a briefcase in the other, I scurried across Trafalgar Square with the other commuters, tired, harassed and anxious to make their connections. The wind swirled rubbish, men's coats and ladies' skirts adding frustration to the melee and impeding progress. Flashing lights and blaring horns with the traffic adding a cacophony of sound to this busy scene. Eyes darted in every direction as we swerved and weaved to avoid people, the traffic and obstacles in order to traverse the complicated pattern of crossing from Whitehall to Charing Cross Station. My eyes, normally concentrated on this ritual, rarely deviated, apart from possibly that of a particularly pretty girl crossing my path. On entering the station there was a billboard with the headlines "Naval pilot ploughs through caravan site". Hurriedly, I purchased the evening paper and dashed through the gates for the train. I deposited the book and briefcase on the luggage rack and clutching the corner of the seat with one hand I attempted to read the newspaper with the other. The train jolted, jerked and swayed on the circuituous journey of south east London to Bromley in Kent. Shattered, my mind suddenly becoming a blank, a naval fighter plane had attempted a forced landing at a quiet second

149

line training airfield on the south coast. It overshot the runway and veered off out of control through a small caravan sight, killing the occupants whilst they were having their lunch. As I read further they were identified as Chief Aircrewman Ewing and his wife. Jock had been my crewman for over two years in 849 squadron. As the packed train careered along making its various stops, with the maelstrom of other trains, whistles and announcements accompanying the journey, my mind drifted back to those squadron days. Jock was quiet, serious, intelligent and reliable with a stable and pleasant personality. We shared many hours in a blacked out compartment in the rear of the Skyraider. It was commonplace not to see the outside world from take off to landing during a four hour trip. We had developed a camaraderie and respect difficult to explain.

On completion of the Mediterranea Spring cruise, he requested transfer to a shore job. He had been away from his wife on and off for many years and although sorry with the prospect of the break up of our crew, I thoroughly endorsed his request and was delighted to learn subsequently, that he was with a training squadron on the South Coast.

The train shuddered to a halt and I was jolted back to reality. The paper slipped from my hand and was soon lost and trampled as dreamily and sadly I left the train. The irony of fate, respect for no man, as life continues its uneven journey.

Their eyes now closed and may they rest in peace.

Chapter 30
Fading Times

My spell of two and a half years at Admiralty soon slipped away and it was essential that my next appointment should be to a carrier as an operation's officer if I was to stand any chance of promotion. I was relieved by a very old friend, Jimmy Thackwell, married to an attractive Norwegian girl, and the father of delightful twin girls. He was enthusiastic about the job and the opportunity to see more of his family having just completed a two year tour in a front line 'Sea Venom' night fighter jet squadron. Dramatically fate was to intervene again in its cruel and ironic fashion. In the 70's, it was reported, but without details, that having recently retired he was employed by a company based in Oslo and was killed when flying as a passenger to an oil rig in the north sea. What an end, having survived a career in aviation, a major proportion of the time exposed to the hazard of flying in night fighters.

A month's leave followed my tour at Admiralty with still no confirmation of when my operations appointment would materialise. Meanwhile, I was to officiate as a briefing officer in H.M.S. Bulwark, a light fleet carrier, for NATO exercises in the Norwegian Sea. My life was to experience a dramatic change. An early retirement scheme had been introduced to streamline the officer structure of the services. An attractive redundancy payment and basic pension was to be provided. It was anticipated that this would be achieved largely by volunteers.

It had become necessary to have a home base for the family, the children growing up, with the consideration for their education. At the end of the war there was a flood of marriages followed by children requiring education. In the 1950's there were not enough schools or teachers. The primary schools in Bromley were unable to provide my boys at the age of 5 and 7 a place in their schools particularly when they understood that I may have to move again within a year or so.

Although I could ill afford private education, there was no alternative. On completion of this indeterminate sea appointment I could be based again in Cornwall, Ireland, Scotland or Admiralty. Bromley was a central location well served with trains. An attractive house, ideal for our needs, came on the market. It was at a low market value because it had been inadequately maintained and required a great deal of attention. It was a touch and go situation to raise the money for the down payment andthen meet the mortgage repayments. On April Fool's day 1956, the services received a long awaited and reasonable pay increase. Another crisis survived.

The Navy had been my life and prior to the Admiralty job, civilians and businesses were remote entities. A particular friend of mine at the local cricket club who had served in the RAFduring the war assisted me with the purchase of our house and had a profound influence on my interpretation of a possible future. He was 45, the age at which I would retire if I was not promoted Commander. He was a Director of a company, dynamic, wealthy, with children of similar ages to mine. At 45, still young anddynamic, would I be happy with some 'backwater' job to supplement my pension? I would join the throngs of middle class soulless people, commuting daily to London, awaiting the day of retirement. Civilian life of which I knew nothing, provided appealing thoughts of a life ashore with my young family. The challenge of a command in the Navy or as a controlling director in a business were the ambitions — the alternatives soul destroying. As a subterranean stream that finally emerges there was an underlying desire for the challenges of the business world percolating and undermining my mind. It was the age old problem that confronts the ambitions at an age when they are most needed in all respect by their family. My wife and I agreed mutually on the decision. I set off the following day, the letter in my pocket, to spend the night with my mother in Portsmouth before joining the Bulwark for the NATO exercise. My mother had been a tower of strength and I owed it to her to explain our decision. My mother so proud, her son a Naval officer, the epitome of success. Although sad at my decision, my happiness and future were the principal prevailing factors. The love and loyalty of a mother is the most dedicated and cherished attribute in life. It was a dull and depressing evening in late September as I strolled to the post clutching a letter that was to change my life.

Portsmouth was where it had all started at the tender age of 16.

Confused thoughts went rushing through my mind. Was I mad to consider turning all this in? Would I change my mind after meeting old friends in the comradeship which I valued so greatly with the challenge and invigoration of this still young and vibrant Air Arm of the Navy? It will be farewell to the travelling,the glamour of foreign ports, the entertaining, the pomp and ceremony of the massed bands of the Royal Marines Beating the Retreat on a floodlit flight deck. I suppose my command, albeit of only a flight, but of expensive aircraft with advanced electronics, had provided a contribution to the fleet, and rewarding privileges for me following a background of grind and servility.

I slipped the letter into the 'box' — maybe their Lordships wouldn't release me! It was likely to be six months before I would learn my fate.

My only significant memory of my spell of duty in Bulwark was the serious threat of an epidemic of Asian 'flu which struck the ship and indeed the fleet when we sailed from the Moray Firth at the end of August 1957. Sailors were still sleeping in hammocks in those days but in an effort to isolate those afflicted, mattresses were laid out on the deck in a separate mess deck not particularly comfortable in a heavy sea when the ship rolled.

The physical training instructor under the instructions of the medical officer had all officers and ratings still on their feet on the flight deck performing keepfit exercises, inhaling clean cold Artic fresh air. I was fortunate having incurred only a mild attack which I suppressed with rum and aspirins. I left the ship at Belfast in October on completion of the exercise and returned to London. The sea appointment for which I was earmarked was delayed — maybe a coincidence!

Meanwhile, I was to serve on an investigation called for by Lord Louis Mountbatten 'Fighting a war in fifteen years time'. A most fascinating and efficiently organised project. The participants were of a variety of ranks, specialisations, and experience. The final presentation was attended by senior officers of the three services including selected foreign representatives. Lord Louis introduced us as a cross cut of the cream of the officer structure of the fleet. Ironically, that morning many of us received a letter from their Lordships terminating our engagement, although without any indication of the final release date.

Fortunately, I was able to spend the remaining days prior to my release in Admiralty to prepare for tackling the civilian world.

PART II
THE CIVILIAN WORLD

CO-OPERATION

IS BETTER THAN CONFLICT

"FIVE STAGES OF A PROJECT"

stage one
EXCITEMENT - EUPHORIA

stage two
DISENCHANTMENT

stage three
SEARCH FOR THE GUILTY

stage four
PUNISHMENT OF THE INNOCENT

stage five
DISTINCTION FOR THE UNINVOLVED

WE TRAINED HARD, BUT IT SEEMED
THAT EVERY TIME WE WERE BEGINNING
TO FORM UP IN TEAMS WE WOULD BE
REORGANISED.

I WAS TO LEARN LATER IN LIFE THAT WE TEND
TO MEET ANY NEW SITUATION BY
REORGANISING, AND A WONDERFUL
 METHOD IT CAN BE FOR CREATING THE
ILLUSION OF PROGRESS WHILST PRODUCING
CONFUSION, INEFFICIENCY AND
DEMORALISATION.

CAIUS PETRONIUS AD65

Chapter 1
Metal Packaging

In 1958 there was a cut back in defence expenditure and therefore little demand in the areas of my expertise. Was all this training to be wasted? Vacancies in the civilian employment market were scarce, certainly no place for ex service officers. The attitude of the average employer in those days was what do they know about business? Will they be prepared to put up with the grind and start at the bottom?

I attended, soon after retirement, a well presented business course for retired service officers at Woolwich under the auspices of London University, providing a useful background for management, the structure of industry, the professions including the trade unions. It became obvious how isolated and ill informed were service officers. As a salve to my conscience that I was preparing for this new world I also attended an adult education course at Bromley in the evening for two nights per week. The tutor provided me with certain long lasting principles, not quite apparent at the time. He was of the Jewish faith and fled from Germany prior to the war. He taught fundamental elements of psychology as they applied to business. A worker with even limited intelligence sought employment that would provide an income for his/her necessary immediate needs recognising that a business only existed if it realised a profit. As part of the profit making system then the worker should receive a proportion either in pay or bonus.

The philosophy appeared simple and obvious but provided a need for thought and self examination. I experienced difficulty in appreciating and accepting my own limitations and also to be able to recognise my attributes and weaknesses. I realised that I would be unable to alter myself fundamentally and furthermore, nor would my competitor. I acquired the ability to recognise the abilities of my employees and to weld them into a cohesive force. Large companies with unions were unable to utilise such flexibility. It has been apparent that since the war management has not benefited as it should from experience. The tribes in the past always consulted their elders. In my experience, the directors of public companies have not built their companies on this foundation. They are particularly prone to being isolated in their own particular field, ensuring that "I am OK Jack" combined with the overall weakness of short term results in order to satisfy shareholders.

A vacancy occurred through the Ministry of Labour for a representative in a company in the metal packaging industry. Experienced representatives were not available at the pathetic remuneration offered. Arthur, the Sales Manager, an excellent type, conscientious and hard working, returned to the firm after serving in the Navy during the war. As with many of his contemporaries, he was on a low salary, with a mortgage to pay and young children to support. Recognising the potential of an ex Naval Officer, available at a minimum salary, I was offered the job on a six month probation, providing my own car for which expenses would be paid. The lump sum received on retirement, which initially sounded substantial, was stretched requiring a subsidy to compensate for a drop of two thirds income. I purchased a second hand Ford 10, certainly not man enough for extensive driving which would include London traffic. A representative reflects the status of the company and an antiquated vehicle certainly did not enhance this reputation. I would park in a side street some way from the firm to which I was called to avoid such embarrassment.

During my appointment at Admiralty, I had worked closely with a scientist at Royal Aircraft Establishment Farnborough. It was necessary to visit firms producing equipment for the services. Anxious to obtain these contracts, we were well entertained and only seeing the glossy and efficient aspect of these companies. These dreams were soon shattered with the reality of small and medium sized companies tucked in back streets operating with antiquated plant. Training was 'in house' learning from a fellow operator. Safety was a hazard with antiquated machines not adequately guarded. Gloomy buildings and inferior lighting provided inadequate working conditions. The attitude was "use the cheapest labour available" which provided a breeding ground for dissatisfaction justifying the need for unions. Prewar practices continued; a lethargy existed, rationing ended, but the goods now available, were too expensive to buy. These early impressions were to prove invaluable. A commercial company, regardless of its activity, exists purely on its ability to make a profit - Survival! Employees at all levels, factory and office, must contribute to this survival each forming a piece of the jigsaw puzzle. A company is incomplete without all the pieces. Management requires the trust and teamwork of the employees of the company who in return, must provide trust, faith and goodwill. History reflects the political and industrial problems that can mainly be attributed to the manipulation of people. Management failed and still fails to recognise this fundamental point. Good service and the working for customers was generally talked of but not practised. Training was only provided by the large companies. A salesman was recognised by the public as a 'smart boy' in a street corner market. Industry was low in the social scale. We had nothing to compare with Harvard School of Business Studies. There was no concept of marketing or forward planning. It was not till years later that I attended a Sales Course provided by the Tack organisation. When a market has been established for a product it must then be introduced to the customer. It is vital to ascertain the nature of the potential customers business so that he may be advised why the product is essential to his needs. Selling has been a dirty word and not a career for gentlemen. The professions still remain the fashion for security and wealth. The creation of wealth must emanate largely from industry which must be the spearhead supported by the professions and service industries. Just as the role of a warship is to seek and destroy the enemy and not as a cruise ship for its sailors. A customer recognises his supplier initially by the representative and the person who answers the telephone, perhaps a female with a pleasant and reassuring voice will provide a vital link. How many firms with adequate management training and P.R. overlook this vital communication link?

Obviously with some trepidation, reminiscent of a child starting at school, I reported in at 8 a.m. for my first job in the civilian world. Fortunately, having been at Admiralty where we wore suits, I arrived suitably attired. Life is composed of many memories of anxious events and this was certainly one of them. I parked in a side street (no yellow lines in those days) and announced myself to the gatekeeper, a friendly guy who said "Carry on mate" when I explained my position with the company. Tin Box factories always had a pervasive and obnoxious odour;

161

a cocktail of gas ovens, heated solder baths and printing inks. I suppose a reason why the gentry went into the professions, industry being a dirty word'.

I was warmly welcomed and soon put at ease by Arthur Rumbold, the Sales Manager (tins) and Alan Fellows (drums). Alan had served successfully in the Army during the war, becoming a Major. He likewise had found it difficult to settle down with a family on a low salary. They were both most professional, sound managers with a natural selling ability. The Sales Director, Mr. Coleman, was over 60 and a gentleman of prewar days, diligent, dignified and experienced, someone who inspired trust and respect.

Tins certainly held little appeal to me at that time as they were usually thought of as something rusty which contained paint and with a lid that was difficult to remove. National Dried Milk on which my sons were fed in their babyhood days, the decorated tin at Xmas holding biscuits or sweets, in other words something in life that was generally taken for granted.

It invariably requires a war which creates the need to innovate. Apparently Napoleon in his wars experienced the need to preserve food so that the troops may be fed. It was discovered that this could be achieved by cooking the food and sealing it in a tin for an indefinite period. It was revealed some hundred years later that the soldering resulted in lead poisoning. The tin went out of fashion until the means of folding tinplate had been developed and the tin could e externally soldered which excluded any contamination. Subsequently a whole new industry was created and we now accept as commonplace food, beer, wine and beverages in this basically simple sealed container.

There was no training and for the first two weeks it was left to me to learn all I could. I read diligently the technical literature and regulations available regarding metal containers and toured the factory endeavouring to follow the intricacies of tin and drum manufacture. The line foremen were most helpful and instructive describing the process and my early naval engineering proved invaluable. 'Francis' was an old established family factory and post war became a public company. Roger Francis, the technical director, a son of the original F. Francis, was a fine engineer who had also served in the Navy during the war so this was a help.

A tin, manufactured from tinplate or aluminium, could be of various specifications according to its purpose. There are principally three types; a slip lid where the lid fitted over the outside of the body, a biscuit tin being a good example; a full aperture where the lid filled on the inside, providing a straight uninterrupted body internally, ideal for mastics, putty, etc., but the most common tin is the lever lid where the lid is either a lever or flush top fitting into a ring seamed to the top of the tin. Tins can be supplied round, square or rectangular, each requiring separate tooling. This story is about the manufacture of tinplate containers often referred to as tin or metal bashers. Tinplate is produced from an iron core extruded into sheets of varying thickness and coated by an electrolytic process with tin. Prewar, the sheet was dipped in tin and possessed a much heavier coating than is the case today with the electrolytic process. The tin provides a coating resistant to corrosion, is shiny and resistant to bacteria. It can be soldered providing it with a sound strong and watertight joint. Prior to welding, this was the standard specification for containers for food, beverages, paints, chemicals and oils. Tins containing food were found recently to be in perfect condition in the base camp used by Captain Scott during his expedition to the Antartic. The contents were found to be perfectly edible.

Tinplate in the prewar days was supplied as a box consisting of 100 sheets weighing about 180 lbs, capable of being manhandled by two men before the days of fork lift pallet trucks. In the 1950's in the interest of economy with the advent of lifting equipment and lorries capable of carrying heavier loads, it was supplied in 1 ton bulks (1000 to 1200 sheets per bulk).

Printing techniques were developed with offset litho providing a medium for high quality printing, ideal for illustrating the contents of the tin, instructions for use and high quality reproduction for promotional packaging. In later years, we developed the technique of screen printing on tinplate. Whilst unable to provide half tones, colour presentation was improved but the principal feature was short runs particularly attractive to retail outlets for seasonal lines, cakes, biscuits, etc. As with every product, the advance in technology required adaptation to the changing market place.

163

BODY BLANK

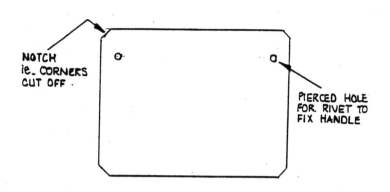

NOTCH
ie. CORNERS
CUT OFF.

PIERCED HOLE
FOR. RIVET TO
FIX HANDLE

LEVER LID TIN

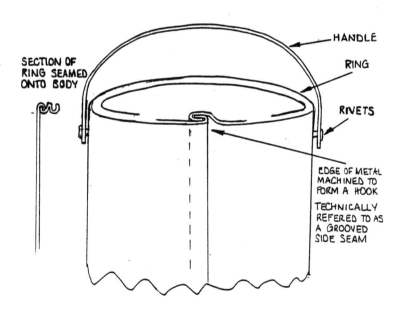

SECTION OF
RING SEAMED
ONTO BODY

HANDLE

RING

RIVETS

EDGE OF METAL
MACHINED TO
FORM A HOOK

TECHNICALLY
REFERED TO AS
A GROOVED
SIDE SEAM

Although plastic and other forms of packaging have made serious inroads to the popularity of the tin, it still retains an image of being clean, firm and robust, fire resistant and when printed, a most attractive container. It must surely retain an important role in the market place in the 21st century.

Francis had wisely invested in new plant to meet the growing demand of the post war economy. Doubtless a contentious point but many companies were subsidised during the war, there was little competition and high profits were achieved. It was inconceivable that Britain's economy could recover substantially having used its overseas investments to finance the war. Undoubtedly, a combination of factors including the Marshal Aid plan enabled a recovery. The fairer distribution of wealth must have been a major factor in enabling the working man to enjoy a greater spending power and an improved standard of living inconceivable before the war.

The first operation in producing a tin is to cut a body blank from a sheet of tinplate by a guillotine. Rotating or gang slitters enable high speed cutting for production to size of a number of bodies simultaneously. The bodies have their corners cut off, technically referred to as notching. The body is then rolled or squared by a machine into its final shape. A seaming machine locks the two edges of the body together, known as grooving. The ends of the body are flanged so that the top and bottom may be fitted by a further machine, the seamer. Ancillaries such as handles are fitted to the finalised tin. Automatic high speed production incorporated the same principles. It was fascinating to observe the tins in their various forms of construction scurrying along runways and finally in a finished form to be packed and palleted. The mastery of efficient production provides a rewarding and satisfying fulfilment.

The creation of wealth must emanate from the earth through an industrial process to serve man's needs. Service industries including the professions provide a necessary supportive function but they must be secondary to the manufacturing and distribution process. There can be no standing still if industry is to prosper, it must be as the tributaries of a river gathering pace to join the main stream.

Initially my sales territory covered the whole country with particular concentration on the London area with the Sales Manager being responsible for house accounts. Results were what counted and I respected the trust as to how my time was employed and that my expenses were paid which were reasonable and not subject to undue scrutiny. Industry was intriguing and I found knowledge of the customers product and its production fascinating as well as vital in the process of ensuring that he was provided with the right package and service. Gradually, close relationships were developed.

By now, after four years of the vital ground work of selling, the lure of business with added responsibility and influence in management was challenging. An opportunity arose in a small metal packaging firm, a subsidiary of a public company, to cover selling and general management. The existing manager was near retirement and the firm planning expansion. During the 1960's, the pattern of industry was changing with asset stripping, amalgamations and takeovers, the small and medium sized firms were being squeezed out.

Chapter 2
The Little Shop 1959 - 1968

Because of the inadequate education system existing at the time, my wife and I agreed that although our circumstances had changed dramatically, we must educate our children at private schools even though it may involve sacrifices. Life is made up of people with contrasting personalities and our neighbour Mary personified this trait. She was a spinster of Jewish descent with a flamboyant personality, about 60 years of age but with dynamic energy. Singing was primarily her interest and flair, the epitomy of success being a concert at the Opera House in Covent Garden. She had befriended a Maltese during a visit to the island and he returned with her to be a coach for her singing and to tend the garden. As they were an odd pair it was difficult to imagine anything peculiar about their relationship. Mary had obviously inherited money, lived modestly and was considered, in those days, as being a woman of means. Jews have an inherited talent for creating wealth. She had been persuaded some years previously to purchase the leasehold of a sweet shop aptly named the 'Little Shop' in Bromley, just off the High Street. She soon found the commitment to be in conflict with her singing interests and planned to put it on the market. She was aware of our circumstances and suggested that it could provide a rewarding investment. It should only be necessary for my wife to work half daily from Monday to Friday by sharing with the existing lady member of the staff. It all sounded fine but with our limited business experience, we were literally as 'green as grass' particularly concerning the implications involved in the purchase of a leasehold business. We paid an extortionate sum for what really only amounted to the purchase of goodwill. The building was a dilapidated wooden structure about 100 years old, and the oldest shop in Bromley. It was owned by the Church Comissioners who provided a five year lease with the tenant responsible for the maintenance. Security was a nightmare even in those days and to obtain insurance cover on stock it was necessary to have an expensive alarm system connected directly to Scotland Yard. It was a tempting target, particularly as we held large stocks of cigarettes, and 'break-ins' could be attempted from the seclusion at the rear. The combination of real and false alarms would often result in a 'bevy' of police cars homing in from South East London. Fortunately, the drink/drive law did not exist in those days as call outs would invariably occur between 11 p.m. and 2 a.m. The days of the 'Bobby on the beat' were fading being replaced with Panda cars, providing the smart boys with a bonanza.

Routine, discipline and the day to day activities provide the background to life. Unfortunately, disturbances occur, like storms at sea, and the routine pattern cannot be maintained. There is only one way to run a small retail outlet and that is to reside above it. The Indian and Pakistan community have demonstrated this more than adequately with their total commitment. They share the work as a family, opening the long hours required in a low profit margin business providing always a pleasant and polite manner. During the nine years that I owned the shop it became necessary to employ additional staff to cover holidays and sickness. During 1961 my wife required an operation and was absent for some weeks which coincided with my change of job in the packaging industry. Within six months of her recovery our marriage broke up, the children were all at fee paying schools and the need for income overcame the desire for 'Hari Kari'.

I will always remain indebted to the assistance of my mother who looked after my home and the children and the staff at the shop who enabled me to carry over the difficult forthcoming months.

I believed, and still believe, that it is the small business with the entrepreneural spirit that has and will continue to provide the survival in this country. Whilst supermarkets were active in the USA in the late 1940's it was not till the late 1950's that they posed a threat in the UK. It was to form the pattern of the 'Big Boy' enjoying the juicy bits of the prey. High turnover, low margins, with short term profit on cash returns. A supermarket opened nearby in the square in Bromley trading initially in a comparitively leisurely style opening from Monday to Saturday 9 a.m. till 5 p.m. with a late night until 7 p.m. on Friday. The staff were inadequately trained with the manager on some sort of bonus and it was commonplace for customers to be overcharged at the check out, in fact apparently part of an undisclosed policy. We gained business indirectly as we attracted customers who passed our shop with their children demanding an ice lolly or equivalent treat if they were to behave. The parents then discovered that we stocked high quality confectionery in addition to matches and other coincidentals not available at the supermarket. Bromley was an up market area with a demand for more selective and refined gifts than the commonplace box of Cadbury's Milk Tray or Roses. We benefitted by offering additionally the higher priced quality products with the versatility also of selling $2^1/2$ ozs of liquorice allsorts for $4^1/2$d (2p) whilst the supermarket would offer an $^1/2$ lb pack at a cut price of 1/3d (6p) much cheaper, if you could justify the increased quantity.

My new job proved more interesting and demanding. I had remarried and decided that the time had arrived to sell the business. The council, meanwhile, had negotiated with the Church Commissioners, my landlord, to demolish the shop to provide an access road for shops. It was to be named Tetty Way, perhaps 'Petty Way' would have been more appropriate. A relic of the past with its character and place in social history was destroyed to be replaced with the more cold and material aspects of modern life.

It was coveniently phased to coincide with the end of the lease so there was no compensation.

Life is all about learning combined with 'Hard Grind'.

Chapter 3
Metcan

Metal packaging prewar was made up of a multitude of small privately owned manufacturing companies located locally to their customers. The introduction of high speed automatic plant for food cans improved the production output but necessitated capital to provision the plant. A consortium of firms was formed in the 1920's becoming the Metal Box Company and concentrated particularly in this domain in addition to fending off competition from the larger American companies interested in setting up in the U.K.

This story is about General Line which provided tins, drums, and kegs for a very wide range of products including food, oils, chemicals and fancy goods. The larger companies concentrated on the higher volume requirements where standard sizes were required and the smaller on the specialist requirements. During the war it was a reserved industry with tinplate on allocation. The majority of firms were mainly privately owned family businesses; narrow minded, cliquish, suspicious of any outsider, jealously guarding their customer base. Lacking competition during the war their products were expensive, generally of poor quality; demand having exceeded supply for many years and the industry was complacent, providing a very indifferent service.

Improved production methods and plant were being introduced and packaging was to become an expanding, sophisticated and competitive market. Metal, glass and cardboard had met the essential needs for generations. Plastic, a cheap, lightweight, petroleum by-product penetrated the market providing a cheaper product and reflecting the changing scene of the environment. The 1960's was the age of the 'Beatles', Carnaby Street and the permissive society. Supermarkets with mass marketing necessitated the demand for everything to be packaged from a drawing pin to an automobile.

Ten years with this company provided the background for running a small manufacturing company. We exploited the niche market which required flexibility, particularly in production, striking a balance between cost effectiveness and the size of the order. The market place was like 'shifting' sands. A growth market today could collapse the next with new product-development by customers and emerging competition from competitors. Quality and service were the keynote, with the ability to respond to customer demand. A saving of, say, 10% on price was of little value to the customer if the containers were not there when required to fulfil his order. The shrewd buyer would appreciate this and realise that for an alternative supplier to survive required regular business.

People are the cornerstone. T.R. was the boss, an accountant by background, a tall ponderous character with common sense and business acumen. The parent company produced bakery products and we were obliged to provide priority in supplying their requirements at the expense of the outside world. T.R. would spend hours on detailed calculations on costing and statistics, rotating in a circle and finalising at the beginning to confirm the price. Sensitive, he was generous in some ways, and mean in others. A controversial character who found it difficult to accept limitations in others. Metal packaging in those days was renowned for its reputation for paying low wages and yet for complaining bitterly over labour shortages. Production bonus and profit sharing was being introduced by the larger companies in industry but this was too complicated for the smaller firms. Female operators were the mainstay; they came to work to earn sufficient to supplement the family income. They were conscientious, happy with the repetitive nature of the work and preferred part-time work. Mothers with children were unreliable time keepers and therefore not conducive to maintaining a continuity of production. Factory management required experienced operators. Machines were antiquated, requiring continual maintenance and setting for the diverse nature of the sizes manufactured. Short production runs required careful planning and flexibility to ensure cost effectiveness and profitability. Metal Box provided the training and was the source of supply for the technically qualified. A cross section of competent production engineers, not likely to attain the top jobs, but fancying the smaller company with added responsibility and the opportunity to develop their skills, formed the backbone of the smaller manufacturer.

There were many of these dedicated, skilful and loyal people who toiled long hours on a low salary, enabling ancient machines to remain operable, their experience providing flexibility in meeting specialist demands. Whilst efficient mass production must satisfy the demand of the bulk consumer, the smaller manufacturer must satisfy the more specialised requirements and provide research for new product lines for the changing market place.

Survival is the driving force created in business by competition.

Albert and Tom were the indomitable characters at METCAN (Tweedle Dum and Tweedle Dee). Tom, a short, wiry, serious and sensitive individual born and bred in South London; intelligent but with his education limited by the prewar social system which had necessitated him starting work at fourteen. He served an apprenticeship at Metal Box becoming a qualified engineer. He appreciated after the war the limitations of the large company, preferring the prospect of becoming a big cog in a small machine. T.R. coerced him into joining this small company on a low salary but with prospects if he could assist it to become successful. The plant was antiquated and required refurbishment. He was a good engineer with the flair for instinctively turning the right nut to transform a machine into operation with minimum loss of production. As a dog with his master, he possessed an extraordinary servile attitude to the 'boss'. He flourished with self importance and the epitome of his ambition was to appear as the boss as he crossed the road from his home wearing a suit and carrying a brief case. In his local he was the all important manager of this thriving company. Poorly paid, dominated by his wife and family, his life was motivated by the need for appreciation. Management in this country loses so much potential in not understanding people and exploiting their potential. Failing to see "the wood from the trees" we are becoming monopolised by the computer and its inherent bureaucratic tendencies. Technology provides the future providing we remain the master and not vice versa! Loyalty and dedication, possibly a latent feature of our race, correctly channelled could result in untold rewards if converted into profitability.

Albert, a brash cockney from the East End, was the antithesis to Tom, outspoken and single minded. Apart from service in the Army during the war, he had spent his life in metal packaging, albeit in a wider variety of firms, large and small. He had designed the 'stackable' 5 gallon drum, a simple but ingeneous development saving considerable space in storage and transport. The company he worked for was taken over by Metal Box, the production rationalised necessitating a move from Kent. The increase in sales meant that Tom needed assistance. Albert a dedicated production man joined us in the early 1960's. He possessed a magical influence over people with an inherent and natural style of leadership and the ability to motivate people which is so vital for production. In full way cry, at the end of tea break, he would hammer on the doors of the male and female 'loos' and cry "Come on out you lazy bastards", which would have been unacceptable from anyone else. In this day and age 'ACAS' would be running round like a 'Cat on hot bricks'. Sensitive, moody, a character of contrasting moods he was not blessed with the best of health. He was not the servile type and was never fully appreciated nor understood by the boss.

Sales were developed in niche markets. A growing demand for catering packs for milk powder and instant coffee provided a profitable market shared solely with Metal Box. Production was improved with our investment in plant. Sales were further developed in 10 and 15 litre containers for trade packs where there was an increasing demand particularly in DIY outlets. The company was beginning to thrive but needed more investment. The parent company was in difficulty absorbing the profits to cover up its losses. The principal director died and it was sold off to a large food company. Within a short space of time, as part of a rationalisation programme, they converted all their packaging to plastic. My worst fears were realised. Thanks to our diversified range of manufacture and reputation for service,this provided a minor set back. Meanwhile, being profitable, we were taken over by a Merchant Bank. They promptly and prematurely retired T.R. A director of the previous company took over. Jobs for the boys! The city whizz kids appointed consultants and there shortly appeared a high paid engineer as a director experienced in automatic production but with no concept of our style of activity. Expensive expansionist plans were introduced without the technical backing or consultation with the factory management. Plagued with financial controls and accountants breathing down their necks, loyal experienced administrative staff moved to other pastures.

Ten years of hard work culminated in attracting this modern phenomenon of theories, which had little respect for experience and oblivious to the factory staff responsible for this opportunity for success. Tom, our engineer, replaced by a new Technical Director was moved to a lower grade plant. He suffered terrible humiliation and died from an obscure cancer of the brain, initiated doubtlessly from a broken heart. Progress in the modern age!

I respected my position and responsibility as Sales Director, as without sales, we would collapse. Wrestling with principles, soreness, respect for comrades, security and advancing years, I had a growing obsession to run my own business as flames from a fire fanned by the breeze. Packaging was intriguing and had become part of my life. the smaller company with its dedication, experience and hard work contributed to society and its workers. But where could I find the capital?

Then came a chance remark by a representative that the owner of a small business was suffering ill health and was anxious to retire. Although a member of our federation, I was then unaware of its activities. An appointment was arranged.

Trinity Church Square is tucked behind the Borough High Street, halfway between the Elephant & Castle and London Bridge. An oasis bordered with high rise flats, law courts and office buildings. On a cold autumn afternoon the square provided a sombre but attractive impact. A grand square of Georgian houses cream with black doors, railings, coal holes, brass knockers and scrubbed doorsteps. Trinity Church, a classic London Georgian building with its triangular front, Greek portico, prominent clock tower with the statue of King Alfred on the lawn centred the square. In its grounds, the trees with fading leaves provided a panorama of contrasting colours.

G. Wallin with an office on the ground floor of a corner building, its name on a neat brass plaque, tarnished through a lack of brasso and elbow grease. Deceptive, hardly the setting for industrial premises.

Straightening my tie and taking a deep breath, I raised the large black iron knocker and it dropped with a resounding thud. Mr Barham, a tall, frail, ailing figure, opened this wide and inspiring solid black door. He welcomed me with a genial smile and generous greeting. A short passageway, the floor covered with worn linoleum, led into the office. It was furnished with three grand mahogany leather topped desks, rickety chairs and lit by a single bulb set in a cracked discoloured white glass shade. Dark and depressing, the environment was reminiscent of the Dickensian era. A gas fire was the only source of heating with the electricity supply only wired for lighting. the four upper floors were dank and damp with bare floor boards and used solely for storage. The basement was even more stark, the floorboards, plaster ceiling and walls had collapsed mainly through damp. The front area was used for storage of items of value such as solder and copper bits for the soldering irons. At the rear was the remains of a kitchen, with a window providing a view of the yard above. An iron fire escape from the factory led down into an exit into the road from the yard. A popular anecdote was that the manager could gaze up the girls skirts as they descended or apprehend those who slid out of the factory for a sly smoke. The yard also housed the foreman's lavatory, a decrepid wooden shack jealously maintained. Rarely used and unheated, its privacy offset by the discomfort of being exposed to the elements.

The factory was located in Cole Street running parallel to the square in a warehouse type four storey building still common at that time in London. Hatches on each floor opened out allowing goods to be raised or lowered to the road by a rope pulley.

The ground floor of the factory housed the heavy presses required to provide stampings for the fittings for the tin. Low ceilings, uncoated dirty supporting beams, wandering leads, with the only lighting from bare bulbs suspended over the presses. Uneven wooden floors had tinplate with razor sharp corners stacked indiscriminately. Whilst possibly acceptable in the 19th century, production and profitability could not be sustained under these conditions and a visit from the factory inspector could close the works down.

The tinplate store and cutting shop, the heartland of a metal container manufacturer, was congested with one ton bulks of plate stacked precariously to the ceiling. A 'Heath Robinson' hand operated fork lift was the only lifting appliance available.

Wooden stairs, the steps split with wear and age, led to the three upper floors. At one end of the top floor a beam was sagging, corroded by the flux from a solder bath. Prompt action was necessary to prevent this one ton machine collapsing on to the floor beneath. Fortunately, later on my advice was heeded and the machine dismantled and moved. The presses, and tools in the toolroom such as the lathe, were operated by a clutch that moved a leather belt from a rotating shaft running the length of the factory to the individual machines. An electric motor provided the power to rotate the shaft. Apart from the hazards of leather belts, and the inefficiency, it took up considerable space, was dirty and uneconomical - a momento from the Industrial Revolution. Many of the machines and presses in the factory were fifty or more years old. Spares were not available necessitating the costly purchase of custom made parts or time consuming work for the ill equipped and overworked engineers.

Tinplate, components, cartons, etc. were taken up from the ground floor by a lift operated manually with a rope. Surely a museum piece even in the 'Dickensian' era. Maybe suitable as a 'keep fit' muscle developing exercise but not conducive to modern manufacturing methods.

During the blitz, a landmine had destroyed a large paint factory on the opposite side of the road. Our factory having wooden supports and joists apparently swayed like bamboo but with no apparent significant damage. Incendiary bombs landing on the roof had been extinguished by staff who obtained access through a trap door, which also served as a fire escape. There was a retaining wall with the gutters running on the inside which took the water from the sloping slate roof and along which it was possible to walk. It is amazing how so much of this part of London escaped during the blitz considering its closeness to the river, Surrey docks and the Bricklayers Arms, a vast railway goods terminus.

Following the factory tour, Alf outlined the background to the business established in 1888 by George Wallin. Alf was his nephew who joined the business straight from school as a factory hand at the age of fourteen. Jobs were at a premium in those difficult days. An intelligent practical man with common sense he lacked the zest for business, leadership and the complicated intricasies of handling a factory workforce. With the changes in the market place, competition and lacking a salesman, the business had become lethargic and was beginning to flounder. Earlier in the year he had suffered with a bad bout of influenza and had not properly regained his health. He was 62 and relished the thought of retirement. Owing to the complicated nature of the structure of the company, it was not possible for me to invest in it, become a director and eventually take over the ownership. In order to realise his investments in the business, he must sell out to another company so that his company could be liquidated. A faint hope in those days as leasehold property in a residential area offered little prospect. Since leaving the Navy, educating my children and remarrying, my capital was at a low ebb. Nevertheless, there was this obsession for my own company. An infusion of sales would resotore profitability, although shortly investment would be necessary to replace plant most of which was ready for the scrapheap. Wages would also have to be increased in line with local rates. I left with a copy of the latest balance sheet revealing still a modest profit.

Many private firms I approached with regard to backing for an acquisition were interested initially, but because of taxation, the risk was not considered worthwhile. An experience I shared in later years.

Discussions continued with Alf but with little progress. I was able to provide contacts for work not within my firm's capability and this proved mutually beneficial. Meanwhile, he made inconclusive approaches through our federation. Many firms professing interest were purely inquisitive, and certainly not helpful. Business is not a happy and moral world. Women have an intuition and an influence with an insight peculiar to their sex. Mrs Barham, with whom I later was to become more involved, albeit in unfortunate circumstances, pressed Alf to sort out a deal. Explaining the situation and his declining health, I was offered a position as a Director, for six months, with no fixed commitments on either side. My present contract necessitated giving six months notice of resignation. Therefore, at my age, this must be final. There would be no turning back, with little prospect of any management position if it failed.

The following six months proved particularly difficult. My employers applied pressure on me to change my mind particularly as investment for new plant had been approved to provide increased production on two of our main lines. Unfortunately, during this period, I also suffered considerable pain and restriction with a recurrence of an old back injury.

Chapter 4
Wallins - 1972

Finally the big day arrived and I joined this family orientated company, insular, antiquated, and environmentally opposed to change. Management was an unknown entity with everybody operating their own peculiar system. It soon became apparent that the staff, many long serving, local people, ages ranging from 16 to 80, were poorly paid and beginning to leave. Although there was a labour shortage in the area and they possessed considerable skills at making tins, they were ill-equipped for work available locally. However, when the old hands left neither the work nor pay was attractive to younger people. The first task was to obtain profitable work within the framework that existed. George looked after sales, dispatch, loading of lorries and general administration. He was popular but while providing service to the remaining existing customers he had neither time nor experience to keep in touch with the market place and seek new work. There was no costing system. Prices were reduced to satisfy customer pressure. He also operated on the side, a small non-registered merchanting company providing him with remuneration but not cost effective and beneficial to the firm. Apart from three years conscripted service in the Navy during the war, he likewise had been with the firm since he was fourteen. It is easy to condemn older generations for being narrow minded, reluctant to change, uncooperative to outsiders who may take their job. In the decade prior to the war, work was at a premium. Squirrels hoard their nuts to sustain them through the winter. Survival, a dominating biological force, correctly applied is healthy, creative and competitive, but when under threat, dangerous like a spreading disease. It was logical that George wouldtreat me with suspicion, jealousy and distrust. Nevertheless, he must appreciate his inability, intuition or desire to risk his protected position. He must learn to accept therefore that being 58 and knowing the state of the business, cooperation was essential to assist in its survival.

During the first week, the full implications of what I had done began to strike home. After all the hard work, in the other firm, through trials

TIN MAKING IN THE 1920's

and tribulations, I had achieved a reasonably secure position as Sales Director. Was all this to be lost, my training and experienced wasted? Joining this new firm was akin to going back 50 years in time. My family still required financial backing, my wife was a pillar of support with her encouragement.

Motivation and a task however dreary prevents morbid thinking and self pity. A challenge existed, a firm at risk, like a ship floundering in an angry sea. Revitalised and determined after considering the problems, I set out to find profitable work. I must exploit sales in the sizes of tins that could not be mass produced by the large companies and where a more profitable price could be obtained. We must provide quality and service still sadly lacking in the market place. It was also important to ally ourselves with other smaller companies and establish confidence that we were not out to poach on their territory.

Fate was to take a cruel twist. In mid October at the end of my second week and still utterly bewildered with the organisation and factory practices, Alf called George and I into his private office. He explained that his health had not recovered since a bad bout of influenza in January. He was feeling very tired and intended having a few days off. Mrs Spencer, who worked part time, normally prepared the wages and maintained the sales and purchase ledger. Unfortunately, she had been absent for over a month after an operation. Meanwhile, Alf had been looking after the wages. He explained that they were complete and a cheque signed for them to be drawn from the Bank on the following day.

I drove him to Fenchurch Street Station and saw him on to his train for his home in Southend. During Friday afternoon, he 'phoned to say that he felt better having slept solidly for twelve hours and hoped to be in on Monday. At noon on Saturday, the 'phone rang and it was his daughter with the news that he had passed away in his sleep during the night following a heart attack.

Religions provide various reasons for life on earth, the journey to heaven all of little avail to those left behind at its termination. The circumstances were to result in dramatic changes. The following Monday I announced the news to the factory with a plea from Mrs Barham for patience and forbearance until matters could be resolved. Factory working people become closely knit and are basically loyal and sentimental even though of diverse ages and backgrounds. However, a newcomer was suspect, can he be trusted, why is he here - to exploit us? Difficult days were to follow until confidence established.

Mrs Barham, advised by her trustees, was under no illusions of the difficult financial position of the company. At the age of 50, I had no desire to return to a public company. A sensible, generous and attractive agreement was formulated. I was to form a company to take over the existing company providing my company was successful and the debentures settled, Mrs Barham would be able to liquidate and realise the investments providing an income for her retirement. Unfortunately, like a minefield, the way ahead was strewn with obstacles. The Bank manager was not easily convinced and was far from cooperative. The landlord having enjoyed the rent and upkeep of the premises since 1888, was to prove dictatorial and a 'thorn in the flesh' for the lifetime of the company. Crippling conditions and penalties were imposed including a staggering list of dilapidations to be completed before the lease could be transferred.

The laws regarding property, rents and leases are certainly not conducive to encourage the smaller manufacturing company which survives by hard work and loyalty to its staff. Southwark, the local authority, always pleaded it had no money and was never able to contribute assistance in any shape or form. It was bureaucratic and a hindrance.

Politicians of all breeds provide only lip service to small companies, their vested interests being with the public and state-owned monopolies. Small firms provide employment, their own capital and are generally strike and race discrimination free. ACAS, unions, professional bodies, (surveyors, accountants, lawyers) thrive on bureaucracy and act as a drain on their resources. The cost of staff and time in providing returns on PAYE, National Insurance and taxation provide an enormous and crippling burden.

However, notwithstanding these hurdles, there will always be those in whatever aspect it may apply who will rise to the challenge in overcoming the obstacles to attain the 'quest for success'.

Experience is a vital ingredient to success. Tribal chiefs would always consult their elders before embarking on a fundamental change to their way of life. Practices established over time cannot be altered without considerable consultation, perseverance, understanding and patience. Old habits die hard. Wallins wallowed in the past and methods to improve output became the most daunting task.

Profits had to be produced at all costs to realise the payment of higher wages, refurbished plant, satisfy the requirements of the factory regulations and demands of the lease for dilapidations. Each section of the factory operated independently like a separate cell, a relic of the past; survival, protect your own particular function. Teamwork and cooperation to acquire cost-effective production was an unknown quantity. Fortunately, the outside world was equally inefficient, in particular, metal packaging. A breathing space was established and slowly there were glimpses of sunshine through the gloom.

Mrs Spencer was a lady employed part time as a wages clerk and to maintain essential books. She had suffered from appendicitis and had been off work for the month previous to Alf's death. Fortunately, she returned the week after he died and could look after the wages. Undoubtedly her illness and absence must have added to the pressures that he was under and contributed to his heart attack. Mrs Spencer had not fully recovered and, combined with the changes being introduced, found the pressure too great and tendered her notice. It was essential to have a qualified book-keeper and wages clerk. We used the Kalamazoo system for the accounts. Wages and tax returns are a tedious, complicated and time consuming occupation. Joan who had worked in my last firm was available and accepted the position on a part-time basis. She was qualified in all respects in additon to being a most proficient shorthand typist. She was competent, reliable and a delightful person, respected and liked by all. She worked three days a week travelling to and from Dartford in Kent by British Rail South East network, hardly the most reliable and comfortable journey. She was a tremendous asset, contributing greatly towards our success and my piece of mind. When we finally took over the company in June 1973, it was necessary to recruit a further book-keeper as a back up for wages and accounts. Alf had used his accountant for this purpose but he was shortly to retire and advised that it would be more economical to maintain our own accounts thereby only requiring accountancy services yearly for audit purposes. We placed an advertisement for a book-keeper in an employment agency near London Bridge. The following day, they 'phoned with a cadidate for us to interview. The applicant was a retired army officer, who had run a school in Essex and being over 60, decided it wise to sell, particularly with imminent changes pending in the education system. He, Mr Day, arrived promptly for the interview, smartly dressed in a business suit, with his rolled umbrella; a distinguished and charming gentleman. The part-time terms suited him adequately. Although lacking experience in book-keeping, his natural enthusiasm and intelligence counteracted this inadequacy. He appreciated, both as a military man and from running a school, that accounts must serve as a history of events and be used as a tool. I found our discussions stimulating and productive, helping to formulate our own distinctive and innovative costing system not generally accepted or understood by our bankers or the accountancy profession. It provided a figure for a cost per hour, incorporating all the overheads adjusted according to the wages which were geared to the work ratio. The sole advantage of a fluid staff was that they needn't be replaced if the work rate fell. A selective experienced work force particularly with our operation was obviously the ideal. Joan and Mr Day complimented each other and formed an ideal team contributing considerable to the economic stability and success during the formative years.

Reorganising production was the urgent priority. Alf had advised that the introduction of improved production methods may be accepted more readily from me as an outsider. He had recommended that Ted, the production foreman and line setter, should be given a chance as he was long serving, competent, loyal and enjoyed good relations with the staff as well as being an experienced setter. This was all to be easier said than done. Tin-making methods had not altered during the century. As soon as a supervisor's back was turned, the operators would revert to the old methods. Limited success was achieved by laying out the lines so that tins could only be produced on a flow basis. If an operator went to the 'loo', then the line stopped, everybody operated individually and teamwork was just not understood. Jim though an excellent engineer, was unfortunately unable to cooperate with the line foreman and supervisors. He was disabled, which was later diagnosed as cancer. He suffered considerable pain and was forced to retire.

The engineer's shop was in a wire cage at the end of the press room. There was a single belt operated lathe at least fifty years old, a shaper and a belt operated drill. Jim owned his own tools including verniers and micrometers whichhe treasured and would not loan to others. An asset were the senior female supervisors, four of them and all over 60 who had worked on piece rate before the war. Their individual performance on machines was phenomenal and control over the operators excellent. They possessed an incredible degree of loyalty and their contribution was invaluable. The operation of tin-making machinery, on first sight, appears simple, but to the majority is repetitive and monotonous. However, there are some, particularly females, who possess a flair for this work which is artistic with its flow and rhythm. The integration of these skills to the production was the key and, with patience and perseverance, considerable improvements resulted.

The lack of finance was critical, the only source being from profits. A limited wage increase was introduced as a gesture resulting in immediate support in the faith that goodwill was being offered. Initially a patching up exercise must be maintained on the machinery.

It is an interesting reflection that difficulties create a need to fabricate. New ideas and innovations only emanate during wars when survival is at stake. Peacetime generally provides development and consolidation and the creeping malaise of bureaucracy. Stimulation of thought generated by schools and universities is not generally conducive to a commercial enterprise. Streamlining mass production is necessary to generate increasing profits in the large public company. The entrepreneur invariably finds this environment alien. He gravitates to the smaller company which lacks finance for training to support research. However, the survival factor creates the drive. Unfortunately, politicians, trade unions and the taxation and legal system have not and do not encourage the smaller companies which is unfortunately, a vicious circle.

During the war in the desert, aircraft assembly was temporarily suspended through lack of split pins, although time consuming, regulations were by-passed by bending wire enabling job completion and the aircraft to fly. Historically, we are resentful and distrust change. We only seem to succeed when the odds are against us.

My last company was owned by a Merchant Bank. The controlling executives were well intentioned but without knowledge of the process of metal packaging manufacture. They believed that high speed production would generate increased turnover to provide the return on capital justifying the capital outlay. This necessitated the elimination of the short runs of special sizes which realised a higher profit margin.

They were to compete with Metal Box and other companies geared and experienced in these fields. However, their loss was our gain. My old customers, including names such as ICI, were denied the supply of those special sizes to accommodate capacities of between 1 and 3 gallons. Unfortunately, the tools had been sold to a company in the north who was slow to react to the demand. Unbelievably, it was disclosed that discarded tools over the years had been stored under the floor boards in the Press Shop. A young, thin and wiry volunteer performed a valiant feat crawling under the floor boards with associated rubble and the fear of rats. He recovered sizes many of which could be modified for the purposes required avoiding the cost and delay of new tools. Many of the tins must be soldered as they were to contain paint chemicals and searching products. Soldering a tin 12 inches tall by hand was slow, tedious and not cost effective. My son and his chums at this period were students working part time and they had a brain wave. Copper bits in stock were drilled and filled with adaptors which were heated by calor gas supplied from bottles. A production flow was provided using six experienced solders maintaining a speed of the line at about 500 an hour. The manufacture of the large tins up to 4 gallon capacity was to prove the salvation and mainstay of the company for years to come.

Previously, tins had been loaded on to lorries singly or with small tins in cartons. This was time consuming, expensive in cartons, and resulted in damage to tins. Loading was incredibly slow, the tins brought down from the upper floors in trolleys by the rope operated lift. Whilst this was proceeding materials could not be taken up so there was a continual interruption of production.

We hired two machines which would tie up tins in bundles with string and could be accommodated at the end of the line preserving the production flow. Wooden chutes were constructed and the bundled tins slid down floor by floor to the lorry in the road. Loading was still labour intensive but could be scheduled with minimum disturbance of production. Office staff, including the Managing Director, frequently became involved. I found it a useful pastime enabling me to witness at first hand what was happening on the lines. We all work more efficiently if we believe we are being overlooked.

The increase in sales, particularly with larger tins occupying more space, required the constant use of our dilapidated 20 cwt Commer vans. They were frequently breaking down with bizarre results. An extra driver was recruited from the Department of Employment. It was difficult to obtain any background of the person to be employed, a clean driving licence the only legal requirement. A driver was a representative of the company, requiring honesty, a pleasant manner, responsibility for his load and discretion regarding disputes on the count. He must be prepared to work inflexible hours and be able to find his way, often a difficult and hazardous task, with some firms being tucked away in inaccessible places. We worked as a family with teamwork as a keynote. So he must load and unload his and other vehicles.

Time and a quick turnover was a prerequisite delivering relatively small quantities of 'empty air' at low value. Many of the larger companies introduced bureaucratic times and conditions for unloading. Frustrating and costly for a vehicle to be behind one or two 40 foot vehicles and delayed for two or three hours. We sold a service which often backfired with these situations. Bill Cooper who joined us in early 1973, can only be described as an extraordinary character. He was highly strung, a depressant, impatient and suffered with insomnia and would often be on a customers doorstep at 4 a.m. Driving high powered vehicles, cars or motor bikes, was his passion. Fortuitously our vehicles were governed and their maximum speed limited to 40 m.p.h. Nevertheless, we soon learnt, to our cost, that engines were worn out in rapid succession. In a strange way, he was loyal, persevering with an endearing personality. Whilst difficult to control, his merits, properly utilised, could offset his costs. Providing he was thoroughly briefed with the overtime that he could claim, the responsibility for his vehicle and awareness of the running costs, he moulded into the family character of the firm.

Bill's mother, a cantankerous old lady in her seventies, would 'phone complaining that her Billy was being ill treated. On numerous occasions she would call at the office reporting extraordinary and ill-founded stories about the staff. She was jealous of Bill's girl friends and would 'phone saying that he filtered petrol from the van for his motor bike. The latest 'lady love' had six children and on a day out it was an expensive occupation with treats to Southend and the funfair. He was married when he joined us and his niece, Debbie, worked for us as soon as she left school at sixteen. Although her home life had been virtually non-existent, she had a delightful honest and loyal personality. Highly strung, impatient, demonstrative but naturally intelligent, she developed into one of our best operators. It takes a lot to make the world.

It was this utilisation of assets that enabled us to produce a cost-efficient and flexible output of short runs to compete in the market place with the lumbering giants. Whilst working to ensure survival of the company was the paramount priority, the factory domestic problems could never be ignored. Visits or 'phone calls from relatives whilst at times amusing, became a time consuming occupation. Mothers would 'phone that their 'little girl' was being victimised or ill treated, invariably based upon a misguided story to disguise devious activity. Timekeeping and absenteeism were also a mixed blessing, responsible and conscientious because they needed the money, the problems of sickness and lack of childminders proved another long term problem. Historically, families tended to work in metal packaging firms in the London area. We employed over the years a number of families including grandmothers, mothers and children. One of the steadiest and most reliable press operators was over eighty.

The increase in sales necessitated the employment of a second driver. The Department of Employment with all their wisdom despatched Fred, disabled with a glass eye. The fact that it was illegal, escaped their otherwise efficient bureaucratic requirements. He was an enormous, ungainly and endearing personality, a widower in his mid-fifties. During the D Day invasion, he had been involved in a mortar attack and badly injured. He lost an eye and suffered severe burns leaving permanent horrific scars. Nevertheless, when he smiled his face permeated generosity and kindness. He was a lonely man living in a single room in a tower block in Brixton. As it was observed that he drove a lorry and was away by day, the premises were frequently broken into. Finally, when his unique collection of brass-band records, which were his particular treasured collection, were stolen, he had a minor mental breakdown. The council had ignored his pleas for security so regrettably, he terminated his employment with us and left to live with his daughter.

He was a moody individual and when something upset him he would threaten to leave, slump off round the block and report back for the next trip without any malice. He was a steady and reliable driver, even with one eye. There was an unfortunate accident when he was stopped in a traffic hold up on the feeder road to the A2. A coach unable to stop, hit his vehicle from the rear with such force that he ended up unconscious in his vehicle facing the other way. He was taken by ambulance to Woolwich hospital and when we visited him in the evening, he was conscious and not suffering any pain. He had suffered concussion and was released after a couple of days and duly reported back to work. The van was a write off but with no witnesses, we received virtually nothing from the insurance and vague promises from the coach driver who admitted liability but was without funds.

Profit at all costs was the prime necessity for survival. the black clouds were gathering, staff problems requiring higher wages, maintenance of plant, tooling to meet the market requirements for more profitable outlets, the payment for the debenture.

It was the habit of the Factory Inspector to make an impromptu visit. We had devoted the maximum priority, with our limited resources, to ensuring that the presses were securely guarded and inspection cards up-to-date with the factory act and insurance certificates prominently displayed. Sure enough, the dreaded day arrived. My son in those early days was a student working weekends and holidays. Fortunately, the day the Inspector called he was available as I was out visiting a customer. Notwithstanding their reputation for pettiness and toughness we were fortunate. The advice and recommendations were practical and beneficial and we were given six months for them to be incorporated.

Whilst the terms of the sale had been agreed and payments of the debenture initiated, the landlord would not permit the transfer of the lease until the list of dilapidations they had drawn up were completed to their satisfaction. They provided an estimate of £30,000 to fulfill the list of requirements as per the schedule. Ernie was a talented nephew of my wife, who was self employed and needed funds to complete the reconstruction of his Georgian house. We instituted a programme where the initial work would combine to satisfy the dilapidations but provide a profitable contribution. As part of our service, we would supply a complete range of tins to satisfy the customer requirements. We would purchase and stock tins not within our range of manufacture. The rooms above the house were suitable for tins in cartons. Paint and emulsion was purchased at a discount from our customers. Ernie, with the assistance of his father, rapidly rendered a cheap but satisfactory job. A cable (unauthorised) was run from the factory so that points could be installed in the house for electric fires and other appliances. The floorboards in the factory were broken and uneven. Hardboard was laid hiding the damage to flooring and saving the costly replacement of boards. It also provided a smooth surface whereby tins stacked on wooden trolleys could be wheeled about the floors to the loading chutes and tinplate and materials wheeled on a pallet truck to the lifts.

Fortunately in 1973 the demand exceeded supply and we were able to build up manufacturing and merchanting sales. Meanwhile, Jim, our engineer, who had worked so hard and loyally under difficulty with his health was advised he must shortly retire. My mother always said that as "one door shuts, another opens". During the previous month, Henry, an engineer in my last company, 'phoned explaining that he had been made redundant and was very unhappy working for a firm outside of the industry. A loyal, conscientious, experienced and first class engineer, he had spent a lifetime in the tin box industry. I explained the financial situation at the time, but would keep in touch. I was most anxious not to coerce staff from one disaster into another. He met Jim and was thoroughly acquainted with the problems. He accepted the offer to match his current salary and my promise that it would improve with the fortunes of the firm. He was to prove an invaluable investment and a cornerstone to the success of the company. Henry required help as the machinery was in a very dilapidated condition and now he was on his own.

Whilst of different backgrounds and practices, Henry and Jim worked well, their combined skills fulfilled an invaluable contribution before Jim regrettably was forced to retired with his ill health. He maintained a keen interest and provided useful advice during my visits in his fading life. An engineer of the old school he was stubborn, frank, thorough and highly skilled. A breed who formed a vital background to the engineering companies of this country.

In 1973 we recruited many West Indians who were keen to work and were reasonable time keepers. Luke was sent to us from the Job Centre as being intelligent and interested in engineering. He was tall, thin and very athletic, good looking and of a cheerful disposition. Although of different temperaments and a disparity in age, they formed a remarkable partnership. It soon became apparent that he was unstable and involved in scrapes with the police particularly over his attractive girlfriend. I backed him assuring the police of his value to the company. He was loyal and appreciated the support. His proficiency as an engineer grew rapidly. Suddenly he became ill, taken to hospital and within a matter of two or three weeks, died of stomach cancer. A tragedy that struck the factory: a young man not yet in his prime of life, a delightful and refreshing personality. Although only with us for about a year he left an indelible mark.

Chapter 5
Owning a Factory

June 1973 was a further landmark for the company. My wife and I, as controlling Directors, were to be responsible for G. Wallin & Company Limited with the old company acting as Guarantor for the lease until our worthy landlord deemed the dilapidations saitsfactory and the lease be transferred. The results for 1972 to 1973 turned out to be confusing indicating a loss of £10,000 for the year ended. I was confident that this was for the early part of the financial year and that our current sales should be yielding a profit. Nevertheless, with all at stake and the deed of our house as guarantor for the Bank overdraft, the situation was not conducive to celebration but more in fact sleepless nights. Whilst not a religious person, I had a faith, as in my flying days, that we would survive. The senior sister of my wife's family was deeply religious and extols that life is a journey. The memories in life generally recall the peaks and troughs.

In November the 'oil' crisis struck. Panic reigned, prices soared, queues stretched at filling stations. The needs of the public was for petrol to run their cars, joyrides, take kids to school and the distribution of goods. The lifeblood of the country became second place. Whilst pleading with the Department of Employment and M.Ps produced no assistance, we must queue with our small lorry at the filling station often to reach the head of the queue and find that the fuel had run out.

Somehow we managed to deliver. Tinplate prices escalated which happily we were able to pass on. Plastic, a petroleum by product, suddenly became in short supply and their prices also increased appreciably. Suddenly the sun glimmered through the clouds and our horizon lifted with the prospects of the restoration of a more secure base for metal packaging. Whilst the demand increased so did the problems. Apart from the cost, it was virtually impossible to obtain tinplate to the specifications required, load times for delivery were extended and were unreliable. A cartel existed between the major tinplate manufacturers in Europe, and the smaller companies were restricted to purchase from British Steel through its agents. A few firms managed to purchase plate cheaper and of superior quality from South Africa or even Japan. Whilst the Welsh were delightful people, they were very narrow minded, the manufacturers and unions insular in their outlook that there would be an indiscriminate demand. The political system must surely be largely responsible, capitalist organisations squeeze out competition and support conservatism. Trade unions are dependent upon large capitalist and nationalised industries with the mass labour market where they wield their power. As a small manufacturer, we suffered from the worst of both worlds.

Labour shortage was another particular problem. During 1960 and 1970, the shortage was acute and consequently wages rose. Since our manufacturing methods were not geared to mass production, the work was less repetitive and the environment more friendly and family orientated. Nevertheless, our running costs, provision of plant, dilapidations and overheads must all come out of profits therefore our wages were still relatively low. Consequently, the younger employees we attracted were of low mental attributes, many of them unable to read or write with an unhappy and deficient home background. Timekeeping and sense of responsibility was a nightmare. However, with patience and perseverance, they gradually acclimatised and found a stability in this more family orientated company.

The survival of metal packaging in my estimation was, and still is, largely dependent upon printed tins. Tinplate provides an excellent base for the reproduction of print for product presentation, fancy goods, signs, combined with the preservation of the container from the elements, then fortunately, the presentation on plastic containers was, and still is, inferior. The offset litho process was in those days expensive and labour intensive. The large companies such as Metal Box had their own printing plant but smaller manufacturers must contract out with the small specialised offset litho companies. It was difficult to accommodate the extended dead-line for deliveries and high costs which many customers found prohibitive. Unfortunately, market forces often in the long term reduce customer choice and more specialised products become unavailable. Notwithstanding these problems, this enabled us to establish a base in more specialised containers particularly the larger sizes where the demand did not justify mass production and with lower overheads we had the edge on the larger manufacturer.

Man is part of the biological process striving for survival often to the detriment for the future. Whilst collectively we can best harness our resources, in reality even with all the bureaucratic barriers, the individual resorts to basic instincts. Small companies innovate, are more efficient and flexible and yet must operate with outdated and unproductive plant.

The professions, unions, civil servants must justify their living with the constant introduction of bureaucratic controls across a wide spectrum from engineering, health, environment, quality control, taxation and vehicle operations. Whilst at times they proved a stranglehold on our profitable activities, in many instances, being smaller and more flexible, they could be by-passed, often an impossibility for the larger companies. The guiding light was service and quality. It was of little value for a firm to have orders for a product without the containers available at the right time and place.

It is significant that the war produced the need, and money was provided for scientific research. Revolutionary contributions were produced in all aspects of science. In order to coordinate many of these projects, the Government introduced the Ministry of Supply which post-war developed into a bureaucratic sponge. I worked closely on a project with a scientist whose talent and motivation was in providing answers to our electronic requirements. We developed a harmonious and productive relationship. I attended the meetings selling our requirements and reporting progress, working wherever possible more closely with the manufacturer. It is said today that since 1980 the Government has cut back on research and to qualify for what appropriations are available the scientists must waste their time and talents on budgets and selling their ideas to justify their existence. Unfortunately, in large companies, quick returns on investment are the order of the day. Shareholders require dividends now and not in five year's time. The small company attracts the entrepreneur and innovator, but the opportunities are limited because of the lack of financial backing. The far sighted firm must be the winner in the long term foreseeing future demands and drawing on the experience of the past. Why do other nations recognise the need for science and engineering for industry? This country has always encouraged literature and the arts, science created as the plumber. When I entered industry in 1958, selling was a dirty word with remuneration less than that of a road sweeper. Apparently this attitude is even more prevalent today. There are apparently more accountants per capita than in any other country in the world. My impression generally over a span of forty five years, is that the Americans in particular have this refreshing young and enthusiastic enquiring mind over most matters of civilisation and progress, whether it be history, engineering, aviation, business or the livelihood and habitat of the individual. Generalisation is obviously dangerous and all individuals resort to protectionism and isolationism.

The Tin Box Federation was formed to enable manufacturers of tins and drums to discuss common problems, agree specifications and generally provide a concerted body to represent the views of industry to the Government and other large organisations. In the 70's it was appreciated that the packaging industry covered a wider field and its membership extended to include merchants, printers and other organisations. The name was changed to Metal Packaging Manufacturers Association. Representation was included with SEFEL, the European counterpart. A particular problem emanating in Europe was the carriage of dangerous goods. The problems which were particularly serious for this country involved mass produced containers such as the lever lid type tin produced economically and to a standard and quality satisfactory to the customer. This tin would not however fulfill the specification for transportation by sea of inflammable and toxic materials such as chemicals and paints. The 'Herald of Free Enterprise' disaster in the 80's demonstrated the potential threats. Similarly, imagine a 40 ton vehicle spilling its load on a motorway. Legislation, albeit on a short term basis, was negotiated to reduce the impact on the existing market. A considerable investment would be necessary to produce a standard container to meet the regulations. Customers for the home market would remain on the existing container. Meanwhile, other countries particularly Europe, manipulated the legislation to a large extent to utilise their current full aperture container. We have therefore for some years been forced to import containers from Europe to package products for export to conform with the regulations. The result to this country was increased import costs with business lost to UK manufacturers. Large companies would not invest shareholders' money in plant where there was still only a limited market. Small companies were without the resources to be able to finance such a development. I suppose this is the story of British industry and the supposed free market economy. Manufacturing, particularly of labour intensive products, will be lost to countries with cheaper labour markets.

At Wallins, in order to survive, we had to find specialist markets for tins which required the development of ideas and ingenuity. Although we were not endowed with brilliant brains or scientific degrees, enthusiasm and experience generally enabled us to solve the problem. Why does the large corporate company not set up this small research and development units that can economically exploit the future requirements?

The retail industry have an increasing influence on packaging which may well encourage the development of new ideas and investment.

Quality control was a vital factor particularly as we manufactured a wide range of food containers. The production line being non-automatic enabled a much closer scrutiny of the tins during manufacture. We supplied a very large and famous food company with slip lid tins for packaging a powder product for a catering outlet. They were packed with the lids fitted, strung in bundles, and loaded on to a large contract hire vehicle virtually following manufacture and delivered to a factory near Liverpool the following day. The union in this company was renowned for being aggressive and non-cooperative and we complained regarding the problems experienced and the delay in unloading. A few weeks later, a letter arrived demanding the visit of a representative to inspect a tin from this consignment containing 'urine'. My representative duly visited the company and explained that as the offending tin was in the middle of the bundle it would have been impossible at our factory to remove and then replace the lid without the bundle collapsing. The explanation was not accepted and this contract for about 20,000 tins per annum was lost. It was admitted two years or so later that it was done 'in spite' by a member of their own workforce over a pay dispute. Whilst complaints were often received regarding tins delivered damaged, usually in transit, the complaint was invariably amicably settled and fortunately, this was a one-off episode.

Nevertheless, it was costly and very upsetting to our staff.

Shortage of staff was a constant problem. There has always been strong pressure to employ disabled people and a form of legislation existed requiring an explanation if it was not offered. This proved a difficult problem particularly as the factory act and insurances were most severe should there be an accident. There were virtually no jobs available which did not involve operating presses or rotating machinery. We developed a close liaison with their organisation. Epilepsy could be a particular problem if we were not aware that the illness existed. We employed a young man who was a particularly good operator although a bad timekeeper, the excuse was oversleeping usually due to over-indulgence. At 8 a.m. one morning, he collapsed in the yard with a fit. The ambulance arrived from Guys and the paramedics were excellent and the man soon revived. I worked closely with the specialist at St. Thomas Hospital who assured me that providing he followed the prescribed routine and treatment, he would not have further attacks. I also cooperated with his mother who was anxious that he maintained his employment. However, being mentally unstable, he suddenly left, attracted by a less secure but a more remunerative job. He lasted two weeks before being dismissed. Unfortunately, there are many people in similar circumstances who eventually end up requiring social assistance.

The fear of accidents was a prevailing nightmare. Fortunately, during the twenty years of running the firm, we only experienced two really serious accidents. The first was horrendous.

It was a Friday afternoon when inevitably there was a slow down on production. John, a quiet, likeable young man but unfortunately rather simple with a mental disability, was leaning on a bar serving as a safety barrier across a hatch in the factory opening to the road 15 feet below. The bar was not adequately closed and leaning out to chat with his chum, the bar collapsed and he fell on a broken wooden box and was impaled through his lower abdomen by a sword shaped broken wooden supporting member. Charles who had recently joined us on a part-time basis heard the scream and dialled 999. He had served in the merchant navy and was familiar with first aid. He acted magnificently, chatting and comforting the poor fellow until the ambulance arrived.

John was taken to Guys Hospital and their prompt action and expertise saved his life. They informed his parents who were naturally shattered. I drove home in the evening like a zombie, and maintained regular touch with the hospital. Unable to sleep, my mind was pervaded with nightmarish thoughts with an horrendous guilt complex. Safety was a prime priority and it was inconceivable that a commercial enterprise could justify such an accident. How could such a thing occur to an ordinary person with loving parents pleased that their son had a job? My wife and I visited him the next day and met his parents. Delightful people who bore no malice. He was on the crucial list for a week and eventually recovered after a year in hospital.

The only investigation was by the insurance company who were exacting and frustrating, forcing us to introduce fatuous and impractical precautions. The amount of compensation paid was never disclosed. My attitude hardened toward the pressure by authorities on employers to employ the disabled.

Charles who had acted so magnificently provided valuable support to the management and was popular with staff, versatile and capable in our many complicated and diversified activities.

Although only in his early thirties he was an alcoholic and unable to maintain employment. He had a loyal and supportive wife and after leaving, they acted as managers in a local pub but again his addiction had the upper hand and they moved again.

The second accident occurred a year or so later. Mary, a senior supervisor of considerable experience and an outstanding operator, had filled in to work a machine to complete the production line. Whilst correcting an operator on an adjacent line, her concentration was distracted, the body of the tin which she was making skidded and cut a main vein in her wrist. Fortunately at that time we were employing a medical student who administered first aid by applying a pressure pad using some rag. This prompt action certainly contributed in saving her life. Although supported, she had to descend four flights of stairs prior to the ambulance arriving. On returning to work, she continued to provide valuable service until her retirement a few years later.

Tin-making to this generation was a way of life, providing

comradeship and satisfaction in addition to a living. We were favoured
with about four ladies of this ability in those early days who contributed
considerably to our survival.

Chapter 6
Domestic Matters

The danger period in any business, particularly manufacturing, is when their is an upturn especially when combined with the acquisition of new business. Tinplate must be provisioned and, if the tin is decorated, then it must be printed and to obtain an economical run, stock must be provisioned to cover three to six months. The customer normally takes two months credit and therefore cash flow can be a nightmare. Even with a supportive Bank manager, interest rates when overdrawn soon absorb the profits. In order to meet the extra production additional staff must be recruited.

Experienced and reliable managers were at a premium. Whilst the engineering side had been reinforced, a general manager was needed to coordinate production and the multitude of day-to-day necessities to run the firm. I contacted the forces resettlement who advised that Dave King, a Chief Electrical Artificer, would shortly be retiring. A quiet serious character with a dry sense of humour, he had joined the Navy early in the war qualified in electrical engineering and apart from a short break after the war, had served over 30 years mainly at sea. He lived at Gravesend and the prospect of employment in a small firm within travelling distance was appealing. He was to prove a bulwark, kind, trustworthy and with a talent for obtaining willing cooperation from the staff. We were indeed fortunate, and he served loyally and painstakingly until the bitter end. He lived a couple of miles from the station and if necessary, would walk, rain or snow, to catch the train. Regardless of rail strikes, Dave would somehow always turn up. He soon picked up the rudiments of tin-making and frequently acted as production manager. A most valued attribute was his knowledge of electrics. The wiring was unsafe and archaic but somehow Dave kept things going, the bureaucrats would have thrown a fit, but as a small company with these marvellous people, we cut corners and provided a valuable contribution to society. We provided many tins for food so essential during the many strikes in the 70's and 80's that nearly paralysed the nation.

In early 1974 as a precaution, following the fuel crisis, and a miners' strike, industry was placed on a three day week. the immediate public reaction boosted by the media was doom and gloom. Loss of exports, prospect of food rationing. In fact, as in the war, the workforce of the country rallied, fear of unemployment combined with a purpose resulted in improved production which to a large extent offset the loss of the two working days.

Whilst law abiding and patriotic, we needed to echo Nelson and place our telescope to the blind eye. The Government provided us as an authority to manufacture tins essential to the nations needs, such as for food. These were essentially special sizes in small quantities, labour intensive in production, and only manufactured by small firms such as ours. During this period, power was cut on the closed days. Fortunately at that time the factory was on the same power circuit as Guys Hospital. We would make the special tins on those days and standard work on the permissible open days. The office being situated in the square was on a different circuit and necessitated working initially by candlelight when the power was cut. Eventually, we ran a cable from the factory to the offices for lighting and would work with the old fashioned wooden shutters closed across the windows. Consequently, we were able to fulfill our obligations with the containers for the Government emergency requirements, maintain employment, service our other customers and remain in business. Doubtless this was not recognised as comparable to Nelson and not included in the 'Honours List'. The sense of drama, and intrigue, enhanced by the media, motivated the work force, created a closeness, sense of purpose and comradeship probably never obtained in the monotony and humdrum of a normal day's work.

People of all sexes and ages respond to being appreciated with support gained rather than alienated by simple acts of consideration. The factory was built in the 19th century, a wooden structure and consequently not affected by extremes of temperature as more modern thinly built brick buildings. The central heating was primitive, with 6" diameter bore cast iron pipes running round the floors and secured to the ceiling and most inefficient in reflecting the heat. Furthermore, over many years they became furred up. The gas boiler was of modern design and reasonably efficient but the timing mechanism temperamental. Frequently on a freezing cold Monday morning it failed to light up. Foot stamping and moans, but an early brew of tea, a few electric fires, a joke and an extra jersey soon dampened ill-humour and production commenced. Conversely in the hot weather we opened all hatches, sought the sympathy of local neighbours to suffer the additional noise from machines and presses. Fortunately, after midday when the sun was at its hottest, the building was shaded by the tall blocks of flats opposite on the south side. We provided fruit squash drinks which was distributed to the floors. A local shopkeeper provided ice daily and early afternoon 'ice lollies' which always proved a 'winner'. These simple and economic measures provided considerable response and maintained production even in the most extreme conditions. We were fortunate that the great majority of the factory staff lived locally. During the various strikes that prevailed in the 70's and 80's, we always kept going. Providing people got to work they were paid from 8 a.m. and until 5.30 p.m. even though they may leave prematurely. There were many who would walk from Peckham or New Cross in all weathers.

Staff cooperation was mainly initiated during the three day week and it is a good adage that success often stems from adversity. Throughout my 20 years Londoners formed the principal majority of staff combined with an increasing number of different nationalities. A collection was made for any member of staff who was ill, in difficulty, or suffered a bereavement. Such generosity is peculiar to the working class.

The increase in factory output with tins of increased capacity resulted in the necessity for delivery by larger vehicles. We developed a link with a privately owned haulage company from Manchester and another from Hull who were anxious to obtain regular return loads from London. A competitive rate, of mutual benefit, was established and the relationship continued until the business was sold and moved to Norwich. The combination of extra production, overtime, extra machinery and the additional loading resulted in complaints from neighbours. They mainly used this as an excuse to complain to the landlord, trying to manipulate the circumstances as a means of obtaining a rent reduction. There was a particularly difficult neighbour whose house backed on to the factory where there was a window which was of opaque glass. We bricked it up but duly received a letter from the landlord with a complaint of noise and movements in the night as though we were surreptiously moving plant. He proved to be very difficult and had been a Southwark councillor. He was intelligent with an active mind and retired, generally interfering with any activity in the square. We were anxious to obtain the support of the local residents and held a meeting one evening in the office, preceded by a tour of the factory. We served sherry, beer and snacks and asked for questions individually which could then be discussed by the assembly. The only complaint was against the rate increase by the council. Whilst sympathetic, it was explained that this was not within our jurisdiction and he must complain to the council. He was difficult to placate being intoxicated having consumed a bottle of sherry. As a meeting, it was a shambles, impossible to maintain logic or sensible questions. Nevertheless we all parted on good terms and obtained valuable support.

There were further complaints brought to us by the landlord from residents not even neighbouring the factory. Again, an effort to obtain a rent reduction. Nevertheless, although the complaints were unjustified, it drew attention to our activities and provided ammunition for the landlord at a later date for not renewing the lease.

Unfortunately, the many revolutionary inventions and developments created become counter productive and man becomes the slave. The potential for the computer has never been completely realised being used particularly by financial organisation as a cash register. Transport has produced a similar history. As an island, towns were always congested with narrow roads particularly in large towns. Instead of using railways and our inland waterways, industry was encouraged to move to undeveloped areas requiring motorways for communication. Goods partly fabricated such as tins would be taken from London to Scotland, filled and transported back to London. Instead of encouraging established firms to remain and use small vehicles to transport short distances to the bulk carriers, we have 40 feet vehicles careering round small roads in London and other large towns. Furthermore, the infrastructure created by Queen Victoria - sewers, water mains, cables, etc. were for light loads such as horse and cart and not 40 ton loads.

My son a keyholder living in Bromley twelve miles away was called out by the police in the middle of the night. A manhole cover for the electricity supply in the road adjacent to the factory had blown twenty feet in the air with a sheet of flame. Fortunately nobody was around. The cable was alight and adjacent to the gas supply pipe leading into the factory.

Fortunately, the fire was soon extinguished but we were without electricity for most of the following day following repairs by the Electricity Board. The factory wall adjacent to the manhole cover had been damaged and required rebuilding. The costs were never recovered apart from the loss of production for best part of a day. The cause was never disclosed but suggests that it was caused by the pounding from heavy lorries. We experienced frequent burst water mains which again seriously distrupted production. A constant supply of water was essential for operating the soudronic equipment.

Yellow lines were a nightmare to Wallins. The council refused a dispensation for lorries to complete their loading or unloading if it exceeded 20 minutes. They would have to drive round and round the block congesting traffic until they could position at the loading bay. The Post Office at the end of the road would have large vehicles parked and blocking the road for extended periods. They were permitted special parking bays for their staff but not for ours.

SOUTH LONDON PRESS 12TH FEBRUARY, 1982.

Cracked pavement threat to cellar

A SOUTHWARK businessman claims the cellar of his tin mal ng factory is in danger of collapsing because of heavy lorries driving over the pavement.

The paving stones are cracking and sinking outside the company offices of G. Wallin Ltd., in Trinity Church Street-square.

Managing director Gordon Sabin claims the damage is caused by lorries forced over the pavement since the council introduced new traffic restrictions in the area.

Industrial lorries use the street as a short-cut since a traffic width barrier was put up at the junction of Trinity-st. and Great Dover-st., maintains Mr. Sabin.

He says the lorries are forced over the pavement because the road is too narrow.

"Now, the council in their wisdom have errected a traffic island immediately outside the factory offices, which means the lorries have to go further across the pavement to use the short-cut," he said.

"My cellar is now in danger of collapsing because of the weight of the lorries. I wrote to the council to complain in August, but have heard nothing from them."

A Southwark Council spokesman commented, We are now considering removing the traffic island because we admit there are problems about the turning around the factory from Trinity Church-st. into Globe-st."

■ *SAVE my pavement . . . Mr Sabin on the cracked paving stones outside his factory.*

Fighting Bureaucracy for "Wallins".

Small companies have been driven out of business by authorities and monopolies even in country areas. The individual has to a large extent been forced to shop in a supermarket where car parks are available. The GLC was responsible for the closure of many companies in South East London, many parts became derelict with a consequent loss of jobs. Glorious democracy and freedom. Common sense lost to bureaucracy and power groups. A very expensive and extensive survey was conducted by the GLC to ban vehicles over 40 feet leaving or entering London after 9 p.m.or entering it before 7 a.m. Stranded drivers, out of driving hours, could only park in special parks of which there were only two in South East London. Southwark would not permit the driver sleeping in his vehicle so he became an orphan wandering the streets or sleeping on a park bench in the middle of winter. The M25 was to be the source of salvation for all travellers and authorities. However, heavy vehicles, commuters and buses were restricted to single lanes as they entered the Greater London area because of bus lanes.

The quest for work to generate profits for recovery proved a constant battle. We concentrated particularly on large tins where competition was on more level terms as the demand did not justify the cost of installing automatic plant. A break-through with a very large company producing an exterior finish coating was finally made in the mid 70's when they decided to extend their range and package it in a 10 litre container in addition to the 5 litre. Selling is a painstaking business requiring optimism and hard work. It is frustrating but when 'lift off' is obtained can be an elevating and a stimulating experience, with the trials and tribulations of the past soon forgotten.

The contract necessitated a considerable investment in printed tinplate. At that time, the Bank was accommodating and extended our credit limit. We had maintained a good record and with a high bank rate, the business was attractive to them. It was a harrowing period before the returns matched the cash outlay. The venture was successful and provided the cornerstone for the turnround and success of the company. Although the plastic bucket was cheaper and available in shorter print runs, the printed tin was considerable superior in print quality and presentation vital for the retail trade. The tin possessed the strength to permit the finished goods to be stacked higher in a warehouse, consequently occupying less space than plastic.

As a safeguard against a breakdown, spare tooling was provisioned, a costly but necessary safeguard. The venture was of mutual success - a fulfilment beyond our wildest dreams.

At long last a light shone through the tunnel. The improved Bank balance provided an opportunity to invest in soudronic welding equipment. We were suffering from the inability to provide a leakproof container for penetrating products such as chemicals, oil and certain resin based adhesives and many paint products. A solder machine for soldering the side seam of the tin would have been expensive and cumbersome; a fire hazard which also created an obnoxious and permeating smell. We used gas operated soldering irons which were far too labour-and cost-intensive for the standard production run container. Soudronic welding was a Swiss development. A weld is achieved by passing an electric current through the side seam of the tinplate body using copper wire as an electrolyte. The weld is smooth, clean and strong, providing a narrower margin than with soldering. The welding machine occupied considerably less space than a solder machine, was simple in maintenance requiring a minimum of spares.

Within two years the 10 litre proved a success, a quality product with smart packaging. Our customer was a market leader in cement products and the success of this 'exterior finish' venture was vitally important. The company which produced their own raw materials had grown from the substance of long service and experienced staff. They were not involved in the asset stripping ventures of that period. As a small company, we were brought into their project and developed a unique trust and cooperation, a vital part of their production line. The success produced problems.

A squat 10 litre on a 254 mm diameter was required that would be more stable and enable a decorator to immerse his roller directly into the container. We appreciated the requirement and the potential to be able to provide containers with an increased capacity up to 16 litres, hitherto only available in expensive steel kegs. Furthermore, we would be the sole manufacturer of tins of this diameter. The cost of tooling was extortionate and beyond our resources, but somehow the hurdle must be surmounted.

Surely on the other side of this mountain there must be a land of milk and honey. Not so, man is motivated and survives by constant encounters, as one wave follows another in an angry sea. Thanks largely to the experience, patience and ability of Henry, our engineer, we surmounted the problem. We were able to purchase cheaply some of the tooling from a company that had discontinued manufacturing on this diameter, and the remainder was within our own resources. We had no spare tooling and were fortunate that no breakdown occurred until we had the time and resources to provision them.

Our reputation for quality and service was growing and with relatively low overheads, our prices were very competitive on the larger capacities, used particularly for bulk packing. Welding provided an entrée into the market for packaging food such as jam. We secured contracts with two of the larger companies which conveniently filled our capacity. We could have been tempted to invest in semi-automatic welding equipment available to manufacture the tins more economically with higher output and less labour. The outlook for this market was uncertain and our resources were stretched to a limit. A heart-rending problem, with competition intensifying, particularly from plastic, at the cheaper end of the market. The workforce was our greatest investment with resources desperately required for factory dilapidations modernising and renovating plant. The taxman would grab tax like an 'eagle in the sky' from any asset such as a new machine. Corporation tax should only be levied when money is taken out of the company. The Government would reap its pound of flesh in capital gains tax when the business was sold.

Chapter 7
Factory Staff

During the 1970's, the strength of unions had grown and it became difficult to employ non union staff. A strike of one group such as engineers involving key members, could close down a medium size company not possessing the resources of its larger public counterpart. Dissident workers approached us, many because of the pressure from their wives, explaining that they needed secure pay and employment and were prepared to lapse their union membership. We were never approached by union officials obviously being too small. During the war these very people had wanted security and stability. Man's instinct for lust and greed has, and undoubtedly will, continue to repeat itself. Steve was one who had been responsible for setting and running the cutting equipment in a local medium size company. Whilst skilled at his job he was a wild character, fortunately dominated by his wife who also happened to work for the Inland Revenue. He was a strong finely built man, cheerful, pleasant, willing and popular with his workmates. A fervent football supporter, he would join his colleagues in a local pub and after a few beers, fights with opposing supporters would frequently ensure using broken bottles. He would appear at work the next morning bruised, battered and scarred.

Tony Beadle a workmate and 'buddy' soon followed as he was recently married and required stable employment. They introduced up-to-date cutting techniques and rapidly production output and quality improved. Tony was an equally controversial character, an enormous man of about 20 stone, extremely strong but with a softness and charm to his nature often used in a beguiling manner with his colleagues. An intelligent man, conscientious, honest and reliable. There was a weakness in his character and that was the temptation to perform ill conceived crooked activities. He served a prison sentence having knocked down a policeman during one of these escapades. There are so many intelligent, educated and uneducated, who unfortunately have these imbalances in their character. Tony, in his way, was a leader and although never aggressive, his physique, was sufficient to deter any dissident. He had an extraordinary sense of humour and subtle wit. We were favoured with many Asian customers who purchased our large square tins for curry powders. A regular named 'Gandhi Foods' was waiting to be loaded with these tins and being a small quantity they would collect. The previous day was the momentous tragedy of the Indian Prime Minister, Mrs Gandhi, who had been shot. Tony in his inimitable and friendly manner sidled up to the driver and said "Sorry to hear about your mum". He could use quite disgusting and racist language to the various black nationalities we employed, but they never took offence appreciating this facade behind which lay a depth of friendliness and kindness. These indomitable characters with unusual talents are not accepted in this programmed bureaucratic society of today. If only these talents could be harnessed, what a nation we could become. However, it appears we are moving in the opposite direction.

Ron Strong, a union convenor at 'Francis', was also beguiled by his wife and the need for security of income and employment. With an aggressive facade, the illusions of self-grandeur, obscured a willing and loyal employee. He was strong and experienced; the necessary attributes for setting the heavy press room tools that we were using because of the extra production required for the larger capacity tin. Ron soon capitulated and told me surreptitiously how wrong they often were to the management and workers in calling some of the wild cat strikes.

We were anxious to invest in people trained in up to date methods. Jim was a promising intelligent young engineer at 'Francis' understudying as a production engineer. He was likewise disenchanted; the reality not matching up to his anticipated prospects. I was on good terms with 'Francis' and it was not my intention to seduce their workers away. I explained this to Arthur, my old Sales Manager, and now a Director. He appreciated the situation explaining in a loyal way, that the prospects had not materialised due to the change of management with the instructions from the hierarchy to prune costs, overheads and employees. It could be construed that in fact we did them a favour.

Jim was tall, thin, bald and wiry with a pleasant and kindly nature. Initially he worked under Henry in the engineer's shop. There was a clash of personalities and to a large extent his abilities were wasted. Engineers are a peculiar breed, suspicious, critical and generally not encouraging in passing on their skills. This obviously stems from prewar when jobs were at a premium and there was always somebody in the background ready to step into the job. Production management had been a constant problem, a specialist breed an essential link with management to effect a profitable sales output, the likes of Albert were hard to find. Jim was keen on production and its objective and in terms of planning, line setting and the ability to remedy breakdowns provided a valuable contribution.

The care for the workforce was essential to obtain their unity. We lacked every acceptable facility in a dirty wooden factory. With low beams, dark, inadequate lighting for toilets and canteen. Individual security lockers were provided and the incidence of theft over twenty years was neglible. These were proud people and the odd instance proved very disturbing.

In the early years, an evening party would be organised before Christmas by the staff but paid for by the firm. 'Ghetto blasters' provided the music. During a memorable evening, and one which was to be the last, everybody appeared to be enjoying themselves so we continued on after 10 p.m. Suddenly, as if the touch paper had been lit, the party exploded into a maelstrom. A sudden reaction to the alcohol rarely consumed in quantity converted normal rational people into lunatics. People were rushing round the factory yelling abuse and some girls pulling the hair out of another. Dave, together with my son and I, experienced in handling drunks, were unable to deal with these tribal type activities. We were also anxious not to upset the neighbours with the noise or provide them with ammunition for complaints. A young fellow, proficient at his job, in trouble with the police and on probation, handled the situation in a quiet and extraordinary manner by calming down the ringleaders. Fortunately, everybody finally dispersed in a reasonable manner.

During the following years we provided a more refined lunch time party on the day that the factory closed for the Xmas recess. It was a sad reflection on the times that in the later years of the company that the young girls in particular would spend the Xmas break on an alcoholic spree. We employed a particularly appealing and reliable group of West African ladies, of a firm low church belief, who spent it with their families.

Our efforts with leisure activities were of limited success. Coach outings to Portsmouth and Southend proved rather alcoholic and disorganised. Surprisingly we produced a reasonable football side which became popular until the lack of availability of pitches terminated the initiative.

Families have always provided an important contribution to the staff of Metal Packaging manufacturers. Cliques were a problem as inevitably people grouped themselves according to age, sex and colour. In fact, it often proved beneficial providing that management, including line supervisors, remained unbiased. Leadership is an inherited gift and developed with encouragement and training. It has always been a problem to take charge of your own workmates. In the Navy a rating was invariably moved to another ship or establishment upon promotion. Unfortunately, small companies cannot enjoy this privilege.

The Beadles were a close knit Bermondsey family comprising seven sisters and a brother, all of whom worked at Wallins for varying periods including 'Doll' the mother. The father was a kind and generous character who worked as a refuse collector for Southwark council until he was made redundant in the 1980's. The living conditions were poor and difficult particularly when the children were young. The established local people always seemed to have the worst deal. Priority for accommodation seems to be awarded to foreigners down and outs and drunks.

The sisters were all attractive, sensible, hardened by their environment but blessed with attractive, generous and engaging personalities. During the years the majority became supervisors.

Sharon, although treated and considered a sister, had been adopted, her history a mystery. She was a well built girl, attractive, vivacious with a compelling personality, hardened by the necessities of life. She was a person of extremes, not always logical, but straight, single minded and explosive regarding anything unreasonable. She was the mother of a child who she worshipped, the father remaining a mystery. She received support from the D.S.S., a lifeline to which she clung refusing to put at risk by earning tax declared income. Naturally born leaders are a rare breed whether they be Admirals, serve in industry, the professions or as humble workers. Sharon possessed this flair, she quickly grasped the idiosyncracies of tin manufacture and became a supervisor. She soon organised the line

212

to increase the output of tins per hour to a greater extent than previously achieved.

Notwithstanding the offer of a bonus and other incentives, she would not conform to regular attendance becuase of losing the child benefits and reverted to part time and so we lost a fine supervisor. Whilst the black market is still rife in the 90's providing money in hand to cleaners, gardeners and the like, as a small company we could not incur the risk of deviating from the law.

It was a common practice for many of the factory staff to adjourn to the local pub after being paid on a Friday afternoon. Although many under 20 years of age, male and female possessed an insatiable appetitie and capacity for booze including extraordinary concoctions of spirits. Wild parties would continue over the weekend and no doubt with some involvement in drugs. Sharon had become particularly depressed, the family were most supportive and there appeared no cause for serious concern.

It was if a bombshell had exploded when she was discovered dead in her room, attributed to drink followed by an overdose of drugs. Her family, friends and the factory staff were stunned with the tragedy. The cremation was a most moving affair attended by many of the factory staff. The car carrying the coffin was ornamented with a fantastic display of flowers with 'Sharon' in white flowers displayed as the centre piece and highlight.

May she have found PEACE!

Chapter 8
Soudronic Welding

The introduction of soudronic welding as a replacement to soldering had always been my dream. It was a low voltage welding system that welded the overlapping edges of the tinplate together providing a neat, strong, clean and leakproof seam. It was a Swiss invention and in its automatic form was adopted world wide, revolutionising the production of food, beer and beverage cans. It occupied a minimum amount of space, and improved the output considerably with its flexibility to weld the many varying heights and diameters of tins that we manufactured.

John Drummond was an old established family company near Greenock providing a wide range of tins for the Scottish markets together with highquality printed specialities for tobacco, shortbread and food products. They had purchased soudronic equipment in its early days and advanced the application for easy opening for products such as sardines and corned beef, providing an alternative to the hideous and dangerous soldered tin that used a turn key for opening and invariably broke off before the tin was even half opened. There must be memories by many of cut fingers with the frustration of trying to prise out the contents. The venture was successful and business established in Europe. Unfortunately, this success was to contribute to their downfall. The fluctations of the exchange rate reduced their competitive margin to the extent that the business no longer remained viable. Whilst politicians procrastinate over Europe, the lack of a common currency can cause a nightmare for trade in imports and exports. It is akin to two birds fighting over a tasty morsel and meanwhile another predator pops in and flies off with the spoils.

I had developed, over many years, a healthy and understanding relationship with Bill Cooper, their Sales Director. In the early 1970's they would supply the printed tinplate and we would make it up into tins and deliver to their customers in the London area and south of England. It provided us with profitable work, saved their transport costs and reduced the pressure on their stretched production. They kindly provided Nigel with an instructive week of familiarisation with soudronic welding in their works preparatory to our ordering the equipment.

Money, Money, Money, the plague of the small privately owned manufacturing company. Politicians 'waffle' in councils or government about their contribution, unions bleat the age old adage that "The world owes us a living". Small companies provide employment to that fading breed of people of all ages who have pride and require to work to remain independent of the state. Banks have a responsibility to protect their interests. Where there is a will there is a way. The Bank was persuaded to extend our overdraft limit by increasing the value of the debenture levied against the assets of the company. They were fully aware that it was an item of equipment that was only of value in a specialist role, unlike a car or a house or a painting with a resale value.

Fortunately, Nigel had a flair for electrics. He spent a few days in Switzerland where they familiarised him with the equipment. We invested in a minimum stock of spares and maintenance but breakdowns never created a problem. It proved to be a most reliable piece of equipment. Operators were quickly and easily trained and even with a tall tin, production easily matched the line flow output. What a remarkable invention by the Swiss, one of the greats in the post war world.

In 1976, when we purchased our first machine, the pound sterling was low against the Swiss franc and the cost was £35,000. If we were to be competitive and remain in business the risk must be taken. The equipment was ordered and was operating within a day of delivery. It proved a cornerstone in maintaining the profitability and survival of the company: that, and some self denial, for my wife and I took less in salary than many of the factory staff. A slight difference to the huge salaries paid to company directors inthe 90's.

The welding equipment together with improvements in production control resulted in an increase of output. We were able to increase our sales albeit at a reduced profit margin and it became necessary within two years to obtain additional welding equipment. The British manufactured equipment available was not suitable for our requirements. A Swiss competitor had introduced a modern and simpler version of the soudronic more suitable for our purposes and less in price. The Swiss france was low against sterling and we made the purchase at something like 1/3rd of the price paid previously. We had advanced a long way in the past seven years, ploughing profits back into modernising plant, satisfying safety standards, completing the landlords dilapidation requirements, incorporating a three phase supply and maintaining a competitive wage structure.

We reorganised our loading and unloading to accommodate palletised loads, necessitating in the purchase of Fork Lift trucks and a larger vehicle for our own local deliveries. The landlord was exacting in his demands, denying the purchase of the freehold notwithstanding the fact that the factory had been a tenant since 1880. We were restricted in our manufacture within a four storey wooden factory and limited within the terms of our lease to be able to modernise production or be able to move to more suitable premises. The council introduced yellow lines and restricted parking creating the ridiculous situation that a 40 foot vehicle must be loaded within twenty minutes. A request for a 'waiting bay' was declined which would have provided temporary parking should there be a further vehicle awaiting to be loaded or unloaded. The traffic wardens would occasionally have a purge so the waiting vehicle would have to drive round the congested roads until it could be loaded. The bureaucracy of Southwark council would have preferred a neat and tidy residential area with parking meters to provide a job for the traffic wardens. Trade and industry would be eliminated, the demand for accommodation for locally born people would be reduced following the consequent unemployment.

An expression on the lower deck of the Navy was 'if you can't stop a racket then join it'. The trade unions had learnt to practice the blackmail system so we, in our small way, raised a petition with signatures of employees, suppliers and customers that we presented to the Council, the Police and the Press. It was the media that played on the politics and we occasionally obtained some retribution. As a small hard working firm this was a battle we could ill afford, the time and costs proving irritating and serious. History reveals that it is the combination of events, as with the streams that join to form a river, that formulates its path and flow.

Chapter 9
Factory Life

The factory lovelife was a web of intrigue; complex, illogical and frustrating from a management aspect. The belief of Freud was that sex dominates the species by virtue of the overriding need for reproduction and survival. Try and put that one to factory workers! There are many factors that cause temptation and in a factory there is close contact during the often long working day between male and female. A senior officer advised me many years ago during a particularly heavy session in a pub in Malta that "Never on your own doorstep". A similar parallel runs in factories where communities are closely confined. It was necessary to identify the problem but another matter to solve it. In a factory with male and female staff jealousy rules supreme - simply biological. All the laws related to equality and sexual harassment, will never eliminate this problem. Akin to chemistry, mixtures of gases result in explosions. We were fortunate being a relatively small company, closely in touch with the problems before they occurred. Jim was a quiet type, married with children to support but his weakness for the fairer sex was to lead him into unusual and extraordinary situations. He became involved with an operator, the wife of Alex, a line foreman. They had only been married a few months and his previous wife still worked in the factory. A birthday party was held during the week at a home of one of the staff. There were few volunteers for overtime that night and prospects for a full attendance at 8 a.m. the following day remote. During the evening hilarity and boisterousness grew in proportion to the alcohol intake. It was noticed that Alex's wife and Jim had left so a group set off to his house. The pair were in bed together and a punch up ensued. The neighbours 'phoned the police and the following morning four members of the staff were bailed out of the local police station with my assurance that they were normally law abiding types. The sequel was, that soon after, the couple split up and took up other employment. Within a few years Jim was to meet his match.

Joey was about 18 years old when she joined; she was pretty and

217

soon proved to be a first class operator. She was not generally popular with her workmates being bossy and she told tales behind their backs. She developed a resentment to authority and a left-wing attitude. We stamped down heavily on this and made her a line supervisor. She was a hard 'nut' but a worker, ambitious to earn money and with responsibility responded to discipline resulting in a considerably improved output on the line. Whilst good at production planning Jim had little control over the operators and Joey was virtually running the production. Following complaints of bias and unfair treatment, Jim was moved to another job working largely on his own installing lines, runways etc. which provided a considerable contribution to improving production and releasing pressure on our hard worked engineers.

Chapter 10
Steel Strike

Events provide the opportunity in life for success or failure. The tinplate industry an integral part of the steel industry had been plagued with problems which in my limited experience, had been of their own making. 'Wheels within wheels' with personalities jostling and cutting each other's throats for power regardless of whether the results would benefit their customers or for that matter the country. In my experience and consideration, monopolies never realise their true potential whether nationalised or privatised. In 1980 the country was reeling over the suicide tactics of the unions with the winter of discontent which included the futile, unnecessary and damaging steel strike.

The Welsh were a misguided people, they lived in a fairyland and were encouraged to believe that they enjoyed a divine right and come what may the demand for tinplate would grow and grow. The management and unions firmly believed that the market would return to its pre-strike level after the strike and that the wages lost would be recouped from overtime. They could not believe that there was a 'Big Bad Wolf' patiently waiting to pounce like a predator to enjoy the spoils provided by Metal Packaging.

Plastic was the main beneficiary. There were many customers who became weary of the dominance of the steel companies over the years which operated as a closed shop. They required containers to package their product when required by their customers, this was particularly vital for an export order with a target date for shipment. The majority of our customers remained patient and understanding but February and March were busy times particularly for the decorative side of the paint industry. Fortunately, the plastic industry was limited in its capacity in those days. Nevertheless, a tin order lost was never regained.

The industry closed ranks and worked together, particularly the smaller private companies. They were flexible in their activities, entrepreneurs who could react to a situation and provide the ability to overcome what appears as insurmountable problems.

It was 'survival' the alternative being bankruptcy for the small firms wedged in between the giants of industry and the union, neither side really representing democracy.

In anticipation of the strike we had purchased the maximum supplies that funds and space would permit. Although labour intensive we used blanks, offcuts, printers waste reducing scrap to a minimum. Unfortunately, the belief of a short strike failed to materialise and it dragged on for months.

It was not the policy of the large manufacturers to antagonise the unions and they publicly declared that there would be no attempt to block the strike and obtain supplies elsewhere. Nevertheless, the major manufacturers obtained supplies surreptitiously through their subsidiaries. As usual, it was the small company that suffered and long term the tinplate workers.

The tinplate hauliers joined the strike resulting in vast quantities of tinplate sitting in warehouses in Wales. We purchased the bulk of our tinplate from a stockist who was one of the few remaining family owned businesses. He likewise was staring bankruptcy in the face unless he could realise sales and ease his cash flow problems.

It was cold and dark at 4.30 a.m. on a Sunday early in March 1980 when John set off from London in his 20 ton articulated lorry. Speeding along the quiet motorway he reflected on the futile gamble this trip could be. Driving to Wales to uplift 20 tons of tinplate during a steel strike was a risk to say the least. Would there be pickets? Would the lorry be loaded if he got through? Could he trust the metal container manufacturer with whom the deal had been negotiated? It was only a small firm employing 60 people and with limited resources. It had survived a month of the strike and was threatened with closure unless supplies could be obtained to fulfill hard won contracts. Similarly the firm in Wales was small with limited resources. Supplies were not forthcoming from the Mills and the plate being sold was a non standard size and difficult to sell normally. The money realised would provide breathing space for all concerned.

He had calculated these risks, his expenses were paid and there would be a generous bonus for the plate collected and delivered. Times had been difficult with little work, all the good jobs going to the big operators. He needed the money to maintain his owner vehicle on the road and provide for his wife and children.

Dawn was breaking as he crossed the Severn Bridge into Wales, not very scenic on this dull morning. Lights were coming on in houses. He was hungry and envious with visions of food being prepared.

The warehouse was abreast a hill up a side road. As he approached, a police officer signalled him to stop and warned that angry pickets were at the gates. It had been arranged the boss would load him personally on a Sunday morning when it was unlikely that pickets would be out. More likely they would be at chapel or recovering from a Saturday night's drinking. Even in hard times, the British workman must have his beer.

Feeling for the club hidden beneath his seat, John let in the clutch and approached the pickets. Unknown to him, whilst explaining his mission, a picket inserted a block of nails under his inner rear tyre. He closed his window to the abuse and drove into the firm. The boss let him in but declined to load him explaining that he couldn't risk being blacklisted, however gave permission for John to use the gantry and load himself. On completion, he secured his load, drove through the gates and down the road ignoring the bricks and threats.

After clearing the area he 'phoned the boss of the container firm with the good news asking for his wife to be told that all was well. He joined the motorway and settled to the long haul to London. Suddenly the lorry slewed, he wrestled with the wheel and ended up on the hard shoulder. He was dazed, but fortunately no injury. He inspected the wheels to find the nails which had worked their way through the tyre causing the blow out. He hailed a passing motorist who promised to report the accident to the Police who would contact a recovery vehicle and the London firm regarding his plight.

I was stunned to receive a garbled call from the Police in the afternoon about an accident involving a lorry carrying tinplate. Nothing further could be disclosed but I would be notified when information became available.

Nightmare thoughts - I must not 'phone John's wife — what if she 'phones me? The poor chap may be injured. Was the lorry adequately insured? Certainly the tinplate load wasn't. Bankruptcy loomed as a reality. The plate must be paid for and if damaged it was unlikely that it would be suitable to fabricate tins. Sixty workers on the dole, no money for redundancy. Job prospects grim in this area their skills limited to this specialised industry.

All this because of a few nails used for a misconceived purpose. Had the picket considered the ramification of his actions? If other vehicles had been involved there could have been a disastrous pile up with possible loss of life. Was this why only sketchy information was available?

Time ticked torturously by. The 'phone rang — a social call — will call back. The 'phone range again - sorry wrong number. Nails, short and long, burst tyres, mangled tinplate and bodies as imagination went haywire.

The 'phone rang and if as a miracle, John's voice loud and clear "I'm okay, a recovery vehicle is fitting a tyre and I have told my wife; see you in the morning". Profound relief notwithstanding prospects of a staggering bill for the tyre and other costs. The tinplate was satisfactory — orders could be fulfilled with work for the factory.

The next day, the police 'phoned to advise that further trips could not be permitted because of the risks involved with the pickets and that they would be unable to guarantee the safety of the vehicle.

The strike fizzled out in April and supplies were rapidly resumed from existing stocks. Problems and adversity often provide rewards, with the strike realising to us, an unexpected but rewarding profit. A jackal in the form of the taxman was ready to pounce, somehow he must be thwarted. We still faced considerable commitments. Ever changing situations, akin to quicksand, required rapid action, somehow this mini windfall must be preserved, developed and integrated. We approached yet another 'crossroads' — Screen Printing! Is this the right road to take?

Read on.....!

Chapter 11
Screen Printing

Plastic was relentlessly burrowing into our business, the particular threat coming from Denmark and Holland. We became a stockist for rectangular style bottles and a range of polythene buckets. It had been part of our service to supply as wide a range of containers as possible to meet the needs of our main customers to whom we supplied our own manufactured tins. Providing they would make up an economical load or phase in with another delivery in the area, we would supply quantities of as few as a hundred. Nigel and I were invited to visit a large factory that had been set up in the North West of England to manufacture polythene buckets. The automatic production process was amazing utilising virtually no labour on the production line. It became clear that we must diversify if we wished to remain in business. Plastic buckets were screen printed individually round the body of the container at the end of the manufacturing process. Nigel was familiar with screen printing from his college days and suggested it might work on tins. Whilst screen printing had been used for overprinting components and single colours on flat sheets, it had not been found economical for standard production methods. The standard method for tins was to print the sheet in the flat by the offset litho, providing a very high quality print. The printing presses were bulky, occupied a great deal of space and involved considerable investment. Setting up time was lengthy and it was only economical for printing long runs. There was an advantage that the plate could be stored and be readily available to be made up into tins as required. There was a disadvantage that the customer must be committed to a contract and should the business fail. he was obliged to pay for the balance of printed plate not taken up. The manufacturer was also committed to having capital tied up in printed plate, the customer only paying when the made up tins were delivered. We had received many enquiries for printed tins but in relatively small quantities. Presentation is an all important feature in today's packaging and tinplate provide the finest medium against all other packaging materials.

We investigated the market and soon became 'A child for the

223

slaughter'. Whilst the printing world was riddled with unions, screen print was confined to the back street boys doing short runs many of them 'smart Alecs' matched equally by their customers who were usually a poor credit risk. Life is invariably torturous and costly. Our first effort was with the purchase of a machine from the continent that would print a made up tin. We were badly advised and it turned out to be a dead loss. We attracted the attention of Jim, a smart boy, very experienced in screen printing. Nigel and Jim produced satisfactory results screen printing on tinplate in the flat using a hand bench, slow and labour intensive but it was a start. Whilst my interest was solely in printing on tinplate, I recognised that we must invest in more sophisticated plant that would be less labour intensive. Initially we must find work that involved printing on other materials until we could produce enough sales for short run printing solely on tinplate. We formed a separate Limited Company on the advice of my accountant. Jim was made a working Director. He was enthusiastic advising that he could obtain a substantial share of a contract with 'Thorn' for printing a stick on type plastic label. Meanwhile, a small order was placed by ICI for screen printed tins, the quantity too small to be economical for offset litho printing. We had 'lift off', second hand plant was obtained and Jim recruited two of his cronies who were experienced printers. We paid dearly for our learning period for within six months or so, Jim disappeared together with the Thorn order.

The steel strike had assisted the drift to plastics and maintaining the order book for tins was proving difficult. There were 'glimmers of light'. We ventured into the fancy goods and retail food market, obtaining an order from Harrods which developed into business of mutual value. We worked closely with Keith Bonner, who was a partner in Secura Products, and later on was to run Surecan, his own business. He made the smaller tins not within our range of manufacture and we supplied the printed tinplate for the orders for printed tins. We soon discovered that the two printers who Jim had introduced were using our plant for private work. They were also earning wages way above those paid to Wallins staff. It was a bold decision but we gave them both the sack. Nigel then worked full time with the print and together with a young fellow recruited from Wallins staff managed to meet our growing order book. Following a serious bad debt from a customer to whom we supplied a very complicated printed plastic cocktail guide, which was sold to many of the main store groups, we concentrated solely on short run print on tinplate. Operators were trained who had served Wallins for some time and possessed an aptitude and enthusiasm for the work. We developed a reputation for quality and service, sales grew which necessitated the need to purchase equipment that provided increased output. Retail outlets were demanding new style packs with striking presentation. It provided us with many opportunities particularly with D.I.Y. and food and provided to some extent the edge over plastic where there was a requirement for the shorter run. Unbelievably we had cornered a niche market which was to prove a salvation to the company.

As with many business decisions, we had come to a crossroad and fortunately took the right turning. There will always be a place for the small entrepreneur, it requires a number of pieces to complete a jigsaw puzzle. Why cannot politicians recognise this fact and provide encouragement and assistance?

A SPECIALIST SERVICE FOR TINPLATE PACKAGING

Alison Cox

For a small business to survive in the tinplate container industry, or indeed in any developing industry today, it must be especially aware of technological progress and aim to provide a service not offered elsewhere. One small firm which has used such initiative to ensure a slice of the packaging market is G. Wallin & Co., a South London family firm which, rather than challenging the giants, actually includes some of them amongst its customers.

Wallin was set up in 1888 in Deptford, within easy reach of London's main food distribution centre, along with many other tinplate boxmakers of those early years—the very first tinplate can was made nearby in Bermondsey. The firm moved to its present site early this century with a workforce of just over 100, manufacturing lever- and slip-lid containers. The greatest changes to have taken place in recent times have happened since the present owner, G. P. Sabin, took over the company twelve years ago. Following a reassessment of the market situation the firm's position as a manufacturer of non-standard general-line tinplate containers was consolidated. Containers are made for packaging biscuits and cakes, chemicals, paints and oils, with non-standard specifications posing no problems. The firm's present inventory includes manufacture of round containers with slip- or lever-lid closures or open-top ends and square containers to any height from 70 to 457 mm.

Assessing artwork at Wallin Print and Design.

New technology

These years also proved a period of redesigning and up-dating with new technology being introduced where possible and, in addition to traditional methods of seaming using soldered and welded seams, two semi-automatic Soudronic welders are now in operation as well as a SMAG ZS welder. The firm being well established along these lines, further expansion was considered on two fronts. Firstly, extending its established service by designing and manufacturing technical packs. Two challenges ingeniously met were for a tinplate container to hold and protect a plastic bottle containing hydrogen peroxide, designed with special beading in the lid and body to ensure strength and a secure fit, and a two-part pack in which two containers of the same diameter lock together to provide one integral unit. Enquiries for uses have come from manufacturers of resinous materials and paint packs for industrial uses. The reduced head and deep bottom provide an additional stacking feature.

Screen printing on tinplate

The second expansion was in a different direction—printing. For most of the printing requirements, Wallin uses offset litho printers. There remained a gap in the service, however, on which Wallin has successfully capitalised—quality printing for short runs. Tinplate is printed in the flat using the screen print process, the first

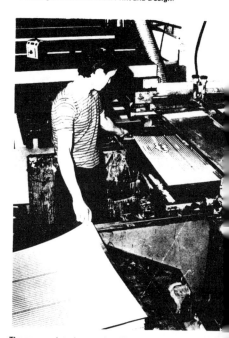
The screen printer in operation. The printed tinplate sheet will be dried in the oven in the background.

No. 145, 1985

ompany, Mr. Sabin claims, to produce decorated ontainers in this way. Although not suitable for fine alf-tone work, screen printing has its own attributes, ving a strong, full-bodied effect which is perhaps even ore effective than offset litho on bold, simple designs ecause of the greater volume of ink which is applied to e surface. The finish achieved is only slightly different to at of a litho print.

he artwork from which the design is to be printed is ade up into filmwork from which the stencil is made hotographically. The stencil is supported by a fine olyester mesh screen through which ink is forced on to e tinplate sheet which is placed underneath. In this way ny design can be printed although each sheet has to be ried before the application of another colour. The ink ries by solvent evaporation in a hot air drier and takes pproximately 30 seconds. Runs of up to 2000 sheets an be economically produced and in as many colours as e design requires.

/allin Print and Design

/allin Print and Design was set up by G. Wallin to roduce all of the screen print requirements as a wholly wned subsidiary of the parent firm and to trade dependently. The flexibility of the screen print process lows a wide range of substrates to be printed on the achinery from paper to PVC and Wallin Print has stablished numerous customer outlets of its own dependent from the tinplate market. However, printing nplate comprises the greatest proportion of its output. he advantages of a short run print facility are enjoyed by nall companies who cannot afford to be committed to rge part contracts and also to the larger firms who wish try out new products and designs for special romotions or test marketing. Wallin Print and Design has s own studio with all the facilities for generating original rtwork and converting this photographically into screen rinting stencils. The company will take on any stage of e process, producing new designs from initial concepts, rtwork from rough visuals and, if required, printed proofs an be made up into finished containers. Wallin's esigners work closely with clients, building constantly on e long-standing goodwill already established by the ompany. Designs will even be produced for containers at are to be printed lithographically elsewhere, and the m also offers its expertise to others on a consultancy asis.

he success of G. Wallin and Co. appears to lie in the ompany's continual evolution, a long-established firm aintaining traditional services but continually taking ock of and up-dating its facilities in terms of new chnology, according to the availability of capital for vestment—and, because such capital must necessarily e limited, selling mostly ideas, experience and quality.

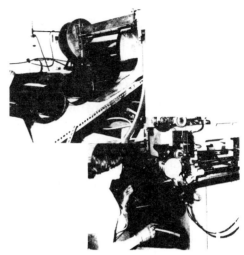

Tinplate is pre-formed into rolls before the seams are welded on the SMAG welder.

Some of the technical packs manufactured by the company.
All I.T.R.I. photographs, courtesy: G. Wallin & Co. Ltd., London.

Tin and its uses

Chapter 12
Traumatic Times

Administration was a vital aspect of the business if we were to keep a step ahead of the vagaries of the tax man, the inquisitive bank manager and the complicated nightmare of maintaining adequate records of wages and salaries and the demands of the D.S.S. The provision and maintenance of accounts requiring the outrageous fees demanded by the accountants who performed the legally necessitated audit were out of all proportion. If I was a solicitor, surveyor or accountant, I would vote socialist, who generally introduce additional laws and bureaucracy. There are apparently more accountants per capita than in any other country, the major predators to the working population.

Mr Day, who had served our purposes so nobly, had passed his three score years and ten and decided that being in his fading years, he should retire and devote more time to his wife. He had been excellent and together with Joan had helped us through some turbulent times. The factory loved him, a relic of the past, as he strode up the square to the office with his rolled umbrella, upright, dignified, smartly dressed in a dark suit.

Jill, a student, had been employed to help us out during the holiday period, a pleasant Yorkshire girl who worked well with Joan. She had a year to wait before entering university so working with us for that period was mutually beneficial. It provided a waiting period enabling us to formulate our future plans for the business. Joan wished to retire in a couple of years when she became sixty. An overlap was required and we consulted an agency explaining our requirements. Sheilagh, an attractive middle aged lady, arrived for an interview. She had been out of work for some time because of an accident. We didn't really stand a chance with her engaging personality and 'machine gun' like rhetoric, so we were bowled over! I depended and trusted Joan entirely over matters of administration, she being utterly reliable, extremely capable, modest and never overpowering. Sheilagh was to be the antithesis with her lilting brogue and feeling and understanding for people. Joan was happy, so we decided on a trial period which continued till the bitter end. She proved a loyal and lovely person earning a great respect from the factory staff combining the role of administration and personnel officer.

Business can be compared to the weather with its constant changes. Blue skies were with us but over the horizon a depression was approaching.

Ray looked after our selling and the purchase of tinplate and had been with us since about 1974. John, an intelligent young fellow, a friend of my son, was taken on to work in the factory while he was sorting out his career prospects. He was adaptable, willing and would drive the fork lift truck to load or unload vehicles, effect deliveries in our own lorry, in addition to dealing with the paperwork. It was pointless making and delivering tins if they were not correctly invoiced. It was remarkable how many large public companies with all their computers and paperwork, still made many errors.

George was the commercial manager, with wide ranging responsibilities peculiar to a small firm. Unfortunately, his wife was terminally ill, he was appraoching sixty and anxious to retire to look after her. He was not in a pension scheme. Apart from three years spent in the Navy during the war, he had been with Wallins since he was fourteen. I worked out a redundancy scheme but because of his age, the state would only pay a minimum amount.

We contributed as generous a sum as our resources would permit. He was able to draw unemployment benefit until he attained pensionable age. After he left we reorganised the office administration with John and Ray looking after the sales and purchasing. My wife was the overseer, typist and general factotum. Business had rallied including the print which was gradually making a contribution. Wallins was back on an even keel.

Blue Circle had become our prime customer with whom we had developed a close relationship. We would supply their requirements large or small whenever required. An ambitious senior director had recently returned from overseas and was appointed to oversee the development and modernisation programme recently instituted. As with so many 'new brooms' he was out to make sweeping changes. Streamlining staff and price cutting is always a favourite pastime. Packaging became the obvious target and by converting our 10 litre tin to a polythene bucket would show a paper saving of many thousands of pounds. The buyer warned me that the switch was ominous and would be within a few months when the contract expired.

I made an appointment and discussed a possible compromise pointing out that polythene containers for decorative products through retail outlets were considered to be the cheaper end of the market. Sandtex Matt was a market leader, its image enhanced by the striking print of the tin. Surely converting to a bucket with its inferior print would be a retrograde step. Storage could be a problem since a polythene bucket when filled and packed on a pallet was not strong and rigid compared with the tin and valuable storage space would be lost.

The arguments were of no avail as he was a determined man and the policy had been finalised. I returned in abject gloom, the prospects of bankruptcy looming if this major contract was lost. What were we to do, all the parameters had been explored and discussed?

Burning the midnight oil, studying every aspect of costs there was no alternative but to attempt to buy time. If we could offer a sufficiently low price to defer the switch for six months or a year, circumstances may change and at least provide us with the opportunity to seek alternative work. It was a difficult decision but we must survive. I 'phoned the buyer with an offer, pitching the price, marginally above that of the polythene contender. There was a stunned silence, it may be too late, but it will receive consideration. Time passed, we must be patient, there were internal politics involved. Employees under threat of redundancy with this turbulent force at work were anxious not to 'rock the boat' it was easier to acquiese.

Meanwhile, Nigel was in hospital having undergone a serious operation on his back and would be away for at least two months. Fortunately, we had reinforced the factory staff with Keith who became a valuable and reliable production manager. Nevertheless, with the increased pressure of responsibilities, my time was a restrictive factor.

Ray, our sales manager, was cooperative and submitted his notice. He considered that his prospects were limited and had accepted the offer of alternative employment. Perhaps he was right even though he had received a fair salary, was in a pension and private medical scheme, a flexible expense account, a firm's car with unrestricted mileage and free petrol of which he made full use. A 9 a.m. till 5.30 p.m. man - not a great loss although a blow at the time. Survival was the motivating factor, price and the responsibility for a loyal, albeit sometimes difficult, factory staff. They were our children, our lifeblood, the means of realising our livelihood.

The customers of many large companies had become disenchanted with their service and approached us with enquiries. It was impossible, with our labour intensive production, to match the prices of our competitors manufacturing with automatic production. However, we were without their overheads and could provide service and delivery in small quantities. Firms found it necessary to label their containers to identify the product packaged should the order quantity be below the economical run for printing by offset litho. Short run print enabled them to provide a superior presentation and for us to enjoy new pastures.

Our dynamic director friend at Blue Circle found the offer difficult to refuse and compromised with a contract for six months at the cut throat price. I also appreciated that their marketing department required time to assess the implication on sales and production before converting to plastic.

The depression passed leaving in its wake debris and problems but we were still alive.

The time approached for Joan to retire and through the agency we were introduced to Hazel. She had been made redundant at 'Courage Brewery' after over twenty year's service. She was familiar with computerised accounts with which we were advised to become involved. She found our more friendly, relaxed way of life strange at first but fortunately, soon settled into our routine and together with Sheilagh, formed a great team.

Coinciding with the departure of Ray, we also lost John who found travelling from Kent too demanding and obtained employment locally.

Christmas approaching with a collapse of the administration. Fortunately Nigel returned, although still weak and restricted in his activities, he was able to resume the running of the factory and its production. My wife and I looked after the sales and purchasing including despatch notes, transport arrangements, etc. Fortunately, we were all interchangeable and it was a matter of 'grin and bear it'. We contacted the staff agency who provided us with a temporary to help with the more general day to day affairs. Bob arrived smart and breezy, willing and intelligent. He had a varied background particularly of sales and commercial administration. Following a trial period a contract was agreed with him to be the Commercial Manager. Bob proved to be most valuable in the difficult days to follow. Maybe we were lucky but observing business today, this vital link between worker, manager and controlling director seems missing. There seems to be no time to consider the human being, everything governed by computer and short term profits dictated by the shareholder. How could a ship like the Q.E.2 sail in early 1995 and on arrival at New York, be found to be unseaworthy by the US authorities? How could there be strikes on the railways with a large percentage of the population unemployed? History repeats itself and few become wiser!

The early 1980's produced problems variant as the weather. F. Francis, who had provided me with my first job in civilian life, was taken over by a city 'whizz kid' epitomising the dirty side of capitalism. Drummonds, our old friends in Scotland, had been included in the takeover. The manager, a previous business colleague, invited me along to explore mutual pastures. They no longer intended to manufacture the 10 litre containers used for decorative paint and food and although it was a market declining to plastic, 'any crumbs' could prove useful!

BUT YOU DONT RETIRE UNTIL 4 O'CLOCK

The bitter cold air struck through me as I walked along the south London street to my car at 6 a.m. Soon after setting off for Heathrow, the snow started falling. Anxiously I peered through the cluttered windscreen, the roads becoming dangerous and speed had to be reduced. Traffic was building up and time becoming tight for the flight. A business opportunity in Greenock to obtain important supplies for the factory. Fortunately, I was ahead of the M4 rush hour traffic but nevertheless it was with relief that I parked the car at the 'short term car park'. After checking in, I relaxed with a cup of coffee. Inevitably because of the weather, the flight was to be delayed. Boarding was eventually announced and dutifully we queued at the gate for the bus, immaculate in our business suits complete with brief cases. The biting wind blew and the snow flurried as we crossed the apron to be herded into the bus. There were a few seats for those fortunate to be first aboard, the remainder standing, clutching firmly the strap as the bus careered its way round the outskirts of the airport buildings and eventually arriving near the aircraft. The queuing process similarly repeated in the prevailing arctic conditions to board the plane. It infiltrated through a numb and already tired brain that this seemed somewhat at odds to the advertisement for the comfort and relaxation of modern air travel. Squeezed in our seats, looking forward to breakfast, a further delay was announced. Because of the weather the wings must be 'deiced'. Somehow I recalled we had coped with this problem 40 years ago in naval aircraft. Perhaps a special 'ICE' akin to the special snow that blocked the lines of British Rail. The U.K. is unique with it special problems.

Airborne, no breakfast, because of the snow, the airport meals had not arrived in time for the flight. Cramped, hungry, tired, dishevelled and hardly prepared for the rigours of the business ahead. Winging our way north gazing down at the dark heavily laden clouds, I reflected on the substance that supported this heavily laden aeroplane. The thrust from the engine providing the propulsion depended upon the intake of cold air heated for expansion and accelerated rearwards by the turbines. Air defined as the mixture of gases we breathe — atmosphere. Supportive to life from the first breath to the last gasp at death. Air temperature changes influencing the weather while man gradually poisons the atmosphere with pollution.

"Captain speaking, sorry for the delay, air traffic control report fog and low cloud at the airfield; fasten seat belts". Miraculously we were guided down through the polluted low lying black cloud by ground control approach to land at Glasgow.

I collected a hired car and set off for Greenock in a sea mist, the polluted wet air reducing visibility to yards. Visions of viewing the beauty of the lower reaches of the Clyde forgotten with concentration directed upon watching the kerb ahead. Greenock, a dour semi industrial town, its buildings blackened by the industrial gases from local shipyards including 'John Browns' where the Cunard Line's 'Mighty Queens' were built. My memories stretched back to sailing fromhere in a convoy early in the war,the post war review of the fleet by King George VI and 10,000 thirsty sailors ashore on a Sunday with the pubs shut.

My meeting at Drummonds proved to be of some mutual benefit. It was sad to see the end of a proud, successful, privately owned Scottish company with a reputation for quality and service become a fragmented offshoot of a 'get rich quick' public company grabbing the tasty morsels, discarding the less prolific slow earners which had been the foundation in the past. Woolworths prewar had made their millions out of the sale of an accumulation of items under 6d ($2^{1}/_{2}$p).

Managing director Gordon Sab in with his unloading problem.

FIRM FACES A YELLOW PERIL

A THIN yellow line, due to be painted in the gutter outside a factory in Cole-st., Southwark, is threatening the jobs of 60 people.

Parking restrictions are about to descend on Cole-st. and surrounding area. The firm of G. Wallin, who have been manufacturing tins for the past 88 years, say that if the massive lorries which regularly deliver tons of sheet metal to the factory are not allowed to wait long enough for the unloading to be completed, the firm may have to close or move out of London.

The firm has asked both Southwark and the GLC for a loading bay to be marked outside the factory, exempting the lorries from the restrictions, but so far there has been no positive response.

Raymond Sullivan, sales representative and buyer for the firm, said the local authorities had suggested that the firm asks the police for an exemption each time a large lorry was due to call, suggesting that traffic wardens would be sympathetic to the firm's problems.

Mr. Sullivan said it was frequently impossible to predict when a supply lorry would arrive since some came from as far away as a steelworks in South Wales.

"No one seems to be aware of the seriousness of our problem," he said. "We only need one of our suppliers to get a parking ticket and they will not come back again.

"There are apparently no plans to exempt us from the general parking restrictions in the area. Consequently we are likely to go out of business if posses of traffic wardens start coming round and slapping penalty-tickets on our lorries.

RIDICULOUS

"We are an old-established business in the borough and it seems ridiculous to me that with the employment situation the way it is our life is made difficult because the bureaucracy cannot bend slightly to accommodate us.

"The police have been very sympathetic but tell us there is no way they could grant us a blanket exemption."

RATES REBEL BOSS RISKS COURT ACTION

A SOUTHWARK firm are refusing to pay rates till parking restrictions they claim are driving them out of business are lifted.

Now the firm, G. Wallin in Cole-st., who employ 70 people making tin cans, face prosecution by the council.

But a yellow line which appeared round the factory two years ago means the firm's two vans and giant 40-foot lorries delivering sheet metal are fair game for the traffic wardens.

Mr. Gordon Sabin is managing director of the company, which has been in Southwark since 1888.

He said, "We are perpetually harassed by wardens who slap tickets on our own lorries and lorries delivering to us."

He said money lost in fines only amounted to £12 or £15 a week. But some lorry drivers drove off when they saw wardens approaching. This, said Mr. Sabin, disrupted production at the company.

Some companies which used to deliver to the firm now refuse to come because of the parking problem.

Mr. Sabin said that although private residents in the area were provided with parking bays, his requests for a loading space was turned down by the council.

He said, "It seems ridiculous that in an area like Southwark, where the council are trying to attract more industry, we are harried by petty restrictions like this.

"In the long term, it means we could close down and our workers would lose their jobs."

Mr. Sabin said he would not pay rates for the firm's premises till "there was some improvement in the parking situation."

Last year these amounted to nearly £5,000.

He said, "I pay rates to get a service from the borough. They have to honour their bargain before I pay."

But Southwark Council say the parking restrictions are the fault of the GLC.

A spokesman for the council said, "We have been fighting a running battle with the GLC to get Mr. Sabin an industrial bay for a number of years, but these things usually take a very long time."

He said Southwark were sympathetic to Mr. Sabin's complaint, but if he refused to pay rates "he will wind up in court."

HARASSED company boss Gordon Sabin with some of the parking tickets his lorries get.

Tea and biscuit on the plane, tensions relaxed with the airborne motion, the white patches of snowbound fields soon to disappear as darkness set in. Memories of bygone days, the Navy, the confusing world of the civilian; workers and employers pulling against each other, the hard fought for freedom of the war with the unity and spirit of the people being eroded by the greed of individuals. Nevertheless, the quality of life had improved, the wealth more evenly spread amonst the people, many of the barriers of sex, class and race disappearing.

A gentle shake, awakened by a glamorous air hostess, the return to reality as the plane touch down at Heathrow. Another humdrum business mission over an away day from the turmoil of the office and factory.

The demise of our competitors, the loss of business to polythene containers for decorative paints and allied products, forced us to diversify into other markets. Whilst the demand for fancy tins for biscuits was if anything in decline, we helped to develop the promotion of fruit cakes, particularly as we could supply a multi-coloured printed tin in small quantities. These were sold through major stores and mail order outlets particularly at Xmas. An extraordinary demand occurred from one of our customers for a sponge like cake mixed with a substantial quantity of rum for export to America. Whilst the Americans could produce equally attractive tins and cakes, the cheap £ sterling combined with the rum being duty free provided a profit margin over the cost if produced in America incorporating the cost of the tax on spirit. There was strict Custom's control in the UK regarding the rum being taken out of bond and the timing of production and shipment became complicated. The venture only achieved limited success because mainly the American client failed to meet the terms of payment.

In the 1980's many privately owned and public companies in the metal packaging, paint and chemical industries either closed down or were taken over. The closing down of shipyards, vehicle manufacturers, together with the competition from polythene containers resulted in the declining demand for metal containers in the old established conventional outlets. The rationalisation of production by the major manufacturers resulted in many of them discontinuing the manufacture of non standard sizes which provided us with a bonus. The gamble with Blue Circle paid off, the storm had passed and our dynamic friend was moved to a backwater. The production manager was anxious to consolidate future production in our 10 litre container at a mutually agreed price, competitive but restoring a more reasonable profit margin. We seemed to be set fair for the foreseeable future.

Problems were looming for in 1985 AKZO took over the decorative paint division of Blue Circle. It was to prove an anxious time, as we had barely recovered from the previous drama of nearly losing the Sandtex business. Our relationship with Blue Circle had been more of a partnership, each appreciating the dependence upon the other. We had, over the years, worked closely together on new developments including the squat 10 litre tin, a stronger and more stable container. We became the sole manufacturer of this tin in the country and with existing tooling on this increased diameter produced a cheap, lightweight, 15 litre container. The take over also involved the redundancy of many of our friends at Blue Circle - C'est le Guerre!

Fortunately, we had supplied AKZO with 10 litre tins for many years and they had benefited with our ability to enable them to convert to the squat version when it had proved successful in the market place. Nevertheless, and notwithstanding our assurances, they were concerned with our ability to be able to provide the combined volume. As with the majority of major sized companies, they were mainly concerned for quick returns to their shareholders. The 'polythene boys were knocking on their door', but fortunately they experienced problems with the manufacture of the 'Sandtex' product thereby providing us with a valuable breathing space.

We were prudent and minimised our overheads, improved the short run print facilities, which assisted towards our survival and maximised our efforts to obtain business less exposed to polythene. We devloped a close relationship with Kalon who supplied the major D.I.Y. outlets with decorative paints that required a high quality container with prestigious presentation and a flexibility of service which we could provide. The retail outlets were 'calling the tune' requiring new packs with eye catching designs for the marketing of new products. We were able to assist Kalon, which contributed considerably, towards the goodwill with their customers.

The problem with these specially designed packs, being custom built, usually ended up with only a single customer outlet. Shareholders require short term profits necessitating industry to rationalise production and limit customer choice. It was only the smaller firmthat could provide this research and development service that was certainly not assisted by the Government in the 1980's.

Chapter 13
Rachmanism

It was during 1985 that virtually all the packaging industry was experiencing difficult times, with increased wages and overheads combined with a varying demand together with the competition from other sources. We required additional space to accommodate the printing plant but the council and our landlord declined planning permission for us to take over the sublease of an adjoining office and warehouse. The existing tenant had moved out and this would have proved of mutual benefit. Apart from the legal costs and time involved in the negotiations, it proved a severe setback. Some months later, our landlord notified the termination of our lease in 1986. Because of our failure to respond within a six month period as stated in the small print we were faced with expulsion, being no longer covered under the terms of the Landlord & Tenant Act. We had deferred in our reply because of the uncertainty of the future and concern at being committed to a further ten year lease. We explored the possiblity of merging with Avon Tin Printers with whom we had always enjoyed favourable relations, stocking many of the smaller sizes of tins not within our range of manufacture. They had grown from a small privately owned family company in Bristol, became profitable and moved into a modern single storey factory on the outskirts operating with semi automatic production lines, printing machines and a prominent position in the promotional packaging field, with growing exports to America. They covered a wide market outlet including the small slip lid tin containing clotted cream, so popular in the past as gifts for holiday makers in the West country. Apparently in the early 70's, Reg who was the owner, had declined a substantial offer from Metal Box. He was rightly so proud of his creation and perhaps fortunately was to die before its demise. The gift market for clotted cream faded and the loss of the lucrative square tin business with Walls, who converted to a plastic container, made a big dent in their sales. They experienced problems with replacing experienced staff due to retirement both in printing and production. There was considerable competition in the early 1980's with small tins from larger companies operating with modern plant. They appointed an agent in the USA to sell fancy goods tins and sales developed considerably. Unfortunately, they suffered many bad debts, which proved, eventually, to be the principle cause of their downfall. There were many temptations for us to merge mainly because of the uncertainty of the future with the lease. The prospect of having to move, with the staff becoming redundant, was difficult to contemplate. The financial aspects finalised the decision. Unfortunately for them, their problems continued and the business was sold to a rather obscure and devious financial group endeavouring to expand their interest in packaging. David, the son of the owner, was deposed and a new managing director appointed. The continuing debt problem in the American market, falling sales and the lack of management in production resulted in a further decline in profitability.

Meanwhile, we negotiated with the landlord and obtained a five year lease but with no promise of renewal. It provided him with an opportunity to seek planning permission to develop the premises for housing accommodation and for us to explore the possibility of moving to more suitable premises or sell the assets to another company. The particularly worrying factor was that we were required to vacate our office accommodation in the Square. What were we to do, there was no space in the factory nor reasonable premises nearby? Whilst 'one door shut another was to open' as fortunately the adjoining premises with which we had previously been refused tenancy, suddenly became available. The potentially profitable client with whom the landlord had been negotiating backed out. Whilst it was to prove costly, and having, no alternative, we obtained a lease running concurrently with that of the factory which included a 'nasty' clause of a rent review after two years. The premises were in an extremely dilapidated condition and hard earned profits were required to renovate the offices and convert warehouse space to accommodate the printing plant. The landlord was of the 'Rachman' era 'take all but give nought'. The premises above the offices leaked and frequently caused flooding after heavy rain, the repairs were always botched and invariably when there were problems he was never available. Relations became insufferable and yet there was no recourse from the law. In 1988 the property market boomed and he took full advantage attempting to quadruple the rent. Following lengthy and expensive negotiations involving professional assistance, we were able to limit it to a 100% increase. The problems of this nature are obscure to the voters and never seem to attract any support or assistance from local authorities or political parties.

We explored every possibility of moving within our own resources, but without success. Southwark Council offered full support since we employed local people and would support a grant, but, since they were bankrupt, there was no money available. The 'black market' in the area was rife, immigrants, layabouts living rent free on social security worked for cash in hand or in crime. The local inhabitants living in council flats who had dutifully paid their rent for years and maintained the property, were always last on the list for assistance. A relation of my wife who, with four children including a baby, lived in a small two bedroom flat with bunkbeds, a coal fire, and with electricity for lighting only. There was a small kitchen with an Ascot providing the only source of hot water for a bath from jugs. There were innumerable cases of this nature ignored by the bureaucracy of the authorities. It is not surprising therefore that these inner London boroughs have become 'Ghettoes', the parks frequented by drunks and drug addicts. There is not a public lavatory, including the railway stations, within South East London. In common with the remainder of London, it has become a rubbish dump, everybody spreading their litter indiscriminantly. We can afford hordes of traffic wardens to distribute parking tickets and yet we are unable to administer the law over depositing litter.

The major British packaging companies were disinterested in our activities, their interests lying in volume markets. Some years previously we had acquired an agent who introduced us to metal packaging firms in France with a view to marketing each other's tins but unfortunately it never materialised. I contacted 'Safet' a French firm who I was advised could be interested in an acquisition. They were a family concern with factories in various parts of France supplying tins to a very wide market. I set off on a cold frosty morning, took an early flight to Paris and was met at General De Gaulle Airport by their representative. The head office and factory was situated on the outskirts of Paris, run by two brothers, who showed me round before we adjourned for lunch. They spoke good English and we soon developed a repartee of common interest. They recognised the requirement to develop an interest in the UK with the anticipated expansion of the common market. Metal Box had recently merged with Carnaud, the largest packaging conglomerate in Europe and Pechiney was soon to take over NACANCO (American owned company manufacturing beverage and general line containers). There appeared a genuine interest and they returned the visit a month or so later. We explained the position with our lease and of the necessity to find a single storey factory ideally within a few miles to preserve our factory workforce. They expressed enthusiasm with the venture and soon after Nigel paid a visit to their Normandy factory to observe more fully their production methods. They reciprocated with a visit to us by their production manager and senior engineer. We exchanged balance sheets and discussed their proposals for a take over. Whilst there would be no cash sum involved for the purchase, they would take over the ownership, provided we could find a suitable factory site. They would finance the move, modernise the plant together with installing additional lines to produce the containers for the outlets they had in mind in this country. It all sounded fine and we investigated all the potential suitable sites. Within six months we found a site satisfying all the requirements and with space for expansion and only a mile from our present factory. Unfortunately, without external financial assistance by virtue of a loan or a grant, it was not possible within our own resources. We employed over 60 people, paid our taxes, in other words were a provider of wealth to the nation.

It has bewildered me in my 33 years in metal packaging of the lack of support provided by the authorities. 'Safet' deliberated and went soft advising that they were reconsidering their policy to operate in this country. It was over a year before they finally 'pulled the plug' on the deal. Meanwhile, they appointed 'Del a Pena' as a merchant for their products and also used them as an adviser. It was pretty obvious that they had been an influencing factor and would like to remain their sole outlet in the UK. We had supplied them with tins over many years but recently with a change of ownership had suffered great difficulty in obtaining payment. It was only a few months later that they became bankrupt and liquidated. 'Safet' had appeared to be genuine and straightforward and this came at a difficult time serving as a severe blow to my faith in human nature. We learnt later that my old employer, Francis, had suffered a similar experience. My friends in the legal, accountancy and surveying professions were the only beneficiaries of these exploits. Unfortunately, we were to suffer further with these setbacks. Avon, under their new owners, financed by Capital Ventures, who at that time had an air of respectability, approached us with a view to a straight purchase. Time was running out and this seemed a last ditch opportunity. Inwardly I was appalled at the prospect of selling my business to a doubtful entity, still dabbling with the risky American market. Maybe it was more the sensitivity of my emotions with the prospect of our staff becoming redundant and being aware that if a buyer wasn't forthcoming when the lease expired and with little or no money available to pay redundancies, the company would have to be liquidated. My son would be out of work and my wife and I would become dependent on the state pension for our retirement, having created a successful company following twenty years of hard work we would become discarded because of outdated property laws and short sighted authorities.

Finally, after meetings and an avalanche of paperwork - budgets, accounts and inventories, the penultimate day arrived. I worked till 10 p.m. finalising figures with my accountant and preparing and agreeing an address with my counterpart at Avon to be announced simultaneously to our factory at 9 a.m. I had already explained the situation to my key staff which was perhaps the most distasteful task I have had to perform. Whilst they had always appreciated the situation, it still came as a harrowing shock. The prospect of unemployment within a declining industry.

At 9 a.m., on the vital day after a night of dreams and reminiscences of the past, still not accepting that as only the third owner of the company since 1888, the year my father was born, I was to end this period of history. Nigel and I toured the factory as usual at 8 a.m., we had plenty of work, it was a pleasant morning and the staff were in good spirits. At about 8.45., there was a 'phone call from my accountant advising me to defer making the announcement as he had not yet received the 'fax' confirming the deal. It was not till later in the morning that the 'cloud burst'. My counterpart at Avon 'phoned me personally. In the afternoon following the pressure from Avon, a senior member of the company called and explained that at a board meeting the previous day, due to a setback in another venture, the Board had voted to cancel the purchase. We were dumbstruck and politely and firmly told him to "bugger off". Apart from the blow to our prospects for the future, it had been an extremely expensive operation in both time and money. My accountant, widely experienced in the affairs of sales and takeovers, was equally astonished, never having experienced the like before.

It was only a few months later that Avon was sold to Lin Pac at a knock down price.

Chapter 14
Deficiency

A deficiency can serve as a haven for predators and vermin. Laws that can be reversed serve to blackmail and degenerate those to whom they are designed to protect. The summer months tended to be difficult being usually a peak time for orders but with a labour shortage due to holidays.

Students with long vacations, at this time of the year, required employment and served as a valuable stop gap proving of mutual benefit.

Bob, our manager, breezed into the office one morning and enquired if we still had any vacancies in the factory. He said that there was a Mr Goona at the door looking for a job. He was short, smartly dressed, possessing a degreee of over politeness combined with a condescending manner. He stated that he was of Nigerian descent, his father being the chief of a tribe, and was in London studying law. He was shown round the factory and it was explained that lacking in experience in tin making he must be prepared to fulfill mundane tasks, such as loading lorries, etc. It was always useful to have staff who could read, write and count. He accepted the terms and appeared enthusiastic. He duly reported in the following morning at 8 a.m. and was put to work with Tony, an enormous 22 stone Cockney, a genial individual with a subtle sense of humour. We operated with a multi race staff, comprising Jamaicans, West Africans, Indians, Portugese, Iranian, Irish, Scots, Welsh and a few English. Outwardly a pretty rough, hard and illiterate mixture but loyal, diligent, responsible and drawn together in an environment that required teamwork to provide production. Tony possessed a leadership flair, subtle and akin to the 'Pied Piper', they all followed him fully appreciating that he was a genial rogue. He possessed that rare ability to use racial language outrageously without causing offence which somehow managed to endear them to him.

I had just returned from visiting a client after a long and tiring journey. It was just before 8 p.m. and the factory was ending an overtime shift when I was greeted by an irate factory manager. Mr Goona had apparently been circulating during the afternoon, amongst the African staff, inviting them to disclose any incidents of racialism. They were confused as to who he was and complained to the foreman of the interference to their work.

The manager explained to Mr Goona that he was employed to perform a job and not set up a political forum. There were adequate facilities and opportunities for staff to represent complaints or suggestions.

On the following day it became apparent that he was a sharp and an incessant talker with a venomous tongue. I called him into the office and explained the complaints which could not be tolerated and that as he was not prepared to work within the terms of his employment, then he must leave. He should call in within a day or so for his money.

He reported in the following day for work as if nothing had occurred. It was explained that he had been dismissed and could collect his two day's pay when the office was open.

The following day he 'phoned threatening to report us for racial discrimination. As he had only been with us for two days, we were not unduly perturbed but kept a note of the incidents.

Some months later, we received notification that we must appear before the Race Relations Board on charges of racialism. In due course, a representative of ACAS called and wasted a day by interviewing staff. Southwark Council had advised, in respect of his investigations, that we were reputed to have the finest record for race relations in the borough. He recommended that if we offered to re-engage him and deal with some of his complaints which included the removal of 'graffite' on the ceiling in the men's toilet purporting a 'Nazi' swastika, the charges would be dropped. Investigating the matter, we found some indiscriminate markings produced by a marker on the plastic tiles which had occurred two or three years previously. My male staff advised that they were not in the habit of sitting in the lavatory, which was hardly a salubrious place, gazing at the ceiling.

There was no way that we could agree to this from of blackmail and so reluctantly, we were forced to pursue the dreary, time consuming and expensive performance of involving a solicitor and barrister. Southwark, a left wing council, lived up to their reputation and declined to give any support.

The hearing day duly dawned some six months later necessitating about eight key members of the staff to appear as witnesses. Taxis were ordered and we arrived well in advance of the scheduled time. Bureaucracy in its glory, the waiting room like a doctor's surgery, packed with people who would normally be involved in the creation of the nation's wealth but instead being held to ransom by generally spurious complaints. There were few seats so we milled around frustrated with our involvement in maintaining the democratic process. Tony, such an extraordinary character, had been so concerned that he turned up in a newly purchased navy blue suit. At first he was not recognised, an event to live in the annals of the company. Whilst this spirit exists in the working population, we must surely survive. Why cannot school teachers, policticians, priests, parents, employers and trade unions, recognise and encourage this feature?

Five minutes before the scheduled time of the hearing at 9 a.m. we were advised that it would be deferred till 11 a.m. Mr Goona had 'phoned and reported a fire in the kitchen of his flat and would be late.

At 11 a.m. we were all seated in the court room including the two presiding judges adorned in their gowns. A clerk appeared and supplied one of the judges with a slip of paper. It was announced that Mr Goona had been further delayed in a bus which was involved in a traffic hold up on Westminster Bridge. The fact that there are no telephone booths on Westminster Bridge did not occur to the judiciary. My barrister suppressed me from making an outburst regarding this incredible situation. He appealed that the case be dropped and that we be awarded costs. The fact that Mr Goona was without money was irrelevant. The political implications of any action were far more important than our claim and it was ruled that he must be given the opportunity for a further hearing at a date to be advised. The disproportionate time involved, our costs and the loss of production were disclaimed. We adjourned to the pub in pure disbelief that we were living in a civilised community and raised our glasses in a toast to British justice.

A few weeks later a terse note was received advising that the hearing had been dropped because Mr Goona had disappeared. I expostulated to the Race Relations Board regarding the disproportionate time and costs involved together with the loss of faith and respect of the judiciary by our staff of mixed ages and races, but to no avail. Similarly, complaints to Southwark Council (Labour) our M.P. (Liberal Democrat) and the Department of Employment (Conservative) were all discreetly ignored. Mr Goona, it was disclosed later, was a failed student, and without money to return home would no doubt be rejected by his family. Apparently this blackmail was a common practice by sharp and devious law students who anticipated that the smaller employer would settle out of court rather than incur the associated expenses, a possible fine and damage of goodwill. Insurance companies always ready to 'jump on the band waggon' offered cover to reduce the hassle and settle with the individual out of court.

Could Mr Goona be the personification of a deficiency or be privileged with the protection of his race?

Chapter 15
Production Management

The conversion to polythene resulted in a declining demand for 10 litre containers and combined with the introduction of legislation on the Carriage of Dangerous Goods, restricted the use of many of our containers for export. The early 1980's were gloomy days generally for the industry. We concentrated our efforts for sales in the more specialised markets where our versatility of tooling and short run print could benefit. Our major competitors had ceased production in these areas because of the low volume so we benefitted to some extent from these 'crumbs that fell from the master's table'. Industry was developing new products for the chemical market, some very searching and inflammable, requiring a leakproof container with a wide neck which we were able to produce with existing tooling. There was a growth in the use of resins for the adhesive industry, particularly in flooring, requiring two part packs, an adhesive in one and a hardener in the smaller pack. Tins provided the ideal package. We manufactured a variety of styles including smaller sizes on the same diameter that could be interlocked with a plastic ring. We gained an award from 'Metal Packaging' for a pack especially designed for our customer to package a high quality flooring sealant. It consisted of two tins on a common diameter that interlocked and provided stacking facilities for storage and fitted with a handle to enable the combined pack to be taken to the site where the contents could be mixed and applied. It provided success for our customer in the DIY market at home and on the continent. We reacted again to customer demand and produced a tin using heavy gauge tinplate that would withstand the pressure required for undersealing motor vehicles. Sales grew for short run printed tins for fancy goods, particularly cakes, biscuits and confectionery, including an order from an American company for a high quality printed tin to pack a jersey manufactured in Italy and sold under a famous trade name. The product sold worldwide although the order for tins was relatively small.

These developments were rewarding, not only financially, enabling the firm to survive, but provided to all those involved, a spirit of pride and satisfaction from the success which could not have been achieved without their combined skills and enthusiasm.

These containers were produced with antiquated plant requiring technical skills in maintenance and setting. Nigel had become more involved in the company administration, planning the production for the print and the factory, together with the processing of artwork and printing orders for offset litho. He also purchased tinplate for the factory and the raw materials for the screen printing.

We required a production manager capable of providing the planned output necessary to meet the budgetary control together with providing flexibility in meeting the changes of customer demand. We had two excellent engineers who had the task of maintaining antiquated plant and ensuring that it satisfied safety standards including something like 29 presses with associated tooling. Additionally, they produced all of our press room dies. It is indeed sad that our nation with such a reputation for engineering has ceased the apprenticeship training that produced these engineers. Whilst computer technology has modernised and improved the methods, trained engineers will always be required to produce tooling in all its aspects for engineering for vehicles, packaging, shipbuilders, aircraft, etc. The requirement for the provision of spares in all these areas must surely remain a further lucrative potential.

Quality control had become a growing requirement in industry for many years. Legislation had become more restrictive. Whilst the protection of the public was essential, bureaucracy stepped in as usual and introduced British Standards 5750. It constituted a form of blackmail since there were firms who would not order from a non registered company. It proved near nigh impossible for a small firm to cope with all the required paperwork. In our case, it would have proved more a hindrance than a method of improving quality standards. It provided a means of image building for the larger companies who could effect it economically with their fewer production lines and high output. Nevertheless, we survived and manged to keep our customers happy! Keith May had worked at Dartford while I was there when he was a young man under twenty years of age. Unfortunately, his manager was forced to take early retirement because of the ill health of his wife. We were at that time installing body making equipment including a high output strip feed press. Keith was quick to learn, possessed a natural gift in handling machinery and coped very effeciently. He moved on later to a small firm producing aluminium membrane tins, on a high output production line, to package instant coffee. Unfortunately, it was for a single customer outlet who eventually installed plant to make their own containers and Keith was out of work. At that time, as much as I would have liked to employ him, we were overstaffed, but I promised to bear him in mind should a vacancy occur. Keith took on a job outside of the industry, worked long hours, but earned good money. He was keen, however, to return to the 'tin making' business which he said "Was in his blood". I explained in broad outline the risks involved in view of the state of the lease; I offered to match his money, and he took on the job. It was very difficult initially, as the foremen of the production line and the cutting department were set in their ways and objected to taking orders from an outsider, sensing it was a criticism of their ability and enthusiasm. We were a close knit community employing basically conscientious people of all ages, sexes, creeds and nationalities but, simple and introvert. They were not concerned with the politics of business of the outside world but purely to perform a job satisfactorily as they understood it to be. My responsibility was akin to that of the Captain of a ship who depended upon his crew to provide all the functions necessary to keep it afloat, operate the weaponry and provide its maximum operational potential. The Captain was then free to concentrate on fulfilling any mission required. The naval discipline act does not operate within the civilian community, who grew up, however simple and uneducated, to react within their own beliefs. Keith with his experience and more open minded approach and with my support, developed the application of the plant enabling us to meet customers' requirements never previously contemplated. He was also able to maximise the use of labour thereby increasing output, appreciate the need for financial restraints and incorporate them successfully and effectively into production. During the final years of the company he remained dedicated, working extended hours sometimes till 9 p.m. to ensure the successful running and production output of the factory. We all have our faults and sensitivities but success in business depends on understanding these limitations and potentials. Keith was to prove a tower of strength during the difficult and complicated negotiations with Safet, Avon and finally Pechiney. It would not have been possible in a small company to handle all the complicated professional requirements together with maintaining sales and other administrative necessities.

It was unfortunate that he found it difficult to accept the changed circumstances when the company was sold to Pechiney and finally moved to Norwich. He had been our right hand man and akin to many in this modern world, became redundant. He, like many of his contemporaries, could provide a forward thinking businessman the opportunity to develop and implement a potential market place. Life is all about understanding people.

We had successfully trained our own operators and Danny Singh, the son of a Sikh, who was still farming in India, became the print manager. When he arrived in England little more than a year previously, he was unble to speak a word of English. He married a girl of Indian descent, bred and born in London. She assured me that if he was provided with a job, he would attend night school and soon learn the language. There were industrious and there were lazy Indians depending upon their religion and background. Danny soon proved to be an industrious worker and very anxious to earn money. He soon developed as an operator and within six months, we offered him a job in the print. He was reliable, cheerful and preferred working on his own and soon became a most valuable asset, cooperated with Keith and their combined efforts contributed considerably to the survival of the company.

Chapter 16
Final Days 1990-1991

We staggered to our feet like a boxer felled by a heavy blow, bleary eyed, the visions of failure looming if the fight be lost. The collapse of the 'Avon' deal had made me bitter and was difficult to reconcile. Fortunately, human beings are mainly resilient, normally motivated by a challenge and particularly where survival is at stake regardless of age. Whilst my dreams had always been to relocate within our own resources, the circumstances dictated it to be an impossibility - but what was the alternative?

We had discussed our situation with most companies within the MPMA, they were interested and sympathetic, but were concerned with their own problems.

AKZO had been our principal customer for 10 litre tins with their sales mainly to trade outlets. Price saving was the prerequisite rather thanquality and presentation and they systematically converted to the 10 litre polythene bucket, a wobbly affair, when invariably the loss of contents in removing the lid largely offset the price savings on the container. In today's computer world these costs are lost (or found) in a different programme! Automatic production incorporating cheaper packaging with closures provides this anomoly, particularly with cardboard containers for fruit and milk drinks, polythene containers with their tamper proof closures on bottled water being just a few examples. Obviously, 'like sheep', we must move with the times. Quantity rather than quality being the governing factor. Shareholders return influencing the product supplied to the consumer.

Fortunately, Kalon, who was our other major customer for the 10 litre tin supplied the major D.I.Y. outlets where quality and presentation remained paramount and the demand remained steady.

It had been appreciated that there was a growing female influence over the purchase of emulsion paints. They were more concerned with the shades and colours that were to be reproduced on the walls in their domain rather than with the initial saving on 5 or 10 litres of the paint.

The product could only be represented by the presentation of the pack, which is obviously why companies, particularly in the retail market, spend so much on TV advertising.

The electricity boards throughout the country would paint their pylons during the summer months as part of their annual maintenance. They used a 5 litre lever lid tin fitted with a tinplate handle which was rigid and strong and could be suspended from the workman's belt so that his hands would be free to scale the pylon. The fitting of the handle had always been a labour intensive operation and with the advancements in automatic production methods, a plastic handle was devised which could be fitted on completion of the manufacturing process. Whilst the major manufacturers would still supply the special tins, they were on a separate line requiring a special run which did not always coincide with the customer's requirements for the tins. fortunately, we were able to match the price and produce them on our standard lines providing the flexible service required. The business became lucrative and helped to fill the gap vacated by AKZO. We had therefore a sound business with some potential to offer the right buyer.

The sands of time were running out fast for within two years the lease would expire and we would be on the streets! Kalon had repeatedly complained of the lack of initiative and short sighted attitude that existed amongst metal packaging manufacturers who concentrated solely on automatic production output. The 'retail boys' were calling the tune with the major D.I.Y. stores requiring new style packs that required variety in presentation.

Shareholders in major companies require a quick return on their investment and are anxious that it does not become speculative.

It is from 'acorns that tall oaks emerge' which has been the perogative of the small but dynamic manufacturer who 'sniffs the scent and hunts the prey'.

J Billig, an old established family owned company, had manufactured tins for General Line for many years. They were competitive and foresaw the potential growth of the packaging industry and opened a further factory with automatic plant lines in Norwich in the late 1950's. Metal Box, the UK packaging giant, had over the decades, resisted the invasion from the

U.S.A. However, industry was modernising and growing rapidly. Crown Cork, an American company, operated a factory in Southall manufacturing aerosols and beverage cans. National Can Company (NACANCO) a major manufacturing company in the U.S.A., required a foothold in the UK and took Billig over in the early 1960's. It was in the aerosols and open top containers used for food, beverages, beer and lagers where the growth lay. In order to supply these vast markets in the competitive world, high speed can making and filling plant was required, necessitating heavy capital investment which could only be provided by the large conglomerates and hence the takeovers.

Although rather complicated, Pechiney, a large French conglomerate, with a Government interest, had systematically taken over control of NACANCO interests in the UK with complete control in 1987, moving them into the No.1 position of packaging companies in the world, in one stroke as it were. The wheels of change often turn in strange directions as it was only a few years before, that Carnaud, the French giant in packaging, merged with Metal Box, the British giant. It was possible through the auspices of MPMA to meet and discuss with fellow members the interests and problems of the industry.

On a day late in August 1990, I 'phoned Bob Clarke, the Managing Director of the then Nacanco Food and General Line Limited. He possessed the reputation of being dynamic and forward thinking with a background of selling experience. We acted as a stockist for some of their tins and had a good rapport with their sales staff. Kalon was an important customer to them for a wide range of tins and we were delighted when shortly he paid us a visit.

Following a tour of the factory, I explained the situation regarding our lease and that with our knowledge of the industry and flexibility of manufacture we could prove complimentary to them with their automatic production lines. We could possibly act as a Research and Development unit to provide ideas and alternative packs for Kalon to represent to their D.I.Y. enquiries. Kalon were aware of our situation and anxious that our activities be continued under favourable hands.

A common interest appeared to emerge with the visit of Gerry Tipple, their Business and Marketing Director together with a Technical Director and we were able to outline the possibilities of a sale. The negotiations that followed were thorough and professional and proved rewarding to be able to deal in an honest and straightforward manner. A feeling of reality existed with the belief that this would prove profitable to each company. The professional constraints were at times bewildering and frustrating with something like 30 pages of faxed material requiring daily attention. It is not possible in this era for a large company to purchase a small one without all the bureaucratic necessities of the legal and accountancy professions obtaining their 'pound of flesh'. It was akin to a fishing trawler spreading all its nets to catch a minnow. It was a 'far cry' from the deal struck in 1972 when I obtained control.

Nevertheless, the deal was struck and on the 30th November 1991, the ownership, only the third in 111 years, was finally terminated. It was indeed a sad moment in my life to proclaim to a bewildered, loyal factory staff, with the recession biting and jobs at a premium, that this somehow anchor like existence in this antiquated wooden factory was to come to an end.

Pechiney were more than generous in their terms and offers toencourage staff to move to Norwich the following year. These were simple ordinary people from South London which was their home and fortunately, many obtained employment in the few remaining packaging manufacturers in the area.

The factory was finally closed in July 1992 with the termination of thelease awating the day when it may accommodate the more refined Guy's consultants and the wealthy gentlemen from the City!

Chapter 17
Leaves

Fallen leaves of various shapes and sizes curled up and lifeless created an air of finality. Yesterday, many were still beautiful on the trees with vivid contrasting colours ornamenting this grand square of Georgian houses with black doors, railings and coal holes, brassed knockers and scrubbed doorsteps. Trinity Church, a classic London Georgian edifice with its triangular front, Greek portico, prominent clock tower with the statue of King Alfred on the lawn, centre the square. In its grounds the bare trees with lace like branches provided silhouettes adding lustre and yet sombre gloom to the scene. Behind the square lay the old 'Tin Box Factory'.

Twenty years of memories crowded these reminiscences akin to nature with the completion of its cycle. The factory a shell, its entrance door and windows boarded up, the bold sign on the wall above printed "G. WALLIN & CO. LTD. Established 1888" casting a ghostlike and eerie spell.

Derelict and without feeling, rubbish swirling on the pavement, gone was the noise of thumping presses, whirring machines and the laughter and chatter of the 'people'. As the leaves, all different shapes and sizes, colours and religions; men and women aged 16 to 80; individually vital to the output - as each leaf contributed to the growth - proud, noble, rough, gregarious, devious, generous or humble, all motivated by the will to live and united with the privilege of enjoying friendship and comradeship in this communal environment.

Voices called out from the past. Hilda, a rare cockney, 60 but still brazenly attractive, dancing eyes, elfish smile, enormous bosom, hips and buttocks: loved by all, a fabulous, endearing and invigorating character. "Come on 'Guv' - cheer up" when spirits were low. It was her nature to be aware of all the activities in the square. Annually, being listed buildings, they must be painted. A kindly lady solicitor offered one of the workmen tea making facilities in her kitchen. The story goes that one afternoon as he went through to brew his tea, she was lying naked on her bed. The temptation irrestible so he raped her. Hilda recounting the story exclaimed

259

"What a fuss — 'dirty cow', what can she expect lying there on a leopard skin rug?".

Sharon, young, brawny, loudspoken, dominating an enigmatic personality. A single mother — drank to excess when the chance permitted. A natural leader who could organise more tins to be produced in an hour than anybody else. A 'swear box' was provided for charity. During tea break her voice echoed 'Guv' — come off it — 'Shit's' not swearing.

There were so many of these great characters who added colour to the scene and as I turned away, with my emotions sensitive to their presence, it evoked memories of long ago as 'Officer of the Day', attending the poignant naval ceremony of 'Sunset'. The sound of the lone bugler reverbrating a cadenza of sound across the erstwhile still waters saluting the flag as it was slowly lowered.

At the setting of the sun, they will be remembered.